STO

FRIENDS
OF ACPL

3 1833 00579 0636

D1506428

The Complete
FAMILY
NATURE GUIDE

The Complete
FAMILY
NATURE GUIDE

BY

Jean Reese Worthley

Drawings and Photographs
by Chris Fastie

DOUBLEDAY & COMPANY, INC.
Garden City, New York

COPYRIGHT © 1976 BY NELSON DOUBLEDAY, INC.

All Rights Reserved

Library of Congress Cataloging in Publication Data

Worthley, Jean Reese, 1925–
  The complete family nature guide.

  Bibliography
  Includes index.
  SUMMARY: Introduces some basic facts about plants and ani-
mals and offers suggestions for observing them in their natural
setting.
    1. Natural history—Juvenile literature.
[1. Natural history] I. Fastie, Chris. II. Title. III. Title: Family
nature guide.
QH48.W92
ISBN 0-385-11609-8
Library of Congress Catalog Card Number: 75-32017

Printed in the United States of America

CO. SCHOOLS
C841515

CONTENTS

Foreword   vii

1. Why Study Nature?   1

2. Are You Tuned In?   3

PART I
General Information

3. Field Trips   13

4. Ways to Raise Your Nature IQ   22

5. Overcoming Fears and Superstitions   26

PART II
Plants

6. Trees and Shrubs   33

7. Ferns and Their Allies   43

8. Mosses and Liverworts   49

9. Wildflowers   53

10. Weeds and Grasses   58

11. Algae and Fungi Including Lichens   64

PART III

Animals Without Backbones

12. Invertebrate Classification and Primitive Groups 79

13. Worms and Other Curious Groups 84

14. Shellfish 90

15. Animals with Jointed Appendages:
Spiders, Millipedes and Crustaceans 92

16. Animals with Jointed Appendages: Insects 98

17. Animals with Spiny Skins 126

PART IV

Animals With Backbones

18. Birds 133

19. Amphibians 143

20. Reptiles 150

21. Fishes 155

22. Mammals 159

PART V

Ways To Enjoy Nature

23. Non-Living Things 179

24. Habitats to Explore 187

25. Projects and Activities 199

Books I Use and Like 218

Index 220

FOREWORD

I WAS RAISED on a Maryland farm and was so involved in various chores —milking cows, cleaning stables, weeding gardens and harvesting crops— that somehow I missed learning much about the common plants, birds and insects on the farm. It wasn't until I reached the ripe old age of twenty-one that I landed in an environment where everyone around me was interested in the out-of-doors and was learning how to interpret it to others. This was at the University of Massachusetts where I went to get a master's degree in outdoor education.

At U-Mass I learned quickly through daily field trips and made up for much lost time. I could hardly wait to get back to the farm to see what plants and animals I could identify with my newly acquired knowledge. When a young Massachusetts man asked me how many kinds of birds there were back on the farm in Maryland I could only think of three: robins, starlings and house sparrows. Later I married him and brought him back to live on the farm. We started to keep a bird list and have added to it every year since then. It now has one hundred and seventy-three species of birds on it.

What has happened to the farm bird list is also true of the farm lists of wildflowers, trees, mushrooms, mosses, ferns, lichens, insects, reptiles and amphibians. Every year we see things that we have not seen before, all because we are using our senses more. Even in a relatively small area such as the one hundred and thirteen acres on our farm, new things are constantly happening. Some creatures, such as bluebirds, which used to be common have disappeared, and a plant, the perfoliate leaved tearthumb, that wasn't there twenty years ago is now a terrible pest.

This volume attempts to do in print what I have been doing on public television for over six years on my series, "Hodgepodge Lodge": interpret our natural environment so that people will understand and feel at home in it.

I want to express my appreciation to the following people: my husband, Dr. Elmer George Worthley for so patiently sharing his knowledge, Dr. William Gould Vinal who introduced us and taught us his philosophy of nature education, and my parents, Waiva Dean and Francis Sydney Reese who instilled in me an appreciation of such nature treasures as hepatica, arbutus, ladyslippers, poke, morels, puffballs, black walnuts and persimmons.

Jean Reese Worthley

Lone Hickory Farm
Owings Mills, Maryland
August 1975

The Complete
FAMILY
NATURE GUIDE

CHAPTER 1

Why Study Nature?

CAN YOU SEE anything that's alive from where you are right now? How about a common housefly or an African violet in your living room? Or a pigeon you can see from your window if you live in the city? If you're in the country you can probably see dozens of living things no matter what time of the year it is.

Have you ever wondered about any of these plants and animals? Or have you just taken them for granted like the bed you sleep in every night? Nowadays there are so many things to do and so many places to go that many of us have forgotten how much fun it can be to stop and wonder about a bird, plant or bug for a few moments. Remember—anything alive is very much like you in that it too is made up of cells. If you're lucky enough to be looking at a drop of swamp water through a microscope you may see some creatures made up of only one cell, but the living things you see on your daily rounds have many cells, just as you do. Think about that and then think back to how every living thing begins very tiny and grows. Think of something very small such as an ant and something very big such as a whale. Each started the same way with two cells uniting; one from the "male" and one from the "female." It's hard to believe but true!

Maybe you have a relative or friend who collects butterflies, grows iris or watches birds. If so, you know they are getting much enjoyment from watching living things, reading books to learn more about their favorite plants or animals, and going on field trips to see new kinds of whatever it is they're interested in.

Have you ever been on a nature walk? Maybe you've been invited but didn't go because it was a little chilly out or you thought it was too hard to tell one bird or plant or insect from another. Well, learning about nature is just like learning about anything else. Once you get started and begin to use all your senses, you'll be amazed how much you learn and how much more fun life is no matter where you are. Your friends will think you know a lot because you can identify several birds or flowers, mushrooms or trees.

On days when you're feeling sad and gloomy, take a walk around the block and see what's going on in the cracks in the sidewalk. Any problems you have will seem minor compared to those of an ant moving piles of dirt and rounding up enough food to last all winter. Once you begin to be a naturalist every trip will be more exciting. When you go to the zoo, instead of just peering at the animals and watching them do tricks you can think about which ones are in the cat family, which ones came from Africa, what they might be doing if they were still in their native habitat or what their ancestors in prehistoric times might have been.

If you can't get out of the house, take a good long look at a house plant. Check the leaves and see if they feel and look the same on the top and bottom. Does the stem have any hairs on it? Lift up the pot to see if some amazing little insects called springtails have moved in to live there and are hopping around. Or if you have a goldfish, examine it carefully

Goldfish, plants and snail in aquarium

and find out some new things. If there's a snail living with your fish see if you can catch it in the act of eating algae off the sides of the fish bowl. You have to look very closely to see rows of minute teeth on a ribbon-like band in its mouth scraping off the tiny plants.

By the way, while you're checking your house plant think about where it might have grown wild originally, for most of our house plants are native to other countries. If you have African violets, for instance, it's easy to think of where they first came from and still grow wild. If you live in a warm place such as Florida, Mexico or Tahiti you'll see poinsettias growing wild outside so commonly that you might even call them weeds. But if you live in a cold place one poinsettia is a real treasure and has to be kept inside in the winter or it will die.

Another thing in nature that's fun to find out about is how various plants got their names. The poinsettia was named after Joel Roberts Poinsett, who was the first United States minister to Mexico from 1825 to 1829 and later was our Secretary of War. He discovered the plant in Mexico in 1828. There are still many things to be discovered and if you really get into this nature study business you might find a new moss or insect and have it named after you! Even those plants and animals that have been discovered and named have mysteries about them to be solved. So try to be a good nature detective. It's just as much fun or more to solve a puzzle in nature as to read a detective story.

To sum it all up there are many, many reasons to study nature and it's never too late to begin! Observing living things will make life much more interesting and make you a much more interesting person. With new labor-saving devices being invented each day we're all going to have more free time and there's no better way to spend it than in getting to know your environment, what's going on in it and how you can help save it before it's too late.

CHAPTER 2

Are You Tuned In?

HAVE YOU EVER sat on a fallen log and thought about all the things that were happening to turn it back into soil? Or have you gone wading in a cool stream on a hot summer day and watched the water striders skimming on the surface, making shadows on the stream bottom with an air bubble under each foot? Years ago these pleasures of country life were enjoyed by many people. But now there are fewer farms and fewer people left living in the country.

The best things in life really are free if you are tuned in to nature and have practiced using all your senses to find out about the world around you. Once you get started—either on your own or with a nature-loving group—and learn to recognize even a few things, such as the song of a chipping sparrow or the shape of an American elm tree, you'll be surprised at the number of chipping sparrows and American elm trees you'll hear and see just because you're tuned in. You may be in a car waiting at a red light when suddenly you'll hear a bird song. Your companions probably won't even hear it unless they're naturalists too. But that's part of the fun because you can teach the song to them right then and there by having them listen while you hold up a finger. When the bird sings drop your finger. Some birds such as the chipping sparrow obligingly sing their song over and over again. After a few times of dropping your finger, ask your friend to hold up his hand when he hears the song and he'll be on his way to being tuned in to nature too. Every time you pass on to a friend something that you know about nature, you learn it a bit better yourself. Our natural environment is fast disappearing and we all need to become interested ecologists to help save what's left. There is much beauty around us even in the cities, but we need to practice appreciating this beauty.

A fringe benefit of being tuned in to nature is that you will feel more at ease if you are the victim of some calamity due to natural forces. If, for instance, a snowstorm or thunderstorm cuts off your electricity for a while, instead of being afraid and upset, take a walk in the rain or snow and see what's happening to your fellow creatures—the birds, the rabbits and the squirrels.

Once the word gets around your neighborhood that you know even a little bit about nature you'll make many new friends who have questions to ask or information to share. You may get letters containing leaves or flowers or bugs to be identified and many other interesting surprises. Here are a few more hints about tuning in: Remember that you're trying to sharpen all your senses. Listening for the chipping sparrow is one way to sharpen your hearing. Try closing your eyes for a few moments and taking note of all the things you hear. First you'll hear the loud noises such as cars and planes but finally the little cricket chirps and leaf rustles will come through. And when you're out walking and don't see any birds, stop and listen and you may hear a woodpecker's faraway tapping or a towhee scratching around in the leaves. Did you know that a woodpecker uses *his* sense of hearing to find food? He listens with his ear close to the trunk of a dead tree and when he hears ants, beetles or other insects chewing or crawling inside, he drills for his meal. After a short time of sharpening your hearing sense you will hear nature sounds wherever you go.

Your sense of sight is the one you probably use the most but you can sharpen it in many ways. Do you remember to look up and see what's happening in the sky? You usually can see a bird of some kind and if not, a cloud or the moon or stars. How about checking under rocks and logs to see what lives there? Always be cautious, especially if you live in scorpion or poisonous snake country, and always replace the rock or log, as it probably shelters dozens of creatures. You can even find fascinating forms of wildlife under an old newspaper, rag or cardboard box that's been in one place on the ground for a while. Turn over a rock in a stream and look for baby dragonflies, snail eggs and the curious homes of caddis fly larvae. If you pass a certain tree every day on your way to school or work you may think you know it very well. But have you ever gotten really close to its bark and noticed what lichens, mosses, tiny spiders or insects are living there? And have you checked closely in the spring to see what kind of flowers the tree has? Or later in the season to find the seeds? Even in winter when the leaves have fallen the buds on trees are interesting. It's hard to believe that all the flowers and leaves for next spring are inside the buds by the end of the summer, just waiting to start growing when the proper time comes.

Besides our eyes and ears we can use our noses to find out what's happening. I never have to look in a book to see when the chestnuts and chinquapins are going to bloom on the farm where I live because when they're in bloom I can smell them as soon as I step out the door. The odor is not a pleasant one but it is unforgettable. It happens to be similar to the odor given off by some curious fungi called stinkhorns but they usually don't appear until summer. So when I smell this odor in the spring I know it's from chestnuts or chinquapins. There are so many things you can find out and enjoy if you have a good sense of smell. Hay-scented ferns and sweet vernal grass give off delightful odors as you walk through them. Most of us have favorite flowers—like roses, lilacs or lily of the valley—whose odor brings back many memories. There are other wonderful scents too. In a barn there is the mixture of animals and hay that smells good. Also there's the wonderful clean smell after a rain. Even the odor left by a skunk is not obnoxious if you understand skunks. If you're out walking in the woods and smell a decaying animal it should remind you of the constant process in nature of living things dying and being returned to the soil by a variety of mechanisms.

You have to be a bit wary while practicing your sense of touch so that you don't end up with a bad case of poison ivy or poison sumac. But there are many things that are fun to feel and also quite safe. Near the water there are smooth rocks and pebbles. Hold one of these in your hand and try to make up a story about it. What might have happened to it since it was broken off a larger rock by a glacier or some other natural force? Practice feeling the bark of different trees and see if you can learn to identify some trees with your eyes closed. Beeches are smooth, tulip trees are rough and the bark on the shagbark hickory peels off in strips. You can feel all these things. Plants in the mint family have

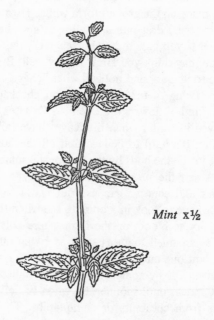

Mint x½

square stems. Feel and compare them with sedges, which usually have triangular stems. There are prickly plants such as cacti and some with sticky juice such as milkweeds. Animals are fun to feel too. Some are soft and furry; others are furrier in winter than in summer; some have curly hair.

Now when it comes to sharpening your sense of taste, you must be very careful. A mushroom or berry that looks delicious may be poisonous. *Don't taste anything you're not sure of.* Start off with a few foolproof things you can taste.

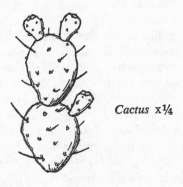

Cactus x¼

Sassafras is an easy tree to identify any time of the year. It's always pleasant to chew on one of its twigs or leaf stems. At any season you can identify it by its clean, refreshing odor. Just break off a small branch or scratch the bark with your fingernail and sniff. Once you've smelled it you won't forget it. During the summer you'll recognize sassafras as an old friend just by the leaves. Sassafras trees of any reasonable size (four

Sassafras x¼

or five feet tall) will have four kinds of leaves: plain with no lobes, three lobes, right-handed mittens and left-handed mittens. Once you see these you can go ahead and enjoy the taste. Chewing sassafras twigs is much healthier for you than chewing gum and doesn't cost anything.

There are many other good-tasting things out in the woods and fields as well as in your own lawn. If you've ever lived in the country you've probably been introduced to sour grass. There are two kinds, neither of which is in the grass family. One is really in the sorrel family and its leaves look something like clover. But it has little yellow flowers and its proper name is wood-sorrel. The other is in the buckwheat family, has leaves like narrow arrowheads and is called sheep-sorrel. Both are refreshing to chew and eat and fun to use in a tossed salad.

Once you start tuning in to nature you'll find that wherever you go you'll hear birds, see new plants, smell interesting odors, want to feel fuzzy leaves or taste new things. You'll see fascinating forms of life no matter where you are, even in the middle of a city. All you have to do is practice as often as you can and be alert and aware. You'll soon know what to expect on your daily rounds and then when something different shows up it'll be a real thrill. It may be a bird that wasn't there yesterday or a moss in a crack in the sidewalk. Whether it's large or small, something new is exciting. And you can enjoy it whether or not you know what it is.

Learning to know trees, birds, flowers and insects is like learning to recognize new friends. With people you remember what color their eyes are or how long their hair is or whether they're short or tall or fat or thin. With trees you have to remember leaf shapes and arrangement and what the bark looks like. Getting acquainted with flowers means learning colors, locations, fragrances and blooming times. Birds are harder because they don't stand still very long but with some practice you can learn to notice quickly bill shapes, sizes, tail length and other important details. Tuning in to nature takes practice, like learning to ride a bike or play a violin. Be alert at all times and keep your senses ready! With your ears open you may even hear a bird song at a noisy party!

Here are a few of the things in store for you once you start using all your senses to tune in to nature:

• What's ugly to some people may seem beautiful to you. Your friends may hate, fear—even kill—spiders, but you'll appreciate them for the valuable role they play in nature and admire their beautiful colors and intricate webs.

• You'll become interested in every living thing, realizing that there is balance in nature and each animal or plant depends on others.

- You may be saddened when you see a tree cut down needlessly or a beautiful farm turned into a housing development or a black spot in a forest along a highway where someone tossed out a cigarette and started a fire, killing many plants and animals.

- You'll understand that it's never too late to learn something new about nature yourself and that there's joy in teaching what you've learned to a friend.

- You'll realize that there are hundreds of interesting things going on in the woods, fields, stone walls, old stumps, logs and cracks in sidewalks all the time.

- You'll meet lots of people who go for walks every day and don't see anything.

- You'll understand what ecology and conservation are all about and want to do something about pollution.

- You'll find that life is a lot more fun when you use all your senses.

- You'll be amazed to hear and see birds even in crowded shopping centers. Starlings, house sparrows and pigeons have become so adapted to civilization that they come where people are to pick up crumbs. Often you can see them behind supermarkets hunting through the old food that's been thrown out.

- You won't consider waiting a waste of time because you can look and listen while you wait. You may even discover a new bird or bush.

- You can make discoveries while waiting for the bus. I know a girl whose school bus was late one morning but while she waited she heard woodpeckers in two different wood lots tapping out messages to each other on hollow trees.

- You'll think back to how busy people were in the old days milking cows, shoveling coal for the furnace, chopping wood, and planting and harvesting. Life is so easy for us now with all our labor-saving inventions that some people get bored and say they have nothing to do. It's important to get interested in things that will keep us busy all our lives and nature study is the perfect answer.

- You'll soon find out that it is impossible to know about everything in nature so you'll never run out of new things to learn. Even people who specialize in one bird or beetle or plant never find out all the answers to their questions in a lifetime!

- You'll begin to think of more ways to get out and enjoy nature. Many chores that are usually done inside can be done just as well or better out of doors and you can have fun with nature while you're working. Things to do when you're listening outdoors might be sewing on buttons, mending, shelling peas, cutting up apples for applesauce, seeding cherries, cracking nuts, husking corn to cook, reading, drawing, painting and writing. It's great fun to climb up an old tree, find a nice branch to sit on and lean against the trunk while you read your favorite story. Try it!

PART I

General Information

CHAPTER 3

Field Trips

THERE ARE MANY kinds of field trips—some last an hour or less, some a day, some a week or more. Of course there are a few wealthy nature lovers who go off for several months pursuing their favorite birds, plants or insects, but most of us have only short periods of time to go afield. Field trips usually take place during the day but nighttime trips are fun too. If you're looking for owls, bats or frogs, toads and salamanders, it's best to go after dark. Some trips can be very specialized. My cousin took a college course in field zoology some years ago and had to walk down the trail through the woods with a flashlight every hour during the night looking in all the holes in trees to see what was happening there. She saw snails, slugs and spiders creeping about looking for food and carrying on their normal activities.

What to Take

First you have to decide when you're taking your trip and how long you have to spend. Then pick out the place and decide what you'll need to take. As a general rule don't take your dog or cat if you're interested in seeing birds. If you're going at night be sure to take a good flashlight. If you're going in a cave you need a carbide head lamp. It's especially important to remember to take a friend if you're going in a cave or wilderness area. In fact it's usually a good idea to take someone with you in any event, for you never know when you may twist an ankle or have some other accident.

You may go on field trips just to enjoy your environment. But there will also be times when you want to bring a little bit of moss, a few rocks or acorns home to study. If you're in a park or sanctuary of course you mustn't take anything but pictures and leave everything undisturbed for the next passer-by. But if you are on your own or on a friend's farm and want to pick up a few things, a knapsack is a handy item to have with you. Small plastic bags are good to have for keeping specimens from getting mixed together or drying out. Little plastic pill bottles come in handy for carrying insects. A small box filled with cotton will protect delicate mineral specimens. If you hear about an old farm that's being turned into a shopping center or a valley that's going to be flooded for a new reservoir, you can take a special trip to rescue any interesting plants that grow there and transplant them to your wildflower garden or to a safer area.

The proper clothes are very important! Wear long pants if you're going in the woods or overgrown fields, boots for wet places, bathing suits or shorts and old sneakers if you're actually going into the water to study plants and animals there. Wear a hat on hot summer days and have a hooded raincoat handy in case of a sudden shower.

If you have an especially good time on a certain day in a certain place you may want to come back next year. So carry a little notebook and pencil in your pocket or knapsack to write down where you were, when you went and what you saw. If you own a bird book, fern book, wildflower book, insect book or tree book that will fit into your pocket, take it along too. And don't forget your magnifying glass for looking into

Magnifying glass

small flowers or mosses. Binoculars are a help too if you're especially interested in birds. Another practical item is a pair of snippers in case you encounter some briers growing across your path.

Binoculars

If you plan to make cross sections of twigs to check their color, shape or formation, take along a pocketknife. It will be useful too for collecting small lichens or mosses from rocks or trees.

If you're going on a short trip add an apple, orange or chocolate bar to your knapsack. Include a sandwich or two if you plan to be gone all day. There are special tropical chocolate bars that do not melt on hot days. Raisins and other dried fruits also make excellent trail snacks. A canteen filled with water is a must, especially in warm weather.

You never can tell when you may get a splinter or brier in your finger while investigating botanical specimens, so keep a small first-aid kit handy and be sure it includes tweezers. Band-Aids are helpful in keeping dirt out of blisters, scratches and cuts. If you're exploring in poisonous snake country put a snakebite kit in with your other first-aid supplies and know how to use it. An elastic bandage in case of a sprained ankle is another good idea.

With a compass and a topographic map of your hiking area you can practice *orienteering* as you travel along and be better prepared to find your way out of the woods if you ever get lost. Orienteering is a Scandinavian sport which has recently become popular in the United States. Individuals, teams or families equipped with maps and compasses start off at intervals to follow a cross-country trail. On the way they find predetermined checkpoints. Orienteering events are similar to sports car rallies in the way that they are set up.

Last but not least, be sure to get permission from the owners of any private property you plan to explore. Most landowners are happy to have you if you're really interested in nature.

What to Do Once You're There

Now that you've assembled your gear and have arrived at the beginning of the trail, or have stepped out the door and are ready to walk around the block, how can you get the most out of your expedition? Well, if you expect any birds, mammals or insects to stay around, be very quiet, talk softly, don't slam car doors or wave your arms wildly about or throw sticks and stones. By moving slowly and quietly you can get much closer to wildlife. If you're out with a group that has a leader, remember to stay with or behind the leader, for if you go ahead you may scare away the very creatures everyone wants to see.

As you wander slowly and quietly down the trail or around the block remember to use all your senses: sight, hearing, smell, touch and taste. Look up and down, near and far, under rocks and trash and fallen branches, always being sure to replace them to protect the tiny creatures underneath. Stop every now and then to listen and keep listening as you move along, even if you're talking quietly with a friend. There are wonderful things to smell: clean air, flowers, spicebush and sassafras twigs, and the woods just after a rain. Walk up to a tree with rough bark and run your fingers over its trunk. Then see if you can find a smooth-barked tree to feel for contrast. Always be careful of thorns and do not touch anything that might be poison ivy. Mint, sassafras, spicebush, wood-sorrel and sheep-sorrel all taste great but *be sure you have the right plant* before you taste it. Remembering to be careful about what you feel and taste is one way of using your *common sense*. Having common sense means you'll be cautious enough to stay away from dangerous situations but enthusiastic enough to try new things under the right circumstances.

While you're out on your field trips using your senses and tuning in to nature, you'll also begin to see how you fit into the balance of nature for better or for worse and how all living things depend on each other. If you turn over a log, for instance, to admire the sow bugs and salamanders and centipedes under it and forget to replace it, you'll upset a *whole* community busy at work enriching the soil and turning the fallen tree back into soil. The entire operation will come to a halt while the animals migrate to the log's new location even though it may be only a few inches away. This is a very small example but it's being multiplied a millionfold every day in this country where whole forests are being pushed aside for new housing developments and shopping centers. Everything we do has consequences and it's far better to think ahead about the results of our activities than to complain later when our lakes and rivers become ruined by all the mud that's washed into them because the trees and other plants that held down the soil have been destroyed.

No matter where you take your field trip, you'll probably see litter. We have misused our environment by tossing cans, bottles, gum wrappers and other trash around in many of our beautiful places. Often the trash is just overwhelming and consists of mattresses, old sofas and chairs that you couldn't possibly pick up and take with you. But if you see just a few gum or candy wrappers, pick them up and tuck them in your pocket or knapsack until you get to a trash can. Every little bit helps and if your friends see that you care and are doing your share to clean up the woods they'll help too. If you do see a lot of large junk items call the public authorities when you get home or get in touch with a scout troop that is looking for a public service project.

If you go for nature walks along country roads where careless people throw things from their car windows you can probably find many bottles and cans to take to your reclamation center. Get your family or friends to go for a nature walk with you and take along several trash bags. Use one for bottles, one for cans and one for paper. If the bags get too heavy to carry because you find lots of litter, leave them behind a tree or telephone pole and come back later with your wagon or the family car. At home sort out the bottles by color, flatten the cans and put the trash that cannot be recycled out for your regular trash collector. Take the bottles and cans along the next time your family visits the reclamation center. This way you'll be helping to clean up the environment and make our natural resources go further. As you get close to the ground to pick up trash you'll see many curious plants and animals that you might otherwise miss. You'll also be setting a good example for others who drive by as you are cleaning up the roadsides.

Kinds of Field Trips

When you get right down to it, any trip can be a field trip. Take a fishing trip for instance; there's a walk involved in getting from the car to the pond or lake or river and all kinds of wonders to be seen along the way. So even though your main objective is fishing don't forget to look up and around for birds, sniff the air for the odor of mint that grows in wet places, and listen for splashes in the water and try to figure out what animals made them. You'll feel some things too. It may be the briers tearing at your clothes or water leaking into a hole in your boots but whatever it is you'll be using one of your senses to become familiar with your surroundings!

Wherever there's water there are many things going on that you can see, and many more that are happening under water where you can't see them. Plants are growing on the banks of the river or pond; insects are flying around and perhaps even laying their eggs before your eyes. Birds may be getting drinks or taking baths or even catching fish, frogs and tadpoles for themselves. Listen while you're baiting your hook or waiting for fish to bite and you may hear a dragonfly zipping by or a kingfisher giving his rattling call from an overhead branch. Remember even if you stay all day and don't catch a fish, a fishing trip can still be an exciting expedition with many happy memories if you're tuned in to what's happening around you.

Even if you've never been on a fishing trip and never expect to go on one, I'll bet you've been on a hike of some sort. Some people go on hikes just to get outdoors for a few hours; others go to look for particular things such as rocks, birds or wildflowers; and still others go to see how much ground they can cover in a certain amount of time. People in this last group often whiz right by many fascinating things going on beside the trail. Because they are in such a hurry, they miss a lot. On the other hand, there are some people who spend so much time looking at things along the path they never get caught up with the group and may even get lost because they're so far behind! It's a good idea when you're with a group to step along but also stay alert so that when you notice an unusual bird, insect or plant you can generate enough enthusiasm to make everyone want to stop a few minutes and enjoy what you have spotted. It might be a beautiful spider web full of dewdrops, an old stump covered with tiny golden mushrooms or a plump toad camouflaged in the leaves.

On bike hikes you travel faster and are apt to miss more but there are still plenty of chances to see interesting flora (plants) and fauna (animals). Look up at the telephone wires now and then to see if there's a sparrow hawk gazing out over the fields in search of a mouse or grasshopper for his lunch. In June maybe you'll be lucky enough to spot wild strawberries on a bank by the road and in July keep an eye out for luscious blackberries in the fencerows. When you stop for a rest, you just might be standing under a sassafras tree. Break off a small twig to chew as you pedal along for the next mile or two and enjoy a most refreshing taste.

If you're lucky enough to have a horse or pony to ride, you'll be higher off the ground and can see more. Of course, sometimes you may make some nature observations on horseback you wish you hadn't! If your horse steps on a yellow jackets' nest in the ground the action can be pretty exciting!

And then there are the hikes you take when you're on vacation discovering new plants and animals that don't live where you do. Even though you may not know exactly what the new things are, you may be able to put them in their proper family because they remind you of some plants and animals you know back home.

Do you like to roller-skate or ice-skate? If you go to an indoor rink the scenery isn't going to be very exciting, but if you do your skating outdoors you'll have many opportunities to add to your store of nature lore. If you're skating on a pond where the ice is clear, look for life under the ice. Algae may be waving back and forth, a painted turtle may be taking a winter walk or a tadpole may wiggle by. Even if you take a spill, lie still on the ice for a minute or two and observe what's going on beneath you. If there's a river or stream nearby with water that isn't frozen, you may see or hear some birds while you're skating. Even in winter great blue herons and kingfishers have to go fishing for their meals.

Around the edges of your skating pond look for winter stages of various plants. Cattails are easy to recognize and it's fun to toss their fuzzy seeds in the wind. In dried clumps of last summer's goldenrod look for galls or the egg case of a nursery web spider as you go skating by. In small trees nearby look for a goldfinch's nest with bits of thistledown in it or the bulkier nest of a red-winged blackbird. Cocoons of some of the giant silkworm moths are much easier to see when there are no leaves on the trees and shrubs.

But suppose you live in California, Florida or some other place where it never gets cold enough to freeze the ponds for ice skating. How about going roller skating? Outside I mean, not indoors in a rink where there's nothing to see except other people. Roller skating is a good city sport. As you whiz along the sidewalk, watch out for interesting things in the cracks. You'll see silvery bryum, a lovely little silvery green moss that grows on every continent—even in Antarctica, where it's hard for any plant to grow. And often there are little ants busy bringing up bits of dirt and sand from down below and hauling crumbs of food back to their subterranean storehouses. There'll be birds along your way too. Look for pigeons, house sparrows and starlings in the city as well as crows, robins, blue jays and song sparrows in the country.

Do you use all your senses when you go swimming? In the old days a trip to the old swimming hole was filled with many delightful surprises. Birds, flowers and insects were everywhere and once you were in the water you could feel the squishy mud between your toes and imagine all the frightening things on the bottom! Modern swimming pools are not nearly as exciting with their concrete bottoms and enough chlorine in the water to kill any small creature that might happen to fall in. But still as you lie floating on your back you can see fascinating birds in the sky and watch the clouds and butterflies going by. Occasionally dragonflies will swoop close to the water. You can learn a lot by studying the insects that fall in the pool accidentally and drown. Swimming pools are good places to find mole crickets which live under the ground and are rarely seen unless you happen to dig some up when you're digging for fishing worms. At night when they come out of their burrows they sometimes fall into pools and drown. Then you can get a close look at their feet adapted for digging and easily see how they were named for their furry counterparts that tunnel around in lawns. If you happen to be swimming in the ocean you'll see and hear lots of birds and get close to many special plants and animals that are associated with salt water.

And don't forget that boats are great for making nature observations. In a canoe you can get into various kinds of habitats hard to reach in any other way. In a sailboat you can learn much about the wind and also make your way to an unexplored island.

A good field trip is one that makes you want to go again. No two trips can ever be the same even though they cover the same trail on the same day. Don't be like a little boy in the comic strips I read once who said, "Once you've seen one field you've seen them all!" And also, don't be discouraged if you're with a leader or others who seem to know every bird, tree and fern they come to. Nobody knows it all and if you pick up one new bit of knowledge on each expedition you'll be doing well. Remember, it's never too late to begin whether you're ten or twenty or older. The important thing is to get out of doors and get started!

Making and Recording Nature Observations

At some time in your nature study career you will begin to realize that it would be a good idea to keep track of things you see and hear. For instance, you may wonder if the bloodroot is blooming earlier this year than last or if the northern (Baltimore) orioles came back earlier or later than usual. Even if you don't have much extra time, try keeping a notebook handy and jot down a few dates and places and names. You'll be amazed after a few years to see how much information you have gotten together. It's fun to compare what goes on in your own back yard this winter with what happened last winter. If you move it's interesting to note the differences in plant and animal life in your new location and to think about why things aren't the same as in your old home.

Let's see what makes a good nature observation and what, when, where and why to observe. First—a good observation is just what you saw or heard—no embroidering on the facts. Write just what you know to be true, for instance: "Today I saw a robin standing quietly on the lawn at 4 P.M." *not*, "There was a robin on the lawn and he was sad because it was cold or because he couldn't find a worm." What you write down should be objective, not subjective.

You can make observations anywhere. Of course, you usually see more natural things outdoors, but if you have an ant, fly or cockroach problem in your home, you can make some interesting observations about them without setting foot outside. You can also see many interesting things going on if you look out the window. Some years ago a man made some important contributions to ornithology by observing redheaded woodpeckers every morning while he shaved and making notes on the birds' nesting activities.

Maybe you do have time to go for walks, but don't think there's anything interesting in your neighborhood. Well, once you start using all your senses every time you go out, you'll become so tuned in to nature that you can't help hearing, seeing and smelling exciting things in *your* environment. There must be a tree somewhere near you that you could watch. Trees are living things and always have something interesting happening in their buds, under their loose bark, around their roots or on their leaves. When you do notice something new, jot it down in a little notebook or a card that will fit in your pocket and be sure to record the date. You may want to copy your notes each day into a nature notebook, diary or journal or just keep them in a card file from year to year. You can also add little sketches of things you see or keep pressed leaves or flowers to help you remember certain field trips. If you like to write poems, put in a nature poem now and then about some special insect or bird or flower you watched.

If you spend a lot of time riding in a school bus, car, or train there are still many nature observations you can make. If you travel the same road every morning and evening, look for birds that are usually in the same field or park. In the spring, each morning keep an eye out for birds that have just returned from their winter homes in the south. If you hear an insect or a bird singing, look at your watch and count how many times it sings in a minute. Or if you have to stand outside somewhere waiting for a ride, you have more golden opportunities to record what's going on around you. Check the cracks in the sidewalk or street; look up for birds; take a deep breath to find out if there are any interesting odors in the air or pick up any litter lying around. Often there are interesting little creatures to observe under or in trash and you're also doing a good deed by cleaning up the trash and putting it in the nearest can. Even if you have the misfortune to get stuck in a traffic jam on a busy highway, it helps to while away the time if you try to find out how many kinds of plants you can spot from where you are stuck and how many kinds of birds fly by. Even in shopping center parking lots there are observations to be made. For instance, have you ever noticed what kinds of birds hang around the trash bins behind supermarkets feasting on odds and ends of food that are thrown away?

On mornings when it feels good to lie in bed, you can at least open your window a crack and listen for birds. You can also hang a bird feeder right outside the window where you can see it as you're waking up. Then you can astound your friends by saying, "I saw six different kinds of birds this morning before I even got out of bed and heard several more down in the woods."

So, if you're asking *where* to make nature observations, the answer is everywhere.

If you're asking *when,* the answer is whenever you're in a position from which you can see something alive.

If you're asking *why,* the answer is because it's fun, you'll learn something new every day and you may discover something new to science.

If you want to know *what* to observe, the answer is anything that interests you.

If you want to know *how,* the answer is to use all your senses and keep records of some kind.

CHAPTER 4

Ways to Raise Your Nature IQ

SUPPOSE YOU'VE ALWAYS liked being outdoors and going for walks and suddenly one day you notice something very unusual. It may be a flower, a beetle, a mushroom or a bird and you really want to know more about it. But after asking your friends and finding nothing in your encyclopedia or at the library, you become very frustrated. At this point you'll probably either forget the whole thing or become very determined to get an answer. Perhaps you live in or near a city where there's a natural history museum. Museum people are often glad to help and even if they don't know the answer to your question they can usually tell you another place to try.

How to Find the Answers to Your Nature Questions

If there's a college in your area, contact its biology department. The Cooperative Extension Service of the United States Department of Agriculture has offices in counties all over the country with experts in various areas to help young people in 4-H, farmers and others with lawn and garden problems. Look them up in your phone book and call or write. If possible, send your plant (carefully dried and pressed flat) or your insect (wrapped in cotton in a small box). If you don't have an actual specimen try to make a sketch and put down notes giving as much information as possible: where and when you found your unknown plant or animal, the names of other things growing nearby that you recognized and anything else you can think of that might be helpful. You may want to send your specimen to the Smithsonian Institution in Washington, D.C., where there are experts in nearly every branch of natural history. This is our national museum but don't be impatient if you have to wait for an answer because people at the Smithsonian are very busy doing research and answering questions from all over the world.

In many neighborhoods there are people who were raised on farms or who used to live in the country, and have kept up an interest in the world around them. If you know people like this you'll find they enjoy sharing their knowledge and experience. They'll look at your specimen and try to help you find out what it is as soon as possible. People who love nature usually love books and often have a good collection they might share with you.

Another way to get help is to join a nature group of some sort. Maybe there's an ecology club in your school or a bird club or junior garden club in your town. You'll learn faster and better with a group than by struggling alone. As you learn more about nature and meet more people who enjoy the out of doors, you'll discover that naturalists are wonderful people who have respect for all forms of life. They're friendly, easy to get along with, and anxious to help beginners get off to a good start.

After you have delved into nature for a while and the word gets around that you're interested in butterflies, beetles, rocks or whatever the case may be, people may begin to bring their unknown specimens to you! You may laugh at this but it can happen. Even if you only know a little about natural history you know more than most people, so to them you'll seem to be an expert. When this happens don't worry about not knowing all the answers and don't be afraid to say, "I don't know." Remember, education means knowing where to look for answers when you need them rather than knowing all the answers all the time.

How Plants and Animals Are Classified

When you begin to learn about living things, you may become discouraged and think it is impossible to learn the names of everything you see. But if you keep at it, you will soon learn how to look things up in field guides. Somewhere along the line you will see that every plant and animal has a scientific name that is made up of two parts, the genus and the species. The most numerous plants and animals have common names, but in each region of the United States and in other countries of the world people use different common names. The scientific names are the same all over the world. For instance, our robin's scientific name is *Turdus migratorius*. If you go to England and hear people talking about robins, they mean an entirely different and much smaller bird.

If you think *you* have problems trying to keep the names of the plants and animals you learn straight, stop for a minute and try to imagine what it was like before things had names, and before all natural objects were organized. The man chiefly responsible for the classification system all scientists use now was Swedish. His name was Carl von Linné, but he is more commonly called Linnaeus, the Latin version of Linné. He used Latin and Greek in naming plants and animals and organized everything into large natural groups. Here's how it works. There are three main kingdoms, animal, vegetable and mineral, just as in the game of twenty questions many children play. The animal kingdom is divided into many groups called phyla (one is a phylum). One large phylum is called Chordata and includes all animals with backbones. These are organized into the following classes: Mammalia (mammals), Aves (birds), Reptilia (reptiles), Amphibia (amphibians), Agnatha (jawless fishes), Chondrichthyes (cartilaginous fishes), Pisces (bony fishes). Each of these classes is divided into orders. In the class Mammalia, for instance, there are eighteen orders. Then each order is further divided into families; the families are divided into genera and the genera into species and the species into subspecies. The plant kingdom is also divided in an orderly way.

Linnaeus' system has held up beautifully since it was published in 1758 although scientists are constantly revising it here and there and new species of plants and animals are added frequently. You might think that everything in the world had been named by now, but there are still some unexplored areas of the world and whenever botanists and zoologists go into these places they find something new.

Using the Socratic Method

Socrates was an ancient Greek philosopher who believed in helping his students find answers themselves by asking certain questions in a particular order. Today this is an excellent technique to use in teaching nature once you've learned a few things yourself and are ready to share your knowledge.

Let's pretend you are taking a walk through a field of Queen Anne's lace with a friend on a lovely summer day. Your friend may pick one of the flowers and ask, "What's this?" If you gave him a quick lecture on the subject you might say, "That's in the Umbelliferae and has three common names but its scientific name is *Daucus carota*." After this your friend probably wouldn't know any more than he did before and what's more he might suggest that you go home! Using the Socratic method you would scrape a little of the plant's skin with your fingernail and have your friend smell it. With a little prompting he would say, "It smells like carrots." You would say "Great—one of the names for this plant is wild carrot and it's an ancestor of the carrots we eat." Then have your friend look closely at the lovely white flowers and ask him what decorations on ladies' dresses they resemble. When he says "lace" then you can give him another common name, Queen Anne's lace. Finally take a look at a plant that's going to seed and teach your friend the third name, bird's-nest. Be sure to conduct a brief review at the other side of the field. You'll be amazed at how quickly your friends pick up new nature knowledge this way.

The more you use the Socratic method the better you'll get. Don't be discouraged if sometimes you can't get your friends to come up with the right answer. Some answers are easier to figure out than others. Just remember to use it as often as you can. When it works it gives the nature teacher and the nature student a real feeling of accomplishment.

CHAPTER 5

Overcoming Fears and Superstitions

THERE'S ONE MORE thing you need to do now that you're all tuned in, have your field trip clothes on, your equipment ready and have picked a good spot to go. You need to get rid of any fears and superstitions about plants and animals that you may have. Many people grow up terrified of the out of doors because when they were children they heard such things as: "Toads give you warts!"; "Bats get in your hair!"; "All snakes are dangerous!"; "All kinds of sumac are poisonous!" You've probably heard all of these and some others besides. Do you really think any of them are true? Have you ever seen a bat get in anyone's hair? And don't you know lots of people who have warts even though they've never touched a toad? This is another time to use your common sense and find out whether a statement is true before you believe it. A library is a good place to find the right answers if you don't have a naturalist friend close by. If you've believed these things all your life it's hard to forget them right away even when you find out they're not true. But keep trying to find out all you can about plants and animals and pretty soon you'll see how ridiculous some of these sayings are. Then you'll be all set to help your friends and family to overcome *their* fears and superstitions so they can enjoy life more!

Let's take a quick look at the four superstitions mentioned above so you can see how they got started. First, the one about toads is based on the fact that toads have bumpy skin. Just look at a toad closely and see that it's covered with big and little bumps and you can see it was easy for someone a long time ago to believe warts must come from touching toads. Warts on people are really caused by a virus and often disappear as mysteriously as they appear.

Now, what about bats? Maybe people are afraid of them because they fly at night, or because they've read too many stories about vampires. Of course there are vampire bats in Mexico and other parts of the world, but not in the United States. Bats with rabies can be dangerous, so it's best not to touch them or pick them up, but observe them from a distance and admire their great mosquito-catching ability. Bats have big ears and send out sounds too high for us to hear. These sounds bounce off people, trees and buildings and back to the bat's ears, keeping him from flying into anything. More information on bats will be found in Chapter 22.

Very few varieties of snakes are poisonous. Learn the identifying marks of the poisonous snakes in your area and you'll realize that most of the snakes you see are harmless. Animals in general and snakes in particular are just as afraid of you as you might be of them and when given the chance, they will leave. Even poisonous snakes play an important role in nature by eating rats and mice and other rodents that destroy farm crops. Another thing to remember is that all snakes *can bite* but the bite of most snakes, such as the black snake or the common water snake you might catch in a pond, is no worse than the scratches you get when you're out picking blackberries.

As soon as you learn to recognize the very few things in nature you should beware of, you can relax and really enjoy every minute you're outdoors. You may even want to make a collection of nature superstitions that you learn when traveling around and meeting people from other parts of the country. Some people think that dragonflies sew people's lips together if they tell lies and others think there's going to be a hard winter if the woolly bear caterpillars have more black than brown on them in the fall. And, of course, everyone's heard that if a black cat walks across your path you'll have bad luck. So why not start a superstition collection just for fun and see if you can find out how some of them got started? For instance, there's a snake that farmers often found in their cow stables in the old days and they thought it was there to suck milk from the cows, so they called it a milk snake. But the truth is that the snakes come in barns to catch mice to eat and do not drink milk at all. But, silly as it sounds, you'll still meet lots of people who will tell you milk snakes stand up on their tails and suck milk from the cows. You may even hear about a hoop snake that is supposed to take its tail in its mouth and roll down the hill!

Now that you are beginning to realize that there's very little in nature *really* to be afraid of, let's find out what is *dangerous* that you could encounter on an ordinary field trip close to home. When it comes right down to facts, poison ivy is the most dangerous living thing you'll meet along the trail. Of course some people are immune to poison ivy and can wade through it without being affected. They may lose their immunity later so they should always be cautious. Others are very susceptible and may even end up in the hospital with their eyes swollen shut. But most of us are just lightly affected with annoying itching. Learn to recognize poison ivy in all its forms, even in winter, and then you'll be safe.

Poison ivy grows in many places, from lawns to forests, and may look like a bush or a vine, climbing trees and fences or creeping along the ground. Its leaves are made up of three leaflets that may be shiny or dull and toothed or plain. In winter, identify it by the buds and the grayish-white fruits which are present sometimes and are good food for winter birds. As a safety precaution, it's a good idea to wash with salt water or good old-fashioned laundry soap after a field trip. Then you'll be even less likely to break out with an itchy rash. You can't be looking in all places all the time you're out and there's always a chance you may brush against poison ivy and not know it.

Many people are afraid of all sumacs just because they've heard of poison sumac. Harmless sumacs have red fruits (most people call these "berries," but to a botanist they are "drupes"), but poison sumac has grayish-white fruits and only grows in wet places. With a little practice you can learn to recognize poison sumac, even in the winter when it has lost its leaves. You can do this by looking closely at the buds and leaf scars (places where the leaves were attached last summer), which are different from one variety of sumac to another.

Be wary of stinging nettles. They are common in some places and grow knee-high. If you walk through a patch of them with bare legs, you will soon feel very itchy and have little bumps all over your legs where the prickly hairs of the nettles touched you. If this happens, it's some comfort to know the itch does not last long. If you run into a patch of nettles early in the summer, put on your gloves and pick them. They are good to eat and lose their prickliness when they are cooked.

As for the other so-called poisonous plants, including poison hemlock, toxic mushrooms, pokeberries, Jimson weed and jack-in-the-pulpit, you'll only have trouble if you *eat* parts of the plants. None of these will hurt you if you touch or handle them.

Of course, there are different things to watch out for in different parts of the country. If you live in or visit places where rattlesnakes, copperheads and coral snakes live you'd better bone up on snake identification before taking off on a field trip. Scorpions, black widow and brown recluse spiders can cause trouble too, so if you know where they like to spend their time, you can stay out of their way. See Chapter 15 for more details on these creatures.

There are various ants, wasps, hornets and bees that bite or sting too. Some people are terribly allergic to insect stings and really have to be careful when they are outdoors. Often they carry antihistamines to use in case they are stung, or they may go through a series of injections which are helpful if they are stung. But most of us, by exercising ordinary caution and common sense, can enjoy our outdoor adventures without fear. Just keep in mind that most living creatures do not attack unless provoked and try to make your nature observations without bothering the animals you're watching!

Besides being afraid of or superstitious about live animals, many of us are afraid of dead animals as well. It's true that dead animals are not very cheerful to look at, but it's also true that you can learn a lot by taking time to make a few observations. Try being a nature detective and see if you can figure out what caused the animal to die. Was it old age, an attack by an enemy, a hunter's bullet or poisoning of some kind? Then look to see what forces of nature are working on the body to recycle it into the soil. An unpleasant odor means bacteria are doing their job of breaking down flesh whether the animal is a small insect or a large deer. Take a stick and turn the carcass over and you may see beautifully colored beetles and squirming maggots. Next time you see a dead animal, don't scream—just remember everything in nature dies sooner or later and, according to nature's plan, returns to the soil.

PART II

Plants

CO. SCHOOLS
C841515

CHAPTER 6

Trees and Shrubs

THE PLANT KINGDOM may not seem as exciting to you as the animal kingdom but if you take the time to become acquainted with some of the plants that you see every day, you'll find them fascinating. They're much easier to study because they don't move around. Though trees are very large plants and mosses are very small, they have some common properties such as their way of making food from air, water and sunlight using chlorophyll. Plants are vital to our chain of food supply. The plants that cattle, sheep and pigs eat eventually become meat for us. Let's take a brief look at plant classification before going into detail on some familiar groups.

Plant Classification

Botanists are continually studying plants and groups of plants, looking for relationships to help in classifying them. In different books about plants you will find differences in classification. But for our purposes let's divide all plants into four main groups. Notice that each group name ends with the suffix "-phyta" which means "plants" in Greek.

1. Spermatophyta (seed plants)

This group includes all plants which produce seeds so this is where oaks, maples, crabgrass, zinnias and most of the plants you know belong.

2. Pteridophyta (fern plants)

Ferns and their allies such as horsetails and club mosses are included in this group.

3. Bryophyta (moss plants)

Mosses, liverworts and hornworts belong to this group.

4. Thallophyta   Algae and fungi and other plants
   (thallus plants)   which do not have true stems, roots
                        and leaves are included here.

Trees

We'll start with the seed-producing plants since those are the ones most of us know best, and work our way down to the lower plants. Trees and shrubs are certainly the largest and easiest to find.

Any time of year is a good time to study trees, so locate one that interests you. You may only have to go as far as your yard, or perhaps to a park. Once you find a tree to learn about, stand back and take a good look at its general shape. Is it round or pointed, or Y-shaped? If it's winter, you may be checking out a tree that has lost its leaves until spring, or you may have picked an evergreen. If it is an evergreen, notice whether the leaves are needle-like or broad. If there are no leaves, you'll have to get closer and carefully look at the buds, the leaf scars and other minute details.

Tree watching is a great thing to do if you're waiting for somebody. For instance, waiting by a black locust tree in early summer when it is in full bloom can be a pleasant experience. The air is filled with the sweet odor of the flowers. Each flower looks like a little white sweet pea so you can tell right away that locust trees are in the pea and bean or legume family. And while you're close to a blooming locust you can pick a bunch of blossoms, take them home, dip them in batter and fry them for supper. After the flowers have fallen you can identify the tree by the little seed pods that form, the paired thorns on the branches and the furrowed bark. You might get another clue from a certain huge shelf fungus that only grows on black locust. Try to follow a favorite tree through all the seasons so you'll know it really well. If you study one tree you'll get to know it like a friend and you'll be able to spot other trees of the same kind in your travels. As you get to know your tree, you'll find out what kinds of birds use it for nesting or food or just resting and what kinds of insects it attracts with its leaves, flowers and fruits. Maybe you'll become interested in what its wood is used for and check the furniture in your home to see if any of it is made from the wood of your special kind of tree.

You may also see some mammals in or near your tree. Squirrels not only get much of their food from trees but sleep and raise their families in them as well. Chipmunks scurry around the bases of trees, often storing their food in holes higher up. Hollow trees make great homes for raccoons, who make scratches on the bark with their toenails when climbing up to their sleeping holes.

With some practice and the help of a good tree book you should be able to identify most trees in your area. If you run into problems, perhaps your tree is an exotic one from some other country. To identify foreign trees you'll need special help. Try asking a tree expert or put a twig, leaves and fruit or flowers in a plastic bag and send them to your city forester, state university, botanic garden or arboretum.

Getting to know trees can lead to many things. Besides learning a common name such as black locust, try mastering the scientific name, *Robinia pseudoacacia,* and finding out what it means. It's also fascinating to find out what trees are in the same family. For instance, once you've gotten familiar with the black locust, look for its relatives, the honey locust and the clammy locust.

Trees from other countries have many stories to tell. Some were brought back by early botanists who underwent severe hardships during their collecting trips in foreign lands. Their stories are real adventures. Even some trees native to the United States have mysterious stories connected with their history. For example, take the *Franklinia* tree named after Benjamin Franklin. Originally it was found growing along the Alatamaha River in Georgia by the Bartrams, early botanists from Philadelphia. They brought back some cuttings and in 1777 planted them in their garden, which still exists. In 1790 the trees were seen in Georgia by another botanist but after that when botanists went back to Georgia they could not find the trees and that's the way the story stands today. All the *Franklinia* trees today are descendants of the Bartrams' original plantings and even though it is a native tree it cannot be found in the wild. Amazing but true!

You'll run into some confusion as you track down trees. Let's take a look at three trees with Norway in their names: Norway maple, Norway spruce and Norway pine. The first two really come from Norway, but the Norway pine, also known as the red pine, comes from Norway, Maine!

There are many interesting things to notice about a sycamore tree but the bark is the most outstanding feature. In trees of any size, the bark is patchy with blotches of brown and white where the outer bark falls off. This sets sycamores apart from other North American trees unless you run into a planting of eucalyptus from Australia, which isn't likely to happen except in Florida and California. The young leaves are fuzzy and fun to feel. The flowers are little round balls, and inconspicuous unless you're really looking for them, but the fruits which hang on the tree all winter are well known to children. If you manage to get one of these balls down from the sycamore you can tear it open and set loose dozens of fuzzy seeds. The leaf shape may remind you a little of a maple leaf but if you remember that all maples have *opposite* leaves then you won't

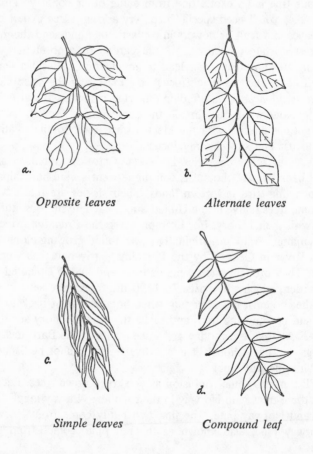

Opposite leaves   *Alternate leaves*

Simple leaves   *Compound leaf*

be confused, for sycamore leaves are *alternate*. In fact, most common trees have their leaves arranged alternately and only a few kinds have opposite leaves. If you remember the words "mad horse" you'll be able to figure out most of the trees with opposite leaves. These letters stand for *m*aple, *a*sh, *d*ogwood and *horse* chestnut. There are two more words to keep in mind if you want to understand trees and their leaves. These are *simple* and *compound*. Sycamore trees have simple leaves and black locust trees have compound leaves (composed of several leaflets). And if you want a tree that's foolproof try the ginkgo, which has fan-shaped leaves and originally came from China. Nothing else looks like it. If you decide to plant one in your yard, be sure you get a male tree, as the females have round, soft fruits with an unpleasant odor.

Tree study in the fall may get you started on a collection of tree seeds. Look for the winged seeds of maples and ashes; the acorns of the various oaks and nuts from hickory and walnut trees. The seeds of many evergreens are very tiny and hidden under the scales of the cones. Bring your cones indoors and let them dry a few days. Then shake them to see the delicate seeds fly out. You'll probably wonder how huge spruces or pines can grow from such tiny seeds.

To begin with why not specialize in one group of trees—the maples, for instance? Some maples are native to our woods and swamps and others, commonly planted, have been brought in from foreign countries such as Japan and Norway. Today in many housing developments a silver maple is planted in front of each new home. It will grow quickly and provide shade but in a few years will become so big it will dwarf the house. Then you may see the owners sawing down the trees and planting slower-growing ones. You can identify a silver maple by its deeply five-lobed leaves which are whitish beneath. Also, freshly broken twigs have an unpleasant odor. Remember that all maples have opposite leaves.

Another common maple is the red maple. It is native to the eastern United States as is the silver maple and is often planted. Its leaves are three–five lobed and whitish beneath but not deeply cut. The leaf stems, twigs and buds may be reddish but you will not get an unpleasant odor from a broken twig. The bark of the red maple remains smooth in old age while that of the silver maple tends to flake off. In the fall the red maple turns red, orange and yellow while the silver maple is usually pure yellow.

Norway maples are quite common on lawns and were introduced from Europe long ago. These trees are often planted along city streets too. The leaf is larger than that of the red or silver maple and turns bright yellow in the fall. One of the best ways to identify the Norway maple is by the milky sap which comes from the base of the leaf when you break it off the tree. One problem with this tree is that it produces many seeds which take root wherever they land so that you soon have many more Norway maples than you want.

In addition to the silver, the red and the Norway maples, one other, the Japanese maple, is commonly planted in yards. It comes in many varieties—some red, some green, some with finely cut leaves and others with shallowly lobed leaves. These maples are small and often have branches hanging down like an umbrella, making great hiding places underneath. The limbs of this very interesting tree grow in a curious twisted fashion.

Another popular type is the sugar maple. This is the most common maple in New England woods and of course the one from which maple syrup comes. Its bark, like that of the silver maple, becomes shaggy in old age and it has large, mostly five-lobed leaves with shallow notches between the lobes. It's fun to try making maple syrup if you have a sugar maple in your yard. You can even make it from other kinds of maples or other trees such as walnuts and hickories. An important requirement is freezing nights and thawing days. This happens in March in New England but may happen earlier farther south or never if you're too far south. See Chapter 25 if you'd like to know how to make the syrup.

If maples don't appeal to you try studying evergreens for a while. Decide on the narrow-leaved or broad-leaved ones so you won't be tackling too many at once. The narrow-leaved group includes many trees such as spruces, pines, firs, hemlocks and larches. The most common broad-leaved evergreens you'll probably find are some of the rhododendrons, the bull bay magnolia, many hollies and some privets.

Many people call all trees with needle-like leaves "pine trees." The first thing to learn is what makes a pine different from a spruce, fir, hemlock or larch. The most important difference is that on pines the needles grow in bunches of two, three or five. When you pull off one needle you get the whole bunch. Pines with five needles are white pines of one kind or another. The eastern white pine is commonly planted and also grows naturally in many places. Different white pines are native to the western United States and other parts of the world. The Himalayan white pine, with drooping clusters of needles, is a lovely one that you may see planted as an ornamental tree. White pines have long, slender cones.

In some pines the needles occur in bunches of two. The Virginia or scrub pine is an example. It makes a rather scraggly tree when many grow crowded together but a nice specimen if planted by itself out in the open. If you take a close look at a Virginia pine you'll probably see three sizes of cones, as it takes three years for the cones to mature and drop their seeds. A good-sized tree will have one-year-old, two-year-old and three-year-old cones. Out West some pines have cones that only open up when there is a fire. Unless the heat of a forest fire makes the

Rough bark of chestnut oak

Smooth bark of gray birch

Persimmons

Poison ivy-(note small fruits in center)

Smooth sumac

cones open and drop their seeds, no new trees of these species will grow. Some fires are started by natural causes such as lightning, others by careless campers, and others on purpose as part of forest management in certain areas.

Spruce and fir needles grow singly. When you pull a needle from a branch you only get one. To tell a spruce from a fir, check the spot where the needle came off. If a little stub is left, the tree is a spruce but if the needle pulled off some bark with it the tree is probably a fir. Spruces have square needles while fir and hemlock needles are flat.

When you look at a larch you'll notice two unusual things. One is that the needles grow in tufts and the other is that all the needles fall off at the end of summer. Only one larch is native to the eastern United States. It grows best in bogs and is also called hackmatack and tamarack.

Dead Trees

How do you feel about dead trees? Many people look upon them as eyesores and don't realize how important they are to many birds and animals. People who understand the needs of wildlife know that many special things are happening in, on and around dead trees. If there is any bark on the tree, many creatures will be living or hiding under it. Walk up close to a dead tree next time you have a chance and pull off a little strip of bark. Maybe a spider or a beetle of some kind will run out. And for everything big enough for you to see there will be many other little creatures too small to be seen without a magnifying glass. Look for different kinds of large and small fungi that will be helping turn the dead tree into soil. You'll probably see holes of many sizes. There'll be small holes made by beetles emerging from inside the tree after completing their life cycles; medium-sized holes made by woodpeckers looking for food; and larger ones leading into cavities made by woodpeckers for their nesting holes. These small woodpecker holes may eventually be used by bluebirds or wrens, which nest in holes but cannot chisel out their own. Bigger woodpeckers such as flickers, red-bellied and red-headed chisel out bigger holes and the pileated woodpecker makes a huge hole which is elliptical rather than round like the others. Holes are also used by sparrow hawks, barred owls, screech owls, great-crested flycatchers, tree swallows and unfortunately by starlings. The latter are so aggressive they often chase out the original maker of the hole and use it themselves.

Among the mammals, flying squirrels and raccoons use dead trees for shelter. If you find a hollow tree with nuts lying around the base, which have been gnawed from both sides, you're probably close to some flying squirrels. And if there's a trail of scratches going up the trunk to a hole, you've probably discovered a raccoon den tree. Red squirrels, gray squirrels and chipmunks like holes in trees too.

In addition to the insects you'll find *under* dead bark and living in dead wood, there are others such as the white-faced hornets who need dead trees. They chew off bits of wood and mix it with chemicals in their mouths. This turns the wood into paper for their nests. Holes in dead or partially dead trees are used by wild honey bees as places to live and store their honey. Many hours can be spent watching the activity at a bee tree—or in trying to find a bee tree by marking bees and following them to their home.

Dead trees are also great places to look for fungi. You'll find some fungi sticking out like shelves, others in cracks of the wood or bark and maybe some puffballs close to the ground. Once in a while you may find a slime mold which has oozed through the tree to the surface and produced its millions of spores, often brightly colored orange, red, pink or yellow.

Once a dead tree has fallen, there are still more interesting things to look for and watch. Mosses, lichens and more fungi appear, and through their growth processes eventually recycle the wood into rich soil. Various insects complete their life cycles in the log and under the bark. Seeds fall or are blown into rotting spots and begin to grow, so soon there are little nurseries for young trees and other plants. Rotting logs are excellent places to find some reptiles such as the worm snake.

If you like to sketch or take photographs, dead trees are excellent subjects. In some ways a dead tree reduced to its bare skeleton is artistically more interesting than one covered with leaves.

Most trees do not remain standing very many years after they die but there is one exception in the forests of the eastern United States: the American chestnut. Most of these trees were killed by the Asiatic chestnut blight around 1920 but today you can still find many standing upright in a walk through the forest. Oaks and other trees have grown up around them and the chestnuts are slowly deteriorating but becoming more interesting to investigate each year. The bark is gone but the wood is a lovely silver gray weathered by the rain, ice and snow. Where the wood has begun to rot it is a rich reddish brown. The chestnut trees do eventually fall over, the branches and trunks becoming rich soil, but often the roots still remain.

Try to think of dead trees not as things to be gotten rid of but as interesting subjects for nature study. Of course a dead tree that is a definite threat to cars, homes or passers-by should be removed. Try to keep an eye on a dead tree and make a record of the plants and animals you see when you visit it. Maybe you can find out how many years it takes for the tree to be completely returned to the soil.

Trees alive or dead can be never-ending sources of interest. Stand in front of your favorite tree for a few moments and try to visualize its root system. Often a tree's roots extend just as far below the ground as its branches reach above the ground.

Leaves on trees come in so many lovely colors, shapes, sizes and textures that they constantly inspire artists, poets and photographers. Leaf colors in the fall are beautiful and the many uses of leaves are fun to think about too. Jumping in piles of dry leaves is one way to enjoy them. Shredding leaves to add to your compost pile helps enrich your soil. You can even make crowns from maple leaves. Bay leaves are used in cooking, adding a special flavor to soups and stews.

Shrubs

It's hard to think of a definition for shrubs. We usually say they're small trees. But then, something that's small in the north may be bigger in the south. A helpful definition is "low woody plants that branch freely from the soil." Think of something you know such as forsythia and you'll get a mental picture of a typical shrub. Many shrubs both wild and cultivated are best known for their flowers and easily recognized when they're blooming. Others are valued for their fruit. Blueberries, for instance, are enjoyed by people and birds. People who enjoy watching birds plant various shrubs to attract them and are rewarded by many species stopping to feast on the fruits in the fall and winter.

Some shrubs are especially pleasing to the eye in winter because of their colored branchlets. The golden twig and red osier dogwoods are in this group. Other shrubs have interesting bark. Among these is the ninebark, with bark coming off in strips. The winged euonymus has corky ridges on its stems. In the dead of winter you can get a preview of spring by bringing in a few branches of various shrubs, putting them in water and forcing them to bloom early. Branches of some shrubs such as the spicebush have a very pleasant odor when crushed. If you take your penknife along on walks, try cutting small branchlets of shrubs to look for interesting shapes and colors of pith. Alders have triangular pith and the round pith of the silky dogwood is brown. Pith is the spongy material in the middle of the stems of most plants. It's usually round and whitish but when it is colored and/or a different shape it makes a good identification feature.

Many familiar shrubs are used in hedges where they are planted close together and clipped to a uniform width and height. Privets, barberries, boxwoods and even forsythias make fine hedges giving privacy to yards. Other shrubs are planted in hedges to provide food, shelter and nesting places for wildlife. Bush honeysuckle, multiflora rose and highbush cranberry are often used in this way.

Certain shrubs such as lilacs, weigelas, and spiraeas are old favorites and associated with houses built long ago. In modern developments low-growing junipers and dwarf arborvitae are frequently planted along the foundations of houses with colorful azaleas in front. Each of us has favorites among the shrubs and bushes we have known as we grew up. I like lilacs and yellow azaleas but don't care for blue hydrangeas.

The one shrub everyone seems to know is forsythia but even if you think you know it you have to be careful, as the winter jasmine is very similar. It blooms even earlier than forsythia, droops more and has greenish branchlets.

There are many other fascinating aspects of tree and shrub study. If you go mountain climbing in New England or out West and get above the tree line, or go north to the arctic tundra, you'll see trees and shrubs only an inch or two tall. And, if you're especially interested in finding good things to eat in the wild, learn about persimmons and papaws and the various edible nuts. Or maybe you are interested in wood. Some woods make better fires for cooking than others. Some fluoresce under ultraviolet light. Others are interesting because of their structure. Some kinds make good fence posts and others are better for whittling. There's something for everyone in the study of trees and shrubs wherever you travel and at every season.

In winter, study bark, buds and shapes of trees. Get to know the vase shape of the American elms that are rapidly being destroyed by the Dutch elm disease. Look closely at willows and see the little "pussies" (male flowers) waiting to emerge from beneath the single bud scale. Search for willows with curiously shaped twigs such as the fantailed willow and the corkscrew willow. These shapes show up best in winter when there are no leaves to obscure them. As spring progresses notice not only the new leaves but also tree and shrub flowers. The flowers on hazelnuts are most interesting. Long yellow catkins dangle at the ends of the branches. These are the male flowers and shed pollen onto the tiny magenta female flowers farther down on the branches. Just remember that all trees and shrubs bear flowers that you can find if you look at the right time. They may not be as showy as garden flowers in many cases but they are just as rewarding to discover.

Summer brings more surprises not only as leaves and fruits mature and trees and shrubs shoot up in height but as birds and other animals large and small make their homes. And of course when autumn arrives, no matter how well you understand how and why leaves change color, it's still magical. In West Virginia whole mountaintops turn red when the leaves of blueberry bushes less than a foot high change color. And in New England the sugar maples with oranges, yellows and reds almost make it seem that the hills are on fire.

Everyone has a favorite season but if you're trying to understand trees and shrubs there's something to learn all the time.

CHAPTER 7

Ferns and Their Allies

Ferns

FERNS AND THEIR relatives are full of surprises once you begin to look into their life histories. At first you may have trouble seeing ferns because they do not have flowers or fruits. But once you begin to look for different shades of green and interesting shapes of leaves, you will find many kinds of ferns and some plants that are closely related, like club mosses, horsetails, spike mosses and quillworts.

There's something lovely and peaceful about ferns whether you're walking in the woods, in a garden or within the glass walls of a greenhouse or conservatory. As a group they're easy to learn. In most places, there are fewer kinds of ferns than of wildflowers and once you know the important characteristics, separating the various kinds is fairly simple. Some, such as the cinnamon fern, are large—maybe as tall as a person if they're growing in a wet place—and some are tiny, for instance the maidenhair spleenwort, which grows in cracks in rocks. The Christmas fern is a good one to learn first; each of its leaflets or pinnae is shaped like a miniature Christmas stocking. It stays green the year round.

In the tropics there are many more kinds of ferns, including some impressive tree ferns similar to those that have been found as fossils.

In the city, you can see ferns all year long in the florist shops and you can even grow one in your living room—an old-fashioned Boston fern in a pot, or a little fern in a terrarium.

If you decide to master the local ferns, you'll soon be able to go for a walk in the woods and say casually to your friends, "See the pretty New York fern!" And then your friend may say, "It looks just like any old regular fern to me, how can you tell it's a New York fern?" Show your friend how the frond tapers at both ends, so he will recognize it the next time he sees it and add it to his list of nature friends. And then in early spring when you come to some baby cinnamon fern fronds unrolling, you can use the Socratic method with your friends. If they don't know the cinnamon fern, say, "See that woolly stuff on the fronds that are uncurling? It's the same color as a spice used in applesauce and cookies. And it has a wonderful odor." By this time, your friends will be guessing ginger, cloves and other spices. When they realize it's cinnamon you can explain that hummingbirds gather the woolly stuff and use it as padding in their nests. There are little tips about most of the ferns that you can learn and use when you're on a fern walk.

One of the most fascinating things about ferns is to find out where baby ferns come from. Some, such as the walking fern, can reproduce in two ways: by spores and by tips of fronds drooping over to touch the ground and producing new plants. This method is curious enough, but when you look into what happens when fern spores start to grow you'll really be amazed. First of all, you'll have to become familiar with spores; what they look like and where to find them. Ferns, mosses, club mosses, horsetails and fungi all produce spores and are called nonflowering plants. All the other plants you know such as daisies, maple trees, dandelions and violets are called flowering plants and grow from seeds.

When you start to look for spores, you won't find them on every fern frond or even on every fern plant. Check the undersides of the fronds for brownish or blackish spots that rub off easily. It may look to you as if there's something wrong with the fern. You may suspect the brown spots are little insects of some kind. But take a close look and you'll see that on each kind of fern the spore-bearing structures are of a certain shape and arranged in a certain order. The spore-bearing structures are called sori and may be round, crescent-shaped or linear and may be arranged on the edges of the pinnae or along the midrib. In some kinds of ferns, spores are only found under the pinnae at the ends of certain fronds. In others, whole fronds are brown with spores with no green pinnae at all. This is true of the cinnamon fern. In the interrupted fern in the middle of some fronds there are several pairs of fertile or spore-bearing pinnae while above and below these pinnae will be the ordinary green pinnae. In the grape ferns spores are borne in a separate structure looking like a small bunch of grapes which rises out of the middle of the frond or comes right up from the ground. Just looking for spores and seeing how different ferns produce them in different shapes and places can keep you busy.

You may think that when one of these tiny fern spores falls to the ground, or is carried away by the wind and lands in a favorable spot, it begins to grow into a new little fern right away. This is not what happens. It is much more complicated. And you'll need to learn some more new terms. "Alternation of generations" is one. This means that when the spore falls to the ground it grows into a little plant that doesn't look anything like a fern. It's called a prothallium and is tiny and heart-shaped. Eventually underneath, little structures grow which produce male and female cells. These unite and grow into a new fern. If you look very carefully in damp shady places in the woods and see baby ferns you may also find prothallia growing with them. Remember, they're small, only about one fourth of an inch across. If you would like to try growing some prothallia, collect some spores from a fern, spread them on damp blotting paper in a dish and cover with a glass in a warm place where there is some light. Keep watching and checking on the spores with your hand lens and in about three weeks you should see some prothallia. If conditions are just right for a while longer, you may even see new little fern plants growing from the prothallia.

There is much folklore about ferns—in the old days some people wore bracken fern in a little bag around their neck to keep them safe and some believed that a sprinkling of fern spores would make one invisible.

You can add vitamins to your diet by eating fiddleheads of varieties such as the cinnamon and interrupted fern. They're crisp when added to a tossed salad and also delicious boiled for about half an hour in lightly salted water.

Once you start on fern study, you'll soon find out that not everything that is called a fern or looks like a fern really is a fern. You may be visiting a friend who shows you her "asparagus fern." You may take a look at it and wonder why it doesn't look like the ferns you've been finding in the woods. The truth is that "asparagus fern" is just a variety of asparagus and is in the lily family. It blooms sometimes with tiny white flowers and eventually produces red berries. Anything with flowers and berries containing seeds cannot be a fern because ferns have spores and no seeds or flowers. Then too, you will come across plants that have leaves that remind you of ferns. Among these are Queen Anne's lace and yarrow. But when you find these you'll usually be able to see flowers or seeds or last year's flower stalks and know they're not really ferns.

Some ferns grow in ponds, floating on top of the water. These are small and really don't look like ferns but are fun to find.

Club Mosses

You may think you don't know what a club moss is, but you probably have seen some. The problem is that most people call them by other names, such as crowfoot, creeping Jenny, standing spruce and ground pine. Club mosses are primitive plants which in the days of dinosaurs grew as tall as trees. The kinds we have now are six inches high or less and in some areas have been nearly exterminated by people gathering them in large quantities for Christmas decorations. There are about fifty kinds of club mosses in the United States, so they make a small but interesting group to study. No matter where you live you can probably find some club mosses, as they grow in a variety of places from rocky, dry mountaintops to watery bogs. The shining club moss, found in damp places, is one that grows well in a terrarium. The most common club moss in eastern woodlands is the one usually called crowfoot. When you pull up one piece you're apt to get yards of it, as the stem runs along beneath the dead leaves on the forest floor.

Club moss x¼

Club mosses are primitive plants which grew as tall as trees in ancient swamps. (It is from the remains of these swamps that we now get our coal.) They are fern allies producing spores as ferns do and also having alternation of generations. Club mosses should be carefully conserved rather than pulled up thoughtlessly. Don't be confused by the fact that they are called different names in different parts of the country. The scientific name of this group of plants is *Lycopodium,* which means "wolf's foot." The spores of some club mosses were collected in the old days and used as flash powder for picture-taking in dark places.

Horsetails

Horsetails, like the club mosses, were tree-like in the Coal Age, 300 million years ago, and are also closely related to ferns. They are a curious and fascinating group and usually there are only a few kinds in any one area. My favorite horsetail is the scouring rush because it is useful as well as ornamental. It's tall (up to three feet), thin, evergreen and like the other horsetails, has a hollow stem and triangular leaves. Also, there is silica in the stem, making it very tough and scratchy to your skin if you break off a piece and rub it on your arm. Pioneers and modern-day primitive campers tie short (two–three inch) pieces of scouring rush in bundles and use them to scrub out pans. You usually needn't worry about using up the supply of scouring rushes, as wherever it grows it grows abundantly. All you need is one tall stem to make your scouring brush. Dried, this plant adds interest to flower arrangements. It grows in open dampish places often close to roads.

Another species, the field horsetail, grows along railroad tracks and in other rather barren places. When you find it you'll see how the name "horsetail" came to be, as each plant resembles a miniature green horse's tail. The plants that resemble green horse's tails are sterile. This means they do not produce any spores. Spores are produced by other plants growing with the bushy green ones. These are flesh-colored, about six inches tall and have a cone-shaped structure at their tips known as a strobilus. In the strobilus are many spores. After the spores have matured and have been blown away by the wind, these fertile plants wither and disappear.

Horsetails, like ferns and club mosses, have alternation of generations. They are fun to discover in rambles about the countryside even though, except for the scouring rush, they're not really "good for anything."

To get an idea of what horsetails looked like millions of years ago when they grew as big as trees, try to visit a natural history museum. In the Field Museum in Chicago you can see a replica of a coal swamp of the Pennsylvanian period with giant horsetails and other interesting plants in addition to some interesting animals. Many museums also have chunks of fossil horsetails on display.

Spike Mosses

The spike mosses or selaginellas are another group of fern allies. They are usually small, creeping plants not likely to attract your attention unless you're out especially looking for tiny green things. One grayish-green kind grows on rocks and is called the rock spike moss. Another sometimes forms solid mats on bare damp soil. So, if you come across some plants in your wanderings that don't seem to fit into either the moss, liverwort or club moss groups, maybe they're the spike mosses.

Quillworts

You are even less likely to find quillworts than spike mosses, as most of them grow in or under water. They are worth looking for because they are different in a delicate sort of way. While you're in a wet place, such as at the edge of a pond, gaze around for some plants that remind you of little onion plants. The leaves are narrow and stiff and spoon-shaped at the bottom. The spore-producing stalks have whitish knobs on their tips and make very interesting miniature dried bouquets.

CHAPTER 8

Mosses and Liverworts

Mosses

As WE WANDER through natural areas or those disturbed by man, we usually notice the biggest things such as trees first, and work down to the smaller wildflowers and ferns, finally to the mosses and liverworts which grow almost flat on the ground. They're so low, in fact, that most people miss them. Even if people do notice mosses they rarely try to see how many kinds there are or notice how they differ from one another. If you take the trouble to try to track down just one moss, you'll find that mosses are a wonderful group to study.

Bryologists (people who study mosses and liverworts) are enthusiastic about these plants for several reasons. First of all, mosses are the only group of higher plants to have the same species growing on all continents, even Antarctica. Two mosses that grow on every continent are silvery *Bryum* and purple *Ceratodon*. Among mosses these two are considered weeds, popping up in cracks in sidewalks and occurring as commonly as dandelions.

If you are interested in living in a healthy environment, check for mosses on the local tree trunks. Many species of mosses are very sensitive indicators of environmental pollution. When the surrounding air becomes foul, many mosses quickly disappear from tree trunks.

Mosses can also tell you much about the soil on which they are growing. Once you get into the study of mosses you will find out that certain ones are usually found in wet places, others on dry soil; some in shady spots and some in sunny spots; and still different kinds on acid, alkaline and neutral soils.

Most people have a pretty good idea of what a moss looks like. How would you describe moss? If you say "small, green leafy plants with spores" you're on the right track. But to complete the definition you should include "without true stems or roots and not having veins in the leaves." The life cycle of mosses also includes an alternation of generation slightly different from those in the ferns and club mosses.

Moss (actual size)

Unfortunately, most mosses do not have common names and the scientific names are often long and complicated. Some, though, are easy to identify and remember. There is apple moss with spore-bearing capsules that look like little green apples; and cushion moss which grows in clumps like fat sofa pillows; and hairy cap moss which has little cap-like covers of hairs over its capsules.

Sphagnum, a common moss in wet places is well known even to children because it's such fun to pick up a handful and squeeze out the water it holds. It has been called "mop moss" by some children because wringing water from it is much like wringing water from a wet mop! This is a good moss to start with as it's easy to find and has a fascinating history. During the First World War it was used as a sterile dressing for wounds. Some Indians used dried sphagnum for babies' diapers. Today it is used for growing plants, especially those in hanging baskets where it helps hold moisture. Peat, used commonly as mulching material, is made up of compressed sphagnum from ancient bogs.

If you find a moss growing where there has been a forest fire or campfire, it is likely to be the burned ground moss, *Funaria,* which is interesting as its stem twists and untwists in response to the amount of moisture in the air. The teeth around the opening of its capsule also open and close according to the humidity.

Once you begin to look for mosses you'll be amazed at the variety of places in which you find them. Often the shingles of old spring houses or sheds are bright green with flourishing mosses. If you happen to find an animal's skeleton in an old field where it has lain for a few years, there may be mosses growing on the bones. Mosses grow also on old antlers and hides and there is even one group that grows only on animal dung. A few live in the water totally submerged.

Have you ever seen a moss garden? In Japan, where space for gardens is scarce, moss gardens are great favorites. Some people in the United States have them too. There is something very peaceful about mosses in various shades of green growing around carefully arranged rocks.

The next time you see a moss, whether it's growing in a crack in the sidewalk, on a tree trunk or a stone wall or on bare dirt in a flowerpot, think how useful this group of tiny plants is: as ecological indicators; for making lovely gardens; to give evidence of air pollution; to help hold moisture in hanging baskets; and to cover up mechanical aids used in flower arrangements. As you go further into moss study you'll find many other ways these little plants have been or are used. Some groups of Indians have used mosses ground into paste for easing the pain of burns.

Have you heard that you can always find your way out of the woods by checking where the moss is growing on the tree trunks because it's supposed to grow on the north side? Well, this is just one of those sayings that has been passed down from generation to generation and the truth is that you can find moss on all sides of trees. Some of the green growth on tree bark is not moss at all—algae and liverworts grow there too. By the way, Spanish moss is not a moss but a flowering plant in the pineapple family.

So much for the mosses—just remember to look for them in a variety of places, take the strongest magnifying glass you have and have fun looking at different kinds even though you may not be able to identify them right then and there.

You may want to start a moss collection. For a live collection make a terrarium, putting in different mosses you bring back from trips. Keep it covered so the plants won't dry out. Of course, you can't keep mosses from too many different kinds of habitats in the same terrarium. If you keep your container wet enough for sphagnum, mosses used to drier places will mold.

To preserve your moss collection first dry all your specimens and shake off as much dirt as possible. Then make packets for each kind from sheets of paper. These can be filed neatly in shoe boxes. On the front of each packet be sure to put the date and place where the moss was collected and your name. Also, it is important to write down whether the moss was growing on rocks, bark or dirt.

For help in identifying mosses, first try books from the library. From these books you can get the names of moss specialists who are usually glad to help in identification. Also, don't forget there may be a bryologist (moss expert) in the botany department at your state university and that you can pack up a moss and send it to the Smithsonian Institution in Washington, D.C., to be identified. Don't forget to include all the important information.

Liverworts

As you spend more time looking at mosses, you will probably soon notice other plants creeping around in the clumps of mosses. These are interesting plants called liverworts. Many liverworts have only two or three rows of leaves. Others resemble narrow, flat green ribbons. True mosses are leafy all the way around the stem. These plants grow in some of the same places as mosses and are often mixed in with them and with lichens. Like some mosses, some liverworts grow in water but most grow on soil, rocks or trees.

If you get to the point where you can recognize a liverwort when you see one, you will have a great feeling of satisfaction. As you become more and more tuned in to nature and your powers of observation increase, one day you may spot a liverwort with little green umbrellas that

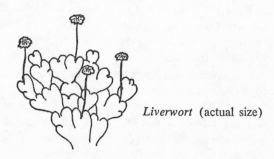

Liverwort (actual size)

are part of its reproductive cycle. Finding these in the wild is really a thrill. When you get down on your hands and knees as you often have to do to get a good look at these tiny plants, you may see some little animals creeping on and under them. These may be mites or tiny insects called springtails. They are just as fascinating as the plants they're climbing on and if you're looking at the scene through a hand lens or microscope it's fun to pretend you're on a field trip in a dense green jungle.

CHAPTER 9

Wildflowers

WHAT'S YOUR FAVORITE wildflower? If you're lucky enough to live in the country, you probably go to the woods early each spring to look for bloodroot, trailing arbutus, hepatica and anemones. A little later, on a trip to the same woods, you may see mayapples, violets and jack-in-the-pulpits blooming. Spring is the time when many people get excited about wildflowers, but there are some to be seen in summer and fall as well. And even if you have to take your nature walks in the city, wild things—including trees—bloom there too. Weeds bloom and grow wild so they also can be included. What may be a weed to you because it is a pest in your garden may really be appreciated by someone else who doesn't have any other blooming plant to admire. Many people hate dandelions, but there's nothing prettier than the golden carpet made by hundreds of them in bloom at once. When you're looking at a dandelion, pick one and notice that instead of one flower on the end of a stalk there are really dozens. There is a whole bouquet in what most people think is one flower.

If you've been used to thinking of wildflowers as only those rare, delicate woodland plants that bloom early in the spring, broaden your definition to include trees and weeds and even skunk cabbage. Yes, skunk cabbage does have flowers, although it is most well known for its huge leaves that give off an unpleasant odor when broken. In fact, skunk cabbage blooms even earlier than the traditional spring wildflowers already mentioned. Sometimes its purplish-greenish hoods can be seen peeking up through thin snow in January and a warm day may even bring out a few honeybees to gather pollen inside the hood from the numerous small flowers there.

It's very important nowadays to realize that wildflowers which were plentiful in the days of Henry Thoreau, John Audubon, Theodore Roosevelt and other early naturalists are fast disappearing. You can probably look out the nearest window and see why this is unfortunately so. There are more and more people who need more and more houses and apartments and more stores from which to buy food and other necessities. In order to supply the stores, more and more factories are being built and wherever civilization encroaches wildflowers are destroyed. At the rate things are going, it may soon be true that eventually the only place you'll be able to see wildflowers is a botanical garden or preserve.

Some people enjoy just visiting wildflowers in their season in the woods. If you go back to the same place each spring to see arbutus blooming, it's like seeing an old friend again. It's fun to make little notes in the margin of your wildflower book of the dates your favorite wildflowers bloom each year. Try to figure out why the bloodroot bloomed later this year than last. Nature is full of little mysteries, some of which are easy to solve. If you like to draw or use water colors, take your sketch pad along and see what you can do on location in the woods sitting next to a patch of hepaticas. Or take your camera and make a record with it.

Sometimes, it's fun to take a tape recorder along on a wildflower trip and just comment casually on the things you see as you wander along. This way, you'll probably have some bird songs and gentle breeze noises as background for your wildflower descriptions. Also, if you come to a flower you don't know, you can record a description of it on the spot which may help you in trying to track it down when you get home or to the library. This way you can identify the flower without destroying it by picking.

One thing to think about when you're exploring in the world of wildflowers is which color is most prevalent in each season. This isn't a very scientific pursuit but it's fascinating. Sometime you may be standing in a field, meadow or swamp and suddenly realize that almost everything that's blooming is yellow or blue or purple or white. For instance, in late summer or fall from one spot you may see several kinds of goldenrod, a variety of sunflowers, some jewelweed and agrimony, all with yellow flowers.

If you decide to specialize in just one group of wildflowers, you will have an interesting time trying to visit and/or photograph each member of the group when it's blooming. Many people decide to make wild orchids their hobby and since some orchids are very rare and many are very small, they spend years tracking down all the kinds that grow in a particular state. And there's always the chance you may discover something new. Orchids are a fascinating group to pursue. Some, such as the pink and yellow lady's-slippers and showy orchids, bloom in the spring; others such as the rattlesnake plantain and puttyroot, in early summer; and still others, including the purple fringeless orchid, in late summer. So this one group can give you something to look for in spring, summer and fall. And even in winter you can find the seed capsules of some of the sturdier orchids. A few orchids such as the Adam and Eve or puttyroot have leaves that last through the winter. Some are only an inch or two tall and others may be three feet high.

Violets are another group that's fascinating to study, especially in the spring. Did you know that besides various kinds of purple violets there are white violets, yellow violets and violets with various stripes growing in the wild? Some grow in the woods, some in swamps, others in yards or open fields. Violets may have two kinds of flowers; the colored ones that you notice and others under the leaves close to the ground that don't open up. These are called cleistogamous flowers. Very few people know about them, but they're easy to see if you look for them. Just lift up the leaves and you'll see short stems with greenish knobs on their ends. These are the flowers that never open. Open the knob and you'll find a pistil and pollen but no petals; or if it's late in the season, you'll find seeds. When the seeds are ripe the three-valved capsule splits open and the seeds fall out.

If you have trouble spotting the orchids and violets because they're small and grow in secluded places, try looking for some bigger plants. The great mullein is easy to see and very interesting to get to know. Even in winter you can find rosettes of fuzzy grayish green leaves growing in waste places and flat against the ground. These leaves feel like baby blankets. If you take out your magnifying glass and look closely at a leaf, you'll see that each hair is star-shaped, making the leaves feel fuzzy. With your fingers poke around in the middle of the rosette of leaves and you may see some tiny black insects—called thrips—keeping warm. Thrips, which often winter over in mulleins, are small but interesting creatures belonging to a special order of insects with feather-like wings. More information on thrips will be found in Chapter 16.

In spring a tall stem grows from the center of the mullein rosette and in summer yellow flowers appear. This flower stalk may be from two to six feet tall. After the flowers have faded and the seeds have developed, the stalks are sought by people who enjoy making winter bouquets. In the same places where the great mullein grows, you'll often find the evening primrose. Its winter rosette has smaller smooth leaves but like the mullein in summer, it has a tall spike with yellow flowers and in the fall an interesting seed stalk which adds much to winter bouquets. Just as learning to identify trees without their leaves can be fun, learning to identify wildflowers by the winter rosettes or old flower stalks can also be fun.

There are other ways to break down the huge field of wildflowers. Maybe you can become an expert on flowers growing in wet places, or keep a list of flowers you see each time you walk through the park. How about watching the local honeybees and keeping track of the flowers they visit at each season? If you are very quiet, you can get close enough to see the colorful balls of pollen each bee packs into little combs on its legs to take back to the hive.

Carnivorous Plants

While most wildflowers are admired for their beautiful blossoms, there are several plants people seek out because of the interesting ways in which they get some of their food. These are the insect-eating plants. One of these, the Venus flytrap, is often sold in stores as a novelty item and with a little care can be kept as an interesting plant in the house. It needs moisture in the air around it, so does better in a terrarium. If you want to see it growing in the wild, you'll have to make a field trip to coastal North or South Carolina.

Some of the flytrap's food is manufactured in the usual way by the chlorophyll in its leaves, but it also digests the soft parts of small insects which are caught by its leaves. These leaves act on the same principle as a steel trap: There are three very sensitive trigger hairs on the leaf. When an insect touches any two of these twice or two adjacent ones in quick succession the leaf closes and the insect is trapped. The leaf will open after a few days and the hard wings, legs and other indigestible parts will fall out. Enzymes secreted by the leaf digest the soft parts. When the Venus flytrap blooms, it has a delicate stalk of white flowers about six inches tall.

Another insect-eating plant is the pitcher plant. It traps its food in a very different manner. There are various kinds of pitcher plants throughout the world, but they all have leaves shaped more or less like pitchers which hold rain water in them. An insect landing on the lip of the pitcher-like leaf may crawl down into the leaf for a drink. But when it tries to crawl back up, it cannot because the leaf is lined with stiff hairs which point downward. The insect eventually falls into the water and drowns. Then the soft parts of its body are digested by enzymes secreted by the leaf. If you remove a leaf from a pitcher plant and empty out the water, you will find various insect remains and possibly some other interesting things. There is a kind of mosquito which lays its eggs in the water in pitcher plant leaves, so you might find baby mosquitoes or "wrigglers." There are several interesting pitcher plants in the United States, all growing in wet places. Although mostly noted for their leaves, they all have interesting flowers too.

Sundews also grow in damp, boggy places and digest insects, which they trap in still a different way. Their leaves are covered with hairs and on the tip of each hair is a drop of sticky liquid. Any insect landing on the leaf is trapped by this fluid and eventually digested by enzymes secreted by the leaf. Sundews have small white flowers.

In another group of insect-eating plants are the bladderworts, which actually grow in water and trap insects and small aquatic animals in little underwater bladders. Botanists are not certain whether bladderworts really use these creatures for food. Flowers of bladderworts are tiny and yellow.

Butterworts are small but curious plants with flat rosettes of leaves and white, blue or yellow flowers. A sticky digestive juice is secreted by the leaves so that insects landing on the leaves adhere to them.

There are other plants which have curious associations with insects even though they do not use them for food. One of these is the sleepy catchfly, an inconspicuous plant growing along railroad tracks and in other barren places. It has a dark sticky spot on the stem which traps any insect which happens to land on it. In another plant, teasel, the leaves on each side of the stem grow together, forming a pocket which holds rainwater. In these little pools interesting insects and other minute creatures have been found, but seem to be there accidentally and do not provide food for the plant.

Milkweeds

Milkweeds are an interesting group to follow through the growing season and into fall. First of all, when the new shoots are a few inches high, try boiling some as you would asparagus and serving them for supper. *Be sure* you're not cooking a similar plant called dogbane. It also has milky sap, but is more slender and not edible. When the milkweeds begin to bloom you may find some kinds with pink flowers, others with orange, some with white and some with greenish flowers. Often on the flowers you'll find a great variety of insects. There's a milkweed beetle that's red with black spots and which will make noises if you hold it up to your ear. There's also a red and black milkweed bug. A search on and under milkweed leaves may yield some striped yellow, green, black and white caterpillars which will eventually become monarch butterflies after spending some time as beautiful green chrysalises decorated with gold spots.

So, think about how our wildflowers have already disappeared in many areas and get out and enjoy them when you can. Remember, it's best to leave them where they are—many are delicate and droop quickly —others are very rare. Take pictures or make sketches instead of picking unless it's something as common as a dandelion or a daisy. Dandelions and daisies are beautiful wildflowers in their own right but many of us don't appreciate them because we haven't taken a close look.

CHAPTER 10

Weeds and Grasses

Weeds

HAVE YOU EVER stopped to think about weeds? Or wondered why some plants are weeds and others aren't? What is a weed anyway? You'll probably think of dandelions, crabgrass and plantains. But instead of naming specific plants that are pests sometimes, try thinking of weeds as plants out of place; or as plants growing where we don't want them; or as plants whose virtues have not yet been discovered. Then if you're really fond of dandelions you can call them wildflowers, and if your friends think they're ugly, they can call them weeds and spend lots of time keeping them out of their lawns. Who said a lawn had to be only one kind of grass? It's much more interesting to be able to find several kinds of grass, some dandelions, some violets, clover and other small plants when you walk around your lawn. Of course, you probably had better get rid of any large, stickery things such as thistles, though even thistles are lovely in a wildflower bouquet. Just let one thistle plant grow in an out-of-the-way corner and you'll have some flowers for bouquets without producing an excess number of seeds to invade the neighbors' lawns. Don't forget that goldfinches depend on thistledown for their nests and thistle seeds for food, so somewhere some thistles must be left to go to seed.

One nice aspect of weeds is that they're tough and grow in many places where more delicate plants cannot exist. So even if you have to take many of your nature walks near railroad tracks, highways or on cement sidewalks you'll probably be able to find a great variety of plants that most people call weeds. One thing that many weeds have in common, besides being numerous and growing in difficult places, is that they are natives of other countries. The dandelion, for instance, came from Europe; Japanese honeysuckle from Japan, and the *Ailanthus* (tree of heaven) from Asia. Sometimes while you are tracking down weeds to find where they came from originally, you'll run across interesting stories of how they happened to be brought to this country. At the end of this chapter there's a list of common plants from other places.

Many weeds are delicious to eat. If you have a garden, you may find that you have better luck growing weeds than the vegetables or flowers that you planted. So you might want to learn which weeds are edible. In many gardens purslane is common and makes a tasty snack when raw or a good dish of greens when boiled. Try chickweed and dandelions in tossed salads or as cooked greens. Lamb's-quarters is excellent and so is wintercress mustard. If you don't have a weedy garden, keep your eyes open as you drive along the road and you may spot a good source of free greens for your table. Much has been written about wild asparagus recently, but unless you know several spots where it grew last year you probably won't notice any this spring until it's too old to eat. Wild asparagus is really not a weed but a plant escaped from gardens. Birds enjoy the red berries and discard the seeds along fencerows and roadsides. It is native to Europe and Asia.

A native weed, poke, usually grows in large clumps. Often at one stop you can harvest enough for a meal plus some extra for the freezer. A good way to spot poke is to look for last year's dead, gray stalks bent over. Check around the bases of these and in season (May and June) you can find the new young shoots several inches tall. When cutting poke, be careful not to use any of the underground portion or the root, and return in a few days to get the new growth. Poke grows best on disturbed soil. If you locate a good clump, there are often others nearby and you may easily harvest and freeze enough in a season to last through the winter. Just use common sense: avoid the roots and don't pick the leaves and stems after they get a foot high. In some areas, people eat pies, jelly and wine made from pokeberries, but this is not good practice as the seeds in the berries are known to cause poisoning in some people. Leave them for the birds. Don't eat them yourself!

There are other common weeds that make interesting nibbles and pleasant additions to raw salads. Try the two sourgrasses. Neither is really a grass. One is an oxalis with three-parted clover-like leaves and yellow flowers, and the other, also known as sheep-sorrel, has spear-shaped leaves and is in the buckwheat family. There are good books on edible plants at your library. Also, try to go out with someone who knows what plants to look for in your locality and where to find them. *Be especially careful to avoid eating any plants or fruits from areas that have been sprayed.* Unfortunately, with the modern practice of spraying weed killers along roadsides, wild strawberries and other good things are often unfit to eat.

Grasses

You know that grass is green, needs to be mowed and is good for lawns and golf courses. Also, it's fun to walk barefooted on the grass in the summertime. But have you ever stopped to think about all the other ways grass is important to us? In some countries, such as India and China, many people live on rice, a member of the grass family. It is just one of the many grains on which we depend, others being corn, oats, wheat, barley and rye. Grains are the seeds of certain grasses and are used in cereals and breads. On farms, livestock eat fresh grass in their pastures; hay (which is dried grass) plus grain during the winter; and sleep on straw which is the stems and leaves of grasses left after the grain has been removed.

To make things sweet, we use sugars of various kinds. Most of these come from sugarcane, a large grass which grows in the South. The juice is squeezed out of the thick stalks and put through many processes before it looks like the sugars we buy.

Take a walk out on your lawn and see how many kinds of grass are growing there. Maybe you think it's all the same kind, but if you take a close look you'll probably see several different ones. Some grow in clumps and others creep along. Usually people like bluegrass and zoysia grass but don't like crabgrass. Crabgrass has a bad reputation because it creeps around and is coarse in appearance. Some grasses are especially good for lawns, some for hay, others for cereals and flours. If you live in the country, you probably know some other uses of grasses. Have you ever pulled out the top of a stalk of timothy to chew on the tender end? And are you one of those lucky people who can take a blade of grass between your thumbs and get a whistling sound when you blow through it?

Once you become interested in grasses, there are many directions in which to go. Try making a lovely bouquet of grasses when they're blooming in the summer and let them dry to keep all winter. Or press some grasses in an old magazine and make a pretty, flat arrangement under glass in a picture frame.

The largest member of the grass family is bamboo that grows in the tropics. Bamboo shoots are edible and have a variety of uses. People living in tropical countries where there are many kinds of bamboo make containers from it, use it for water pipes, fishing poles, fans, in house building and for skewers. In Malaysia there's a tiny bat that lives in the hollow stem of a bamboo. In the United States, there are some kinds of bamboo that are hardy even where the winters are cold. Several of these are very tall and vigorous and can even push their way into your house if you plant them too close! If you decide to plant a bamboo garden, do some research first so you can plant the best kinds for your part of the country and not end up with bamboo taking over your yard. Bamboo occasionally will bloom. This doesn't happen very often, maybe once every sixty years, but when it does it's very exciting, not because the flowers are showy, but because they're so rare. And if your bamboo patch blooms, you will know that all the other patches of that kind will bloom at the same time.

Some Common U.S. Plants
Naturalized From Other Parts of the World

Trees	Scientific name	Introduced from
Empress (also Princess) Tree	*Paulownia tomentosa*	Eastern Asia
Paper Mulberry	*Broussonetia papyrifera*	Asia
White Mulberry	*Morus alba*	Asia
Silk Tree (commonly in error called Mimosa)	*Albizia julibrissin*	Asia and Africa
Tree-of-heaven	*Ailanthus altissima*	Asia

Grasses		
Barnyard Grass	*Echinochloa crus-galli*	Europe
Bermuda Grass	*Cynodon dactylon*	Africa
Bristlegrass (also in error Foxtail)		
Giant	*Setaria faberi*	China
Green	*Setaria viridis*	Europe
Yellow	*Setaria glauca*	Europe

Brome Grass (also Cheat or
  Chess)

Hairy	*Bromus commutatus*	Europe
Japanese	*Bromus japonicus*	Eurasia
Silky	*Bromus tectorum*	Southern Europe
Couch Grass (also Quack)	*Agropyron repens*	Europe
Crabgrass		
Smooth	*Digitaria ischaemum*	Eurasia
Large	*Digitaria sanguinalis*	Europe
Dallis Grass	*Paspalum dilatatum*	Uruguay, Argentina
Goose Grass	*Eleusine indica*	Old World
Johnson Grass	*Sorghum halepense*	Mediterranean Region

Other

Bedstraw, Catchweed	*Galium aparine*	Eurasia
Bindweed, Field	*Convolvulus arvensis*	Eurasia
Hedge	*Convolvulus sepium*	Eurasia
Black Medic	*Medicago lupulina*	Eurasia
Buckwheat, Wild	*Polygonum convolvulus*	Eurasia
Burdock, Common	*Arctium minus*	Europe
Butter-and-eggs	*Linaria vulgaris*	Eurasia
Buttercup, Creeping	*Ranunculus repens*	Europe
Tall	*Ranunculus acris*	Eurasia
Caltrop	*Tribulus terrestris*	Europe
Carpetweed	*Mollugo verticillata*	Tropical America
Carrot, Wild (also Queen Anne's Lace and Bird's-nest)	*Daucus carota*	Eurasia
Chickweed, Common	*Stellaria media*	Old World
Mouse-ear	*Cerastium vulgatum*	Eurasia
Chicory	*Cichorium intybus*	Mediterranean Region
Cinquefoil	*Potentilla norvegica*	Eurasia
Cocklebur	*Xanthium pensylvanicum*	Eurasia
Corn Cockle	*Agrostemma githago*	Eurasia
Corn Gromwell	*Lithospermum arvense*	Europe
Corn Speedwell	*Veronica arvensis*	Eurasia
Corn Spurry	*Spergula arvensis*	Europe
Dandelion	*Taraxacum officinale*	Eurasia
Dock, Curly	*Rumex crispus*	Eurasia
Garlic, Wild	*Allium vineale*	Eurasia
Ground Ivy	*Glecoma hederacea*	Eurasia
Heal-all (also Self-heal)	*Prunella vulgaris*	Eurasia
Honeysuckle, Japanese	*Lonicera japonica*	Asia
Jimson Weed	*Datura stramonium*	Eurasia and Africa
Kudzu	*Pueraria lobata*	Japan and Eastern Asia
Lady's-thumb	*Polygonum persicaria*	Europe
Lamb's-quarters	*Chenopodium album*	Eurasia

Fern fiddleheads

Climbing fern-
(small fronds have
spores beneath)

Pods of common milkweed releasing seeds

Jack-in-the pulpit flower

Skunk cabbage flower with outside cut away to show interior

Japanese honeysuckle

Queen Anne's lace

Turtlehead

Mayapple

Joe-pye weed

Indian mallow fruits

Mallow	*Malva neglecta*	Europe
Mullein, Common	*Verbascum thapsus*	Eurasia
Moth	*Verbascum blattaria*	Eurasia
Multiflora Rose	*Rosa multiflora*	Eastern Asia
Mustard, Black	*Brassica nigra*	Eurasia
Wild	*Brassica kaber*	Europe
Yellow	*Barbarea vulgaris*	Eurasia
Oxeye Daisy	*Chrysanthemum leucan-themum*	Europe
Pepper Grass (also Pepper Weed)	*Lepidium campestre*	Europe
Plantain, Broadleaf	*Plantago major*	Eurasia
Buckhorn	*Plantago lanceolata*	Europe
Poison Hemlock	*Conium maculatum*	Eurasia
Prickly Lettuce	*Lactuca scariola*	Eurasia
Purslane	*Portulaca oleracea*	Western Asia
Ragweed, Giant	*Ambrosia trifida*	Europe
Sheep-sorrel	*Rumex acetosella*	Eurasia
Shepherd's-purse	*Capsella bursa-pastoris*	Southern Europe
Sow Thistle, Perennial	*Sonchus arvensis*	Western Asia, Europe
Spiny	*Sonchus asper*	Western Asia, Europe
Annual	*Sonchus oleraceus*	North Africa, Europe, Western Asia
Stinging Nettle	*Urtica dioica*	Eurasia
Teasel	*Dipsacus sylvestris*	Europe
Thistle, Bull	*Cirsium vulgare*	Eurasia
Canada	*Cirsium arvense*	Eurasia
Russian	*Salsola kali*	Central Asia
Vetch, Narrowleaf	*Vicia angustifolia*	Europe
Water Cress	*Nasturtium officinale*	Eurasia
Water Hyacinth	*Eichhornia crassipes*	South America
Yarrow	*Achillea millefolium*	Europe

CHAPTER 11

Algae and Fungi Including Lichens

ALGAE, FUNGI AND lichens—do these words mean anything to you? If I instead said "slimy green plants that float on ponds; toadstools; and reindeer moss," you probably would know what I'm talking about. Let's take a closer look at each of these three interesting groups of plants.

Algae

Those slimy green plants floating on and waving in ponds are algae. They have chlorophyll, and unlike fungi, they can manufacture their own food. If you're talking about one of these plants you say "an alga" with a hard *g;* but the plural is "algae" with a soft *g* and long *e* ending. Some algae are so small you need a microscope to see them and others are several yards long. The largest ones live in salt water and are called seaweeds. There are small algae in salt water too. We usually think of algae as being green, but there are also red, brown, yellow-green and blue-green kinds.

If you have an aquarium, you may think of algae as pests that grow on the glass and make it hard for you to see your fish—unless you have snails and catfish in your aquarium to clean up the algae. Agar that is used in laboratories where bacteria are grown is made from red algae that grow in the ocean. Some ice cream has an algal product in it. People who like to make their own original stationery use the graceful algae as decorations on plain sheets of paper. Directions for this project are given in Chapter 25.

Much of the green material that passes for moss on the trunks of trees is really a green alga with the interesting name of *Protococcus*. The most important value of algae is as food for all aquatic animals. Even the animals that don't actually eat algae themselves eat smaller animals that do feed on algae. These simple plants also give off oxygen into the water in the process of photosynthesis. The oxygen is essential to the fish and other animals in the aquatic environment.

A few algae are pests. Swimming pool owners don't want slimy green plants in their water and must constantly treat the water to keep algae from growing. In a special group, the dinoflagellates, there's an organism that causes a poisonous red tide and another that makes shellfish inedible.

The next time you see some algae think about their importance and also about the possibility that our modern land plants may have begun to evolve from green algae long ago. With the world population increasing and food supplies eventually decreasing, we may soon be eating many foods made from algae.

Fungi

The fungi are a fascinating group of plants but unfortunately there is much misinformation about them. For example, all mushrooms are fungi *but* not all fungi are mushrooms. As we look into the fungi, remember there are none that are poisonous to touch. Also, that you *cannot* tell which ones are good to eat by using a silver spoon or seeing if the skin peels off easily. Mushrooms, toadstools, puffballs, molds, ringworm, smuts and rusts are all fungi. They cannot make their own food because they do not have chlorophyll. This means both that they must get their food from dead or living plants or animals and that they don't have roots. The rootlike threads you see when you pull up fungi are called mycelia. Let's divide the fungi into four groups: slime molds, algal fungi, sac fungi and basidium fungi.

Slime Molds

The first group of fungi is made up of the slime molds. These don't sound as if they are beautiful, but many of them are. (At one stage in their lives slime molds can move and so resemble animals more than plants, which cannot move. In their movable stage slime molds *travel* through logs, stumps and wood chip piles. But when they emerge into the sunlight, settle down in fixed positions and produce millions of spores, they obviously belong to the plant kingdom rather than the animal kingdom.)

Slime molds are small and come in assorted shapes and colors. You can see them with the naked eye but will get much more enjoyment from them if you take a close look with a hand lens. When I was a little girl, I discovered a pile of old *National Geographics* in the attic and spent many rainy afternoons looking at the pictures. Especially fascinating were some pages that showed beautifully colored shapes two or three inches tall on stalks. Years later, I found out these were slime molds which in real life are only one fourth of an inch high or less! Slime molds have two stages. In one stage they creep along feeding on organic matter and can move right through a rotting log. The other stage is the spore-bearing one. In this stage the slime mold does not move. One common member of this group is "flowers of tan." You'll see it sometimes on the tops of old stumps or on an old pile of wood chips. When it has first emerged from the middle of the log or wood chip pile, this slime mold will be shiny, bright yellow and compact. In a few hours, however, the mass will have dried and the color will be lighter. When touched, the spores will appear on your fingers as yellow powder.

There's a lovely pinkish-lavender slime mold with the scientific name of *Lycogala epidendron*. This means "wolf's breath on a tree." It appears as tiny puffballs which disperse pink spores when touched. Other kinds are maroon, yellow and brown and always fun to discover. With your hand lens you can see that some are on stalks and some flat on the wood and that many have intricate networks surrounding the spores.

In a suburb of Shanghai, China, there is a botanical garden where slime molds are actually cultivated. They are grown on pieces of logs and when at their most beautiful spore-producing stage are taken into homes and admired for several days just as we treasure bouquets of flowers.

Algal Fungi

Algal fungi are all microscopic. On a field trip you're not likely to notice these tiny fungi but you may notice some damage they have done. Maybe you'll be taking a walk around a pond and see a whitish mass floating in the water. It'll probably turn out to be a dead fish covered with a type of water mold, one of the fungi in this group. Other members of this group are the downy mildews which cause blight in potatoes and tomatoes.

Sac Fungi

Now we're coming to a group of fungi that you'll know more about. Have you ever looked in the fruit bowl at your house and discovered a moldy orange, lemon or grapefruit? Well, those bluish, greenish or grayish spots are caused by fungi called penicillia. They are in the sac fungi group and were the first source of the wonder drug penicillin. Yeasts that are used in breadmaking and homemade root beer belong to the sac fungi also. If you've ever been interested in fungi that are good to eat, you've probably heard of morels. They're little brown fungi that look like sponges and appear only in the spring. In our family, we always set out to look for morels the first warm day after the first rain in May. Some years we find as many as a dozen and other years only one or two. Each veteran morel hunter has his own idea as to where the best places to look are. Some people say old apple orchards are best and that if conditions are right you can find a bushel. There's a town in Michigan that has a morel festival each year. Morels are very curious plants with a delicate flavor when cooked lightly in butter, and something to look forward to each spring. They don't grow at any other season and commercial mushroom growers have never been able to raise them.

Other sac fungi are the cause of powdery mildew on your lilacs and roses, and molds that grow on leather in damp places. The famous truffles, fungi that grow underground on the roots of trees, are in this group too. Trained dogs and pigs are used in France and Italy to find them and dig them up. You can buy them canned in gourmet stores, but they are very expensive. Some kinds of truffles grow in the United States but are usually only found by accident when you're digging for something else. Mushroom growers have tried to grow truffles commercially too, but have had no better luck than with the morels.

Another fascinating sac fungus is called *Cordyceps* and grows on dead insects. If you're digging worms to use on a fishing trip and dig up a lump with a stalk sticking out of it, you've probably dug up *Cordyceps* growing on a dead caterpillar or pupa.

Have you ever discovered some hard black finger-like things sticking up out of the ground? They were probably a sac fungus called "dead man's fingers." If you had felt around underground, you would have discovered they were growing on dead wood of some kind. You can also find them growing on dead logs aboveground.

Basidium Fungi

In our last group are the basidium fungi, including the rusts and smuts, jelly fungi, ear fungi, tooth fungi, pore fungi and gill fungi.

Rusts and Smuts: Two of the most noticeable rusts grow on blackberry leaves and mayapple leaves. You may have seen bright orange patches on the leaves of these plants and wondered what was happening. Rusts are parasites on the plants on which they grow and can cause much harm when they spread over a wide area on plants such as white pines or wheat. Some rusts need two different plants to grow on during their life cycles. Corn smut, closely related to the rusts, develops in and ruins ears of corn. If you've ever grown corn, you've probably seen a smut. It grows as a large, grayish boil on the ears of corn, and if left alone eventually bursts, throwing out millions of spores which are spread by the wind to other corn plants. The smut in its young stage is supposed to be edible. Eating it would be one way to make up for its ruining perfectly good ears of corn!

Jelly and Ear Fungi: Another interesting group of basidium fungi is the one in which we find the jelly and ear fungi. Have you ever been in the woods after a rain and noticed a dead branch with bright yellow globs on it? That's the lemon jelly fungus sometimes called "witch's butter." Another bigger, brown, jelly-like fungus growing on dead branches is the "Jew's-ear" and really does look like human ears. When the weather is dry these fungi shrivel and become hard, but when it rains they soak up moisture and become rubbery. These ear fungi are edible.

Coral, Tooth and Leather Fungi: As you walk through the woods in late summer or fall, keep an eye out for some fungi that look as if they should be growing in the ocean. These are the coral fungi, and they may be white, gray, lavender, cream-colored or yellow. Some have just one branch and others have several; some grow on wood and others rise out of the ground. All the coral fungi are edible except one white species.

The tooth fungi are very curious and have strange names such as "bear's-head" and "hedgehog." Some are quite large and grow on dead trees. As you look closely at one, you can see why it is called a tooth fungus. It is made up of long, pointed, fleshy teeth hanging down. It is on these teeth that the spores are borne. Some tooth fungi have the shape of a common mushroom with a stem and a cap, but when you look on the underside of the cap you'll see teeth instead of gills.

Have you ever found something in the woods that looked like a grayish-brown trumpet sticking up out of the ground? It is one of the leather fungi, called the "horn-of-plenty," and is edible, though not very tasty. Turn one on its side and you'll see that it resembles a miniature cornucopia. Thin leathery fungi growing on stumps and logs are probably stereums, although there are many varieties and they're not easy to tell apart. If you pick a thin, tough fungus off a log and can't see any holes or teeth on the underside, it may be a stereum. It'll give you a good feeling to be able to say that much at least.

Pore Fungi: Now for a look into the marvelous world of pore fungi—the ones with holes underneath. You can usually see these holes or pores without any trouble, but it helps to have a magnifying glass along.

The **boletes** are a group of pore fungi which grow on the ground and in which the pore layer is easy to pull from the cap. Several have yellow flesh and in some kinds the flesh turns blue when bruised. The "pine cone fungus" is a brown bolete with dark brown tufts on the cap. It is easy to identify though not very good to eat. Some boletes grow quite large—up to a foot wide, and can make excellent eating. *Several varieties are poisonous* so don't try *any* unless in the company of an expert.

It is difficult to get the pore layer of **polypores** away from the cap. Many of these fungi grow as shelves on tree trunks and can be called shelf fungi or bracket fungi. Where you find one you usually find several. Some polypores are delicious to eat and a few are foolproof as far as identification goes. One of the easiest to recognize is the "sulfur" or "chicken" polypore. When fresh, this fungus is bright yellow and orange so it's hard to miss as you're riding along or wandering through the woods. It can grow very low to the ground on a cut-off stump or fairly high up on a dead trunk. There is usually a large clump of it so you can get enough for a meal and even freeze some for later on. Cooking is simple—just slice thinly and sauté in butter. It is called "sulfur" mushroom because of its color, or "chicken" mushroom because of its taste.

Another polypore that's easy to spot is the "beefsteak" fungus. It's large, fleshy and pinkish-red but unfortunately not very common. If you do find it growing on an old stump, be sure it's in good fresh condition, take it home, slice thinly and fry lightly in butter for a real taste treat.

There are several polypores that attract attention because of their beauty. One of these is the small "turkey tail" fungus. It usually occurs in large numbers on old stumps or fallen logs. When the fungi are fresh, there are bands of lovely colors on their upper sides. With a little imagination, you can pretend the fungi are the tails of a flock of miniature turkeys. The "varnished ganoderma" is another attractive fungus—larger than the "turkey tail." Above, when fresh, it has a shiny appearance very much as if someone had just finished varnishing it. Underneath, it is whitish.

The "artist's fungus" is a prize to find—not because you can eat it, but because you can draw or write on the fresh white undersurface with a sharp stick or similar instrument, and make something that will be a personal treasure for a long time. If you find an "artist's fungus" when you're camping in an especially lovely spot, draw the scene on the fungus and take it home with you as a keepsake of the trip. You'll usually find them on fallen logs, but sometimes on upright dead trees. Often there'll be several of assorted sizes. You have to be very careful when getting them off the log so that you don't bruise the fresh white lower surface.

Some of the large, woody, tough polypores only grow on one kind of tree. For instance, there's one called "Cracked *Fomes*" that only grows on the black locust. You may come across a dead tree with the bark off, but still be able to identify it by the fungi growing from it. "Pine *Fomes*" grows on loblolly and longleaf pines and is important because the red-cockaded woodpecker usually nests in trees infected by this fungus. Another polypore is called the "tinderbox conch" and was used by Indians to start fires.

Other interesting pore fungi are the **daedaleas.** Underneath, instead of small round pores, are irregular openings. If you have ever studied Greek mythology, you may remember that Daedalus was the architect of the maze or labyrinth in which the Minotaur lived. One kind of *Daedalea,* called appropriately "oak *Daedalea,*" grows on old oak stumps.

Gill Fungi: Most mushrooms with which people are familiar belong to the group called gill fungi. The mushrooms in your soup or spaghetti sauce or on your steak are usually gill fungi. Gill fungi often have a stem and a cap. When you look under the cap, you'll see the gills. The spores are produced on the gills and can be white, brown, pink, purple or black. The color of the spores is one of the main ways used to tell the various kinds apart. Telling the color of the spores can be tricky because the color of the gills when the mushroom has just come up is not always the color of the spores.

The **amanitas** are an important white-spored group of gill fungi. Included in this group is the "destroying angel," the most poisonous mushroom in the world. It is pure white and beautiful to see, only causing harm if eaten. A piece the size of your little fingernail could be fatal. Of the sixty kinds of amanitas in the world only six are poisonous. All have white spores; a cap that breaks off easily from the stem; a fleshy ring around the stem; and a cup into which the base of the stem fits. One lovely orange member of this group was relished by Julius Caesar and so is called "Caesar's mushroom" today. It is very similar to the poisonous "fly *Amanita*." Years ago this mushroom, mashed and mixed with honey, was set out in dishes to attract flies. Flies partaking of the concoction became stupefied and so were easily killed. *DON'T EAT ANY AMANITAS!!!* It takes an expert to tell the edible species from the six poisonous ones. Pick them, admire them, photograph them and make spore prints from them (see Chapter 25) but *DON'T EAT THEM*.

The "honey" mushroom grows in clumps on dead trees and is good to eat, as is the "parasol" mushroom.

The "jack-o'-lantern" mushroom, which glows in the night, is bright orange, large and grows in clumps on old stumps. Unfortunately, it is not edible. You'll usually notice it in the daytime because of its bright color and large number of caps. Make a note of the place and try to come back after dark to see the ghostly glow. Not all clumps of the "jack-o'-lantern" mushroom glow, but it's a real treat to find one that does.

The "velvet-footed *Collybia*" is easily identified as it grows in clusters on old stumps. Touch the velvety bottoms of the stems when you find a clump. The name *Marasmius* belongs to some tiny fungi that shrivel when the weather is dry, but revive when it rains. There is a condition, marasmus, which sometimes occurs in babies who don't get enough love and attention. In spite of adequate food their bodies just waste away unless somebody takes the time to cuddle, rock and talk to them. Then they revive just as the little mushrooms do when it rains after a dry spell. There is also a "fairy ring *Marasmius*" that may grow by the hundreds in big circles. Other mushrooms do this too. When you discover a fairy ring of mushrooms, take time to think about it and how it happened. Long ago in the center of the ring there was one mushroom. It dropped its spores in a circle around it so the next year there was a small circle. With the same thing happening year after year the circle increased in size as the food supply in the middle was used.

The "oyster" mushroom is delicious and easy to identify. Look for large white gill fungi without stems growing on trees or logs. Several usually grow close together so you can easily gather enough for a meal while standing in one spot. They're best when fresh before they've been attacked by insects.

The **chanterelles** include bright yellow or orange, often fairly small fungi that make good eating. If you're cooking hamburgers or steak in the woods near a stream, you may see some of these bright mushrooms growing on the stream bank. They have shallow gills that run down onto the stem with dull edges. After you've learned to identify them, a few tossed in with your supper will add a delicate flavor. Either fry lightly or mix the raw mushrooms with your tossed salad.

Sometimes you'll see mushrooms in a lawn or pasture that look very much like those for sale in your supermarket. If you take a close look at these mushrooms and find that the gills underneath are pink, then they are the same as the ones you can buy. Commercial mushroom growers just raise different varieties of the wild "meadow" mushroom. "Meadow" mushrooms are good to eat and sometimes grow in such abundance that you can gather enough to freeze and can. This is a very common pink-gilled mushroom with a conspicuous ring below the cap. The very young ones just poking through the ground are called buttons and since the cap has not yet opened up you can't see the color of the gills. If you slice a button-stage "meadow" mushroom in half you'll see that the immature gills are white. As the cap expands, the gills turn pink and as the mushroom ages the gills turn dark brown. When the gills are still pink the mushrooms are at their best, so try to gather them then.

Another nearly foolproof group of mushrooms is the "inky cap" group. The largest of this group is called the "shaggy-mane." It has been known to come up in a variety of places including cracks in city sidewalks, but more often appears on well-manured lawns. In all the "inky caps" the white gills soon become blackish and slimy so it is important to gather them and use them when they're fresh. Ink really was made from the black spores of "inky caps" long ago. Usually you'll find a lot in the same place so even though they're small, you can get enough for a meal. Remember, though—*DO NOT EAT ANY WILD MUSH-ROOM UNLESS IT HAS BEEN POSITIVELY IDENTIFIED BY AN EXPERT!*

Puffballs: Puffballs are amazing fungi. The "giant puffball" can weigh ten pounds or more and is one of the largest of all fungi. Other puffballs may be only an inch or less in diameter. Any puffballs that you find which are white and soft inside are edible. Just peel, slice and sauté in a little butter and they'll taste much like the "meadow" mushroom. Do not eat any that are gray or dark-colored or hard inside as they may cause illness. The name, puffball, comes from the fact that as these fungi grow old the spores inside became mature and black and in some kinds a little hole appears on top. Through this hole the spores escape and are spread around by the wind. It's fun to find an old puffball on a fall or winter walk and step on it to make puffs of spores come out. Since every puffball contains millions of spores you can usually get several satisfactory puffs out of each one you come to. The large puffballs grow in open fields but there are many kinds that grow on stumps and logs.

Some specialized puffballs are called "earthstars," and look like miniature puffballs with starfish-like arms around them. The arms expand in damp weather and contract in dry weather, folding together over the little puffball in the middle. This activity results in the fungi moving about on the ground as the arms lose or soak up water. If you find a dried-up "earthstar," you can see this for yourself by dropping the fungus in a glass of water and watching the arms expand. When you take it out and put it on a piece of paper, draw a circle around it and check after it has dried. You may find that the "earthstar" has moved out of the circle. One way in which plants differ from animals is that plants do not usually move around, while animals do. So it's curious that "earthstars" move a little due to changes in their moisture content.

Bird's-Nest Fungi: My favorite fungi are the bird's-nest fungi because they're so tiny and such a surprise every time I find them. They grow on sticks, old wood chip piles, old rugs left outdoors for a long time and on old weeds, straw or mulch under other plants in the garden. There are usually many in one small area and they look like little cups with eggs in them. The things that look like eggs have spores inside. Each little "nest" is one tenth of an inch or less in diameter so you can see why most people do not know about bird's-nest fungi. Even if you know they exist, it's hard to find them without an experienced person to show you how to look. Once you've seen them you'll probably find them again because you'll be tuned in to looking in the right places.

Stinkhorns: I'm fond of another group of fungi too because I always find them with my nose! These are the stinkhorns—beautiful and interesting fungi with unpleasant odors! Once your nose picks up the scent you can usually walk right to the fungus. Many years ago when I was in college I found a strange egg-shaped object sticking up out of the ground. I had no idea what it could be so I took it to my biology professor, who didn't recognize it either but cut it open to see what was inside. By the end of the day it had started to grow and to give off a terrible odor! That was my first acquaintance with a stinkhorn. There are several kinds. All are fascinating and grow from egg-like structures. Some are brightly colored, red or orange, and others brown. Some are round and lattice-like and others several inches tall with spongy stalks and pointed or rounded tops. The spores are spread by flies which come to feed, attracted by the foul smell.

The last noteworthy fungi are the imperfect fungi. You cannot see them but you can see the damage they cause. They're responsible for athlete's foot, ringworm and the mildew that appears on clothes left in damp places.

Lichens

Now we come to still another fascinating group included with the fungi—lichens. First, each different lichen is made up of two plants. One of these is almost always an alga and the other is always a fungus. In this very interesting arrangement of living together each plant seems to help the other. The alga contains chlorophyll and so can make food which the fungus cannot. But the fungus makes water and minerals available to the alga and may also keep it from drying out. When you find a lichen and look at it you will not see two different kinds of plants. But if you have a microscope and make a cross section of the lichen, you can see a layer of algae just below the surface of the lichen and fungal threads intertwined. New lichens can grow from little pieces which break off and blow around.

Lichens grow in various places where there isn't much competition from other plants. Rocks, bare soil, tree trunks, stone walls and old fences are good places to look. Some lichens furnish food for caribou and reindeer; some are used in dyeing; and others are treasured as special additions to terrariums or Christmas gardens. Several varieties are used by wood peewees and ruby-throated hummingbirds in their nests. In recent years, due to pollution, certain lichens have disappeared close to urban areas and have therefore become known as pollution indicators. They do best where the air is clean and can be found high on mountains where other plant life is scarce. In tenaciously holding onto bare rocks, lichens may contribute by enzyme action to the process of breaking down the rock into soil.

Lichens are divided into three groups: crustose (crusty), foliose (leafy) and fruticose (shrubby). The crusty lichens grow flat on rocks or tree trunks and are difficult to get off. The leafy lichens are only fastened to rocks or trees in spots, and the shrubby lichens are branched like miniature trees. They usually grow up from the soil or dead wood, but some hang down from branches of trees.

When you set off on a lichen field trip, be sure to take along your hand lens so you will be able to see and enjoy some of the finer details of these little plants. A familiar lichen in the crustose group is the "pink earth" lichen. You can even spot this type from a slowly moving car, as it often grows on bare soil in roadcuts. The pink fruiting knobs are less than one fourth of an inch tall, but a lot of them growing together make a definite pinkish blotch along the road. This is one lichen that adds to a terrarium and is easy to collect. Another crustose lichen is the "script," "writing" or "hieroglyphic" lichen, so-called because it looks as if someone had made black ink marks on the tree trunk. There are some lovely orange, yellow and red lichens in this group too. They are often called "flame" lichens, as they look much like little spots of fire on the rocks from a distance.

Sometimes, the foliose lichens are easier to spot, as they stick up from the surface. One of these, the "smooth rock tripe," can be as large as one foot wide but is usually smaller. The "rock tripes" often grow in large quantities on rocks along wooded trails and are good to know about because they can be eaten in an emergency. You can boil them or fry them but they'll never really taste good. It's just comforting to know there's something in plentiful supply that will keep you going for a while in the wilderness. The name "rock tripe" comes from the fact that this lichen grows on rocks and resembles the portion of a cow's stomach that is called tripe and relished as food by some people. In wet weather these lichens are rubbery, but when it's dry they are thin and papery. The "shield" lichens form grayish green mats on trees and boulders. The "dog" and "lungwort" lichens are others of interest in this group. All lichens have scientific names but few have common names, so this can be a very frustrating group to study.

The lichens most apt to come to your attention are those in the fruticose or shrubby group which have brightly colored fruiting tips. The most well-known of these is the "British soldier" or "matchstick" lichen. It is also called the "scarlet-crested *Cladonia*" and grows about an inch tall, usually in clumps. Similar species have brown knobs. The red tips of the "British soldiers" are especially lovely after a rain and make a fine addition to your terrarium if conditions are not too damp. If there's too much moisture in your terrarium, your lichens will soon be covered with mold.

Another easy-to-identify shrubby lichen is the "pixie cup." This looks like a miniature grayish green ice cream cone. "Reindeer" lichen (often called reindeer moss) has been used for years by many people in Christmas gardens and ming trees. If you take a close look at a clump of this lichen, the branching will remind you of reindeer antlers. Reindeer feed on them in the Far North, finding them in winter by scraping holes in the snow with their hooves. "Reindeer" lichens and their close relatives are very brittle in dry weather but soak up moisture when it rains and become soft and spongy. Another interesting fruticose lichen is the "awl" lichen with little pointed spikes sticking up reminding us of the sharp instrument used by shoemakers in stitching leather. "Old-man's-beard" is the name given to lichens with many fine branches hanging down from trees. This lichen is used for nesting material by parula warblers in areas where their preferred Spanish moss does not grow.

Take a walk around your block or your yard and see if you can find any of these interesting little grayish green plants that are really two plants growing together. You should be able to find some on a tree trunk, a stone wall or rocks unless you live in an area where the air is very polluted.

Bacteria

When I was making discoveries with my first microscope years ago, I noticed some very tiny rods moving in the drop of water on my slide. Because I had soaked a handful of old hay in the water for a few days there were many interesting things living in it. An older friend who was a scientist told me the little rods were bacteria and that I might also find round and spiral-shaped bacteria. I was fascinated and kept looking until I found the other two shapes.

Bacteria make up a large group of microscopic plants. Some are harmful but many are helpful. The harmful kinds are commonly called germs and cause such diseases as tuberculosis, tetanus, diphtheria, pneumonia and scarlet fever. Many plant diseases are also caused by bacteria.

If you would like to see the results of some helpful bacteria at work, pull up a clover plant in your yard. Those tiny white nodules on the roots are filled with special bacteria that can capture nitrogen, thus enriching the soil. Other helpful bacteria are important in the making of yogurt, cheese, buttermilk and vinegar.

Even though we cannot see these tiny plants without a microscope they are important in our daily lives. Every time we clean our fingernails, brush our teeth and take a bath we are getting rid of harmful bacteria. There is still much to be learned from studying these little plants. One man I know wrote a Ph.D. thesis on just the kinds of bacteria found on shoes!

PART III

Animals Without Backbones

CHAPTER 12

Invertebrate Classification and Primitive Groups

THE MOST FAMILIAR groups of animals without backbones are insects and spiders. They are fascinating but before we discuss them let's work our way up in the world of invertebrates from the lowest (most primitive) group to the highest (most complex) group. Zoologists are continually studying animal classification and arriving at new conclusions as to how the groups should be arranged but they do agree that the protozoa (one-celled) animals are the lowest group and the echinoderms (starfish and their relatives) the highest. Following is a brief outline of the most important groups to help you understand the next few chapters. Animals are divided into groups called phyla.

Phylum Protozoa (One-celled and Usually Microscopic)

Phylum Porifera (Sponges)

Phylum Coelenterata (Jellyfish, Sea Anemones, Corals)

Phylum Ctenophora (Comb Jellies)

Phylum Platyhelminthes (Flatworms)

Phylum Aschelminthes (Rotifers and Roundworms)

Phylum Annelida (Segmented Worms)

Phylum Bryozoa (Moss Animals)

Phylum Brachiopoda (Lamp Shells)

Phylum Chaetognatha (Arrow Worms)

Phylum Mollusca (Molluscs)

Phylum Arthropoda (Joint-footed Animals)

Phylum Echinodermata (Starfishes, Sea Urchins)

Protozoa

The simplest animals at the bottom of the invertebrate ladder are those with only one cell. They are called protozoa and you may have seen some of them if you've ever looked at a drop of stagnant water through a microscope. They come in various shapes and sizes. Some move around rapidly in a drop of water and others move along slowly. Some are attached to tiny sticks or bits of leaves. One of these is *Vorticella*. When several vorticellas are grouped together, they look like a tiny bouquet of flowers on long stalks. At the top of each stalk is a little bell-shaped structure with fast-moving hairs which help the animal get food, mainly bacteria, from the water. When something bumps into or disturbs the vorticellas, their stalks snap back, coiling up like little springs. Soon they relax and stretch out again. This action is fascinating to watch. Another one-celled animal is *Amoeba,* amazing because it can change its shape. When it comes to something good for food, it just surrounds it.

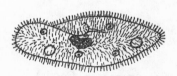

Paramecium x100

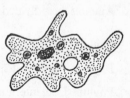

Amoeba x100

I was twelve when I got my first microscope. From then on, whenever I went on walks to the woods I always took along a little bottle and small dipper of some kind. If my friends and I came to an old stump with a hole in the middle containing water, we would dip out a sample and look at it under the microscope when we got home. There was always something interesting to see even though we often didn't know what we were seeing.

Another good way to get exciting things to observe under a microscope is to take a small handful of old hay or dried grass from a field or barn and soak it in water for a few days. When you look at a drop of this mixture you will often see slipper-shaped animals called paramecia.

Protozoa are easy to study if you have a microscope. Their food habits and ways of reproduction are different from most other animals. And you can keep hundreds of thousands of them in small jars ready for study whenever the spirit moves you.

Sponges

Sponges are the next highest group on the animal ladder, but you're not likely to find them on your field trips unless you're walking along the beach where their skeletons have been washed up along with shells and seaweeds. There is one family of sponges that lives in fresh water but they're usually small and inconspicuous—you aren't likely to notice them unless you're actually looking for them in a lake, pond or stream. They grow on rocks or sticks under water and sometimes are green because algae are living in them.

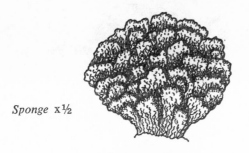

Sponge x½

Most sponges live in salt water and are not easily seen unless you're a deep-sea diver. Occasionally you may see some bright red sponges growing on pilings under a pier. They come in many colors, including black and white. Some are finger-like and others small and round, but they'll remind you of old-fashioned bath sponges. We don't even see many of these any more since men have learned how to make plastic sponges. It's interesting to remember that the part of the sponge we use is really just its skeleton. A live sponge is soft and slimy.

Jellyfish, Sea Anemones, Corals

Next we come to a very interesting group of animals with two layers of cells. Like the sponges, most of the members of this group live in salt water. The only coelenterates in fresh water are tiny creatures called hydras which are barely visible to the naked eye. Hydras have tentacles which expand and contract. In the tentacles are stinging cells which paralyze small worms, tiny fish or other water animals on which the hydra feeds.

Jellyfish, corals and sea anemones are the coelenterates that live in salt water and the ones that most people know about. Everyone who goes to the beach in the summertime hears about or sees jellyfish. And many neighborhood tropical fish stores have salt-water aquariums containing sea anemones. Coral skeletons are familiar as well. All the animals in these groups have tentacles like the hydras and inject poison into their prey. If you've ever been stung by a jellyfish, you know these

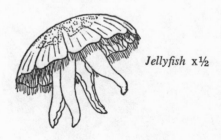

Jellyfish x½

amimals also use their poison to protect themselves from their enemies. Even though you just accidentally bump into a jellyfish while swimming, its automatic reaction is to inject its little poisonous nematocysts into your arm or leg. Have you ever heard of a huge, beautiful, blue jellyfish called the Portuguese man-of-war? It is blown about on the ocean by the wind and has tentacles underneath that may be sixty feet long. The stinging capsules on these tentacles can paralyze large fish and inflict serious injury to men.

If you have a piece of coral in your nature collection, take a close look at it and you will see where the little animals that made the hard limestone skeletons actually used to live. There are many kinds of coral with lovely names. Some have played very important roles in building up reefs and making islands. But they all, when they were alive, were covered with animals waving their tentacles about gathering microscopic food particles from the sea.

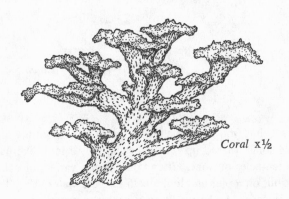

Coral x½

Unless you have the chance to take an underwater field trip in the ocean, you won't get a good look at living coral, but maybe you can visit a tropical fish store and observe some sea anemones in a salt-water aquarium. They really do look like flowers when nothing is bothering them and their tentacles are stretched out. They stay attached to rocks or shells or the sides of an aquarium and can be many pretty colors. When something bothers them or they are digesting food, they pull in their tentacles and scrunch up into rather ugly lumps. It is interesting to watch one of these animals and to remember they are relatives of jellyfish and corals.

Comb Jellies

Next we come to a very small but very interesting group of animals related to jellyfish, the comb jellies. If you live near or have visited the seacoast you may have seen them. Some are only a quarter of an inch long and others can be three feet long. Some have interesting common names such as sea gooseberries or sea walnuts, because of their shape and size. Comb jellies swim around in the water using eight rows of

short hairs called cilia. Many of these animals are beautifully lumines-
cent, shining in the water at night as they move slowly along.

Comb jelly x½

The next time you go to the ocean, keep an eye out for comb jellies.
If you see some washed up on the beach, they'll look like jellyfish with
only two tentacles or none. Often you'll find a variety of comb jellies
you walk out on a pier and look down into the water. They float arour
near the surface. Maybe you'll even be lucky enough to see some th
shine in the water at night.

CHAPTER 13

Worms and Other Curious Groups

Flatworms

THE NEXT GROUP of animals in order of complexity is the flatworms.
Maybe you've never heard of flatworms or realized that there are
different groups of worms in the world of nature. The ones you dig up
to use for fishing trips are segmented worms and there are others called
roundworms which we'll look into later. The flatworms are divided into
three other groups. In two of these groups the flatworms are parasites

living in larger animals. Flatworms in the other group are not parasitic and live in fresh water, salt water and on land, eating smaller creatures or dead organic matter. Sometimes you can attract some of these worms for observation by hanging a small piece of meat or liver in a stream or spring for a few hours.

Common flatworms in fresh water are dark and only about a half inch long. Under a good hand lens they have a cross-eyed appearance. Many experiments have been done with these animals. Some flatworms have the ability to regenerate; for instance, if one is cut in two, the head half will grow a new tail and the tail end will grow a new head. Some kinds have been trained to go through mazes to get food and to remember which way to go. If one of these "educated" flatworms is ground up and fed to another flatworm, then that flatworm is able to go through the maze to the food also.

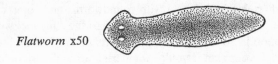

Flatworm x50

The parasitic flatworms, known as tapeworms, are quite a nuisance and can be very hard to get rid of when in a dog or cat. Some kinds even live in people. They have no mouth or digestive system but absorb food right through their body walls.

Roundworms

Roundworms make up another large group. Have you ever heard of hairworms or hair snakes? Well, in the old days farmers would find long, thin, dark-colored worms in the watering trough where their horses drank. They naturally jumped to the conclusion that these worms were simply long hairs that had fallen out of their horses' manes and come to life. What really happens is that the larvae of the hairworms develop as parasites in the bodies of insects such as grasshoppers. When they are mature and ready to emerge they often drop into the water as the insects come near drinking troughs, ponds or streams. Or perhaps the insects drown in the water and the hairworms emerge.

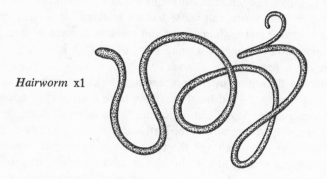

Hairworm x1

Nematodes are another group of roundworms. Farmers know about them because many kinds are pests on such crops as onions, cabbage and soybeans. Some nematodes are also serious parasites in animals. Cats and dogs can be infected with roundworms and some even parasitize people. You've probably heard of a parasite, the hookworm, that is quite common in soil in the southern parts of the United States. It can enter through your skin if you're wandering around barefooted. Modern medicines such as hexylresorcinol easily eliminate hookworm from human bodies. Since this parasite is associated with poor sanitation, higher standards of cleanliness help stamp it out.

Trichinosis is a much worse disease but also caused by nematodes called trichina worms. People can get it from eating pork which has not been thoroughly cooked. Trichina worms are so small that there could be one hundred thousand of them in one ounce of pork sausage! So never eat raw or partly cooked pork. The worms don't seem to bother pigs, who get them from eating infected scraps of meat, but can be very serious and even fatal in humans.

Earthworms and Leeches

Earthworms belong to a group called *Annelida* or segmented worms because all members of this group have bodies which look as if they were made of rings joined together. Most of us know earthworms though we may call them fishing worms, angleworms or night crawlers. They are valuable for several reasons. Many fishermen use them for bait and many birds use them for food. But they are most useful in letting air

Barley

Wild rye

Faber's bristlegrass

Smut on corn

Barnyard grass

Fungi on rotting stump

Puffballs emitting spores

Large earthstar

Curious fungi of the forest floor

Urn-shaped fungi on a lichen-covered branch

into the soil as they burrow around underground. They feed on decaying vegetation and are very helpful in compost piles breaking down old leaves, garbage and other organic matter into rich material for gardens. If you really get interested in earthworms you can spend a lifetime studying them. Some people have worked on them for years finding out much fascinating information about the way these worms are able to regenerate. As with flatworms, if you cut an earthworm in half, the head end will grow a new tail and the tail end will grow a new head. Researchers are trying to find out how the worms know to stop growing when they have grown just the right number of segments.

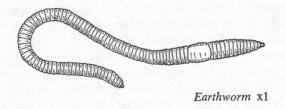

Earthworm x1

It's also interesting to find out that there are many different kinds of earthworms in the world. They come in various colors and sizes. The largest kind lives in Australia and grows up to eleven feet long!

Some other segmented worms called polychaetes live in the ocean under rocks or in tubes buried in the sand or mud. These sometimes have conspicuous heads with big eyes and antennae.

Leeches are also segmented worms. Some are scavengers, but the most well-known are the ones that suck blood. If you've ever found a snapping turtle and turned it over carefully, you've probably seen leeches attached to the thinner skin underneath. They also attach themselves to snails, fish and other water animals. If you go wading in a stream or pond for any length of time, you may come out with a leech on your ankle. When you pull it off, the spot may bleed a little but the injury is not serious. You may have read about how doctors in the old days actually put leeches on their patients to suck out "the bad blood" they thought was causing illness. If you ever find a leech, you might want to capture it and keep it for a day or two to watch. They can stretch out very long and then pull themselves up to be very small. Be sure to put a lid on your leech jar as they can climb right up the sides and escape. Also, be sure to have water in the jar so the leeches won't dry up. They cannot live unless they're in a moist environment.

Leech x1

Rotifers

Rotifers are not considered to be a very important group of animals, but since they live mostly in fresh water, you're apt to see them when you're looking for interesting things under a microscope. If you put a drop of stagnant water on a slide under the microscope expecting to see one-celled animals such as amoebas, you may also find a tiny creature that looks a bit like Mickey Mouse at its front end. He may be moving like an inchworm by attaching his tail end to your glass slide and humping his body along. The things on his head that resemble Mickey Mouse ears are two little wheels of cilia (fine hairs) which seem to whirl around constantly and direct food particles into the rotifer's mouth. Rotifers are more or less transparent so you can see everything that goes on inside them.

If you can't get out to a stagnant pond but have an aquarium, you can probably find rotifers if you scrape some of the green stuff off the sides and put it on a slide. Or, if you have a plant in a flowerpot that's been around for a while, just scrape a few particles from the bottom of the pot, add a drop of water and check it under the microscope. Rotifers are literally everywhere yet very few people know about them. They have the amazing ability to exist for many years in a dried state, but will revive and swim about as soon as they get wet. Many live in places that are only wet once in a while such as rainspouts, cracks in rocks and patches of moss. Rotifers have been spread over the world in their dried state by winds and birds. You can find the same kinds of rotifers in an African lake as in a North American lake, provided similar environmental conditions exist. Some live in colonies, some live in tubes and others float about on the water's surface, but my favorites are those that contract and expand like measuring worms as they travel about under my microscope.

Bryozoa

Have you ever heard of "moss animals"? Think back to the last time you took a walk along the seashore and noticed different kinds of algae or seaweeds washed up on the beach. Remember they were of different colors and some were bushier than others. The bushier-looking ones may not have been algae but might have been many little animals called bryozoans growing together. Their name means moss animals because some of them grow on rocks forming a moss-like mat. Each little bryozoan lives in a protective case and gathers food from the water by creating currents with its tentacles.

Brachiopods

The brachiopods are another little-known group. They are also called lamp shells and all live in the ocean. Many have been found as fossils from 500 million years ago and the amazing thing is that some of the ones we find today look almost the same as the fossils. They resemble clams, but are flattened from top to bottom rather than sideways.

Arrow Worms

Arrow worms are very strange little creatures with bristles on either side of the mouth. Sometimes huge numbers of them are present in the open ocean and look like transparent arrows chasing their prey. They are interesting to know about but you're not likely to find them unless you're out in the middle of the ocean.

CHAPTER 14

Shellfish

THIS very large group is called molluscs or shellfish. If you have a clam shell or oyster shell from the beach or snails in your aquarium then you have something from this group right in your home. And even if you don't have a mollusc shell at home, you could probably find one at the nearest tropical fish store where they sell them to give atmosphere to aquariums. If you don't live too far from the ocean you can buy live clams or oysters at your nearest supermarket. In the country or in a park, you may be able to find a snail or two under a rock or old log if you want to get a close look at a mollusc. Most molluscs belong to two main groups: gastropods, including snails and whelks; and pelecypods, which include clams, oysters, scallops and mussels.

Snails, Slugs and Whelks

You have probably seen several different kinds of snails in your yard or garden. Sometimes you'll find them on the leaves of plants and at other times you'll find them under old logs. These are land snails. There are also several kinds of snails in fresh-water ponds, lakes and streams. In Florida, there are beautifully colored tree snails. Sometimes you'll find just snail shells. You can make a collection of empty snail shells or use them as decorations in a terrarium or around a house plant.

Land snail x1

Slug x1

Have you ever seen a slimy creature stretched out to about four or five inches crawling along your sidewalk at night? If you watched closely, you may have seen that it had eyes on stalks just like a snail and left a shiny trail behind it wherever it went. Some people think these animals are snails that have crawled out of their shells, but they really are relatives of snails called slugs. Slugs come in a variety of sizes. In some areas, particularly in several western states, they are considered pests. Some gardeners kill slugs by putting salt on them, but if you only have a few slugs around, they are fascinating to watch and worth a trip around the yard at night with a flashlight to see what they're doing. Their two pairs of eyes on stalks can be pulled in when the slug is disturbed, but in a little while if you stand still they'll be poked out again. When you go to the ocean and find big whelk shells on the beach, remember they are relatives of your garden snails and slugs back home that have adapted to life in salt water.

Clams and Oysters

Pelecypoda, the second major group of molluscs, contains the animals with two shells, including clams and oysters. Most live in salt water, but there are fresh-water clams and mussels as well. Throughout the world many of these are used as food. Shells of molluscs are used for money and jewelry by many peoples.

Chitons

Another group of molluscs contains the chitons. These odd animals can be from one to twelve inches long and have shells made of overlapping plates. They cling to rocks along seashores and scrape off algae for food.

Squids and Octopuses

Squids and octopuses are molluscs too, even though you can't see that they have any shells. In squids, the shell is inside and is called a pen because it's roughly shaped like an old-fashioned quill pen. In octopuses, the shell may be missing altogether or just consist of a few small embedded bars. These animals live in salt water so you're not likely to see any unless you go deep-sea diving or happen to visit an aquarium. Sometimes you can buy packages of frozen squid in your supermarket. Let them thaw and when you're cleaning them for supper you can take out their pens, admire their tentacles and even see their ink sacs. To protect themselves they squirt dark fluid out of these sacs when they are being pursued.

CHAPTER 15

Animals with Jointed Appendages: Spiders, Millipedes and Crustaceans

You cannot help running into some animals in this group because about 80 per cent of all the animals in the world belong to it. Arthropods live in almost all possible environments including air, water (both fresh and salt) and land (including very hot deserts and very cold places such as Antarctica).

The first class of animals with jointed appendages, Arachnida, includes the spiders, mites, ticks, scorpions and daddy longlegs. All of these animals have eight jointed legs.

Spiders

Spiders, like snakes, are largely unappreciated in spite of the good that they do by eating flies, ants and other pests. Many people kill all spiders they see because they have heard that some are poisonous. The truth of the matter is that all spiders in the world (except for two small families) have poisonous bites but the jaws of most are too weak to penetrate our skin. The bites of the black widow and brown recluse can be very painful but rarely have been fatal. So if you learn to identify these two you can relax and appreciate the rest.

Spider x1

Black widow spiders build webs indoors, particularly in basements, and also out in fields. Some years they are more common than others. I remember one summer in my childhood when there were black widows under every pile of corn ears that we were loading into our big wagon out in the fields. No one was bitten and the spiders crawled off to find new hiding places as soon as we took away the corn piles. The bite of this spider may not be noticed at first but later the victim will have abdominal pain, swollen eyelids and pain in the soles of his feet. After several days of pain the victim usually recovers. Be wary of any shiny black spider about half an inch long with a red hourglass-shaped mark beneath its abdomen. The non-poisonous males are smaller, move around and do not bite, but the poisonous females stay still in their webs, biting if bothered. If you are bitten by any spider, try to capture it and take it with you to your physician.

The brown recluse spider does not build a web, is about one half inch long and may be recognized by a violin-shaped mark on top just behind its head. It lives in houses on the floor or behind chairs, sofas or tables, biting if it happens to get into clothes or towels people are using. The bite may cause no harm or become a deep wound which takes a long time to heal.

Try going out early in the morning to admire spider webs. You may not even see a spider but one can spend a long time marveling at strands of silk hung with sparkling dewdrops. If you find a fresh web and cannot see the spider toss a fly or other insect into the web. This will bring the owner rushing out to wrap up the prey with more silk. If you find a perfect web try collecting it to frame without harming the owner. For this project see directions in Chapter 25.

The golden garden spider is a common, handsome black and yellow spider you may see on a nature walk. It builds a large web two or three feet off the ground and waits for insects to become trapped. The jumping spiders are common too and great fun to watch. They're usually little, very hairy and often have a bright red or yellow spot on them. They live in places such as old birdhouses or empty mailboxes. Wolf spiders are interesting especially if you happen to see a female with all of her hundreds of babies riding on her back. Out West you can find tarantulas which are big enough to be frightening but are not very dangerous as they rarely bite. Some tarantulas in South America are large enough to catch birds and mice for food.

My favorite spider to watch is the spiny-bellied spider whose webs you often run into as you walk through the woods. These spiders seem to spin their webs at eye level right across paths. House spiders spin their webs in hard-to-reach corners of the ceiling where they can catch tiny insects that might be flying around your house.

Crab spiders are well-named, for they look very much like tiny crabs. Sometimes after you have brought home a small bouquet of wildflowers you're likely to be surprised by a spider exactly the color of your flowers. On goldenrod you may see a yellow crab spider and on daisies a white one perfectly camouflaged as long as they stay still.

Spider eggs are fascinating in themselves. Some are carried around in a little sac attached to the mother's abdomen. Others looking like a string of beads are held together by strands of silk and left hanging in the web in a tree. Sometimes on a winter nature walk you'll find a tan silken ball the size of a large marble hanging from a dead stalk. If you open it hundreds of baby nursery web spiders will come tumbling out, having already hatched from their eggs. But left undisturbed, the larger, stronger babies would have spent the rest of the winter eating their weaker brothers and sisters and then when spring finally came would have emerged from the egg sac to begin life on their own.

Many of us have fears about spiders because we don't understand their place in nature. If you're afraid just keep telling yourself that spiders are useful in controlling insect pests and providing food for other animals. They will not chase you and only bite in self-defense. If you find an unwanted spider in your house, try to resist the impulse to step on it. Just pick it up with a tissue and usher it outdoors.

Mites

Mites are tiny little creatures often found as parasites on large animals —one red velvety variety being particularly beautiful. Have you ever sat on a stone wall on a warm day in early summer and noticed lots of tiny red spots moving around on the stones? Well, these are mites and with your hand lens you can see that they each have eight legs, unless they're very young in which case they have only six. During the winter they hibernate in cracks and crevices. There is even a mite, only one fiftieth of an inch long, that lives in the hair follicles on people's faces. There are dozens of kinds of mites that are pests on plants as well.

Ticks

Ticks are just large versions of mites. Because of their bloodsucking habits they are parasites on man and various domestic and wild animals. Ticks, which spread diseases such as tick fever, are actually eaten by some native birds.

Scorpions

Most scorpions live in the warm, dry climate of the southern and southwestern states. By day they hide in crevices under bark, logs and stones, coming out at night to forage for insects and spiders. Scorpions catch their prey with their large pincers and use a curved spine at the tip of the tail to inject poison into their victims. Their sting can be fatal to children but is not dangerous to adults. Be careful in scorpion territory when in places where they might be hiding: they only sting in self-defense. The most dangerous scorpions live in Mexico, South America and North Africa. Those found in the United States are less harmful.

Daddy Longlegs

Daddy longlegs are not true spiders. True spiders have two parts to their bodies—a cephalothorax and an abdomen—as well as silk glands. A daddy longlegs just has one part to its body and has no silk glands. Other names for these little animals are harvestman and grandfather graybeard. They are completely harmless to people, though most people do not like having long-legged creatures walking on them. Just remember that daddy longlegs are useful because they feed on small insects.

Daddy longlegs x1

Centipedes and Millipedes

Because both creatures have a large number of legs, many people do not know how to distinguish between them. If you look closely you will see that centipedes have one pair of legs on each segment of their bodies, while millipedes have two pairs on each segment. Centipedes eat smaller animals; millipedes live on decaying plant matter.

Centipede and millipede x1

You're apt to find both kinds of animals when you pick up a rock or roll over a log. Most kinds are harmless but in the tropics there are some very large centipedes and millipedes with poisonous bites. The main thing to remember about these animals is that as they have jointed legs they are relatives of insects and crustaceans. In spite of their fearsome appearance they are in general beneficial. In fact, the most frightening-looking one you're apt to see is the house centipede which has the scientific name of *Scutigera forceps*. As you can tell from its common name, it lives in houses, where it performs a valuable service by eating ants, flies and other pests.

Horseshoe Crabs

These animals are not really crabs at all but very primitive creatures more closely related to spiders and scorpions. They are fascinating to look at and study because they are so primitive and have existed since ancient times without much change. We often find them during a walk along the Atlantic coast. Live ones are usually weak and dying, having been brought in by waves from their feeding grounds on the ocean bottom where they hunt for worms and shellfish. Horseshoe crabs resemble armored tanks with small eyes and long, sharply pointed tails. In spite of their appearance, they are not dangerous. Underneath are five pairs of walking legs and several pairs of leaflike book gills. They really do look like the pages of a book. When you find a living horseshoe crab, it usually has numerous hitchhikers, such as little boat shells, attached to it in various places.

You may find the empty carapaces (shells) of these creatures in your beach walks, for they are cleaned out by gulls and other scavengers soon after they wash ashore and die. An amazing phenomenon takes place annually when the horseshoe crabs, driven by age-old instinct, emerge from the sea to lay their eggs on the beach at high-water line. A bizarre sight occurs at this time when large numbers of shore birds follow along behind the mating pairs of horseshoe crabs and feed on the eggs after they are laid in shallow nests in the sand.

Crab, Shrimp, Lobster and Pill Bugs

This is a very familiar group, as we eat many of the shellfish in it. Most of them live in water but a few live on land. In salt water we find lobster, crab, shrimp, salt-water crayfish and barnacles plus many smaller kinds. In fresh water, there are very tiny crustacea such as water fleas and larger ones including many species of crayfish.

In general, the members of this group have two pairs of antennae, compound eyes and bodies covered by a carapace, which we usually call a shell.

If you have done much exploring in your back yard, you've probably found some land crustaceans under rocks or boards on your woodpile. They are little gray creatures, less than half an inch long, with ten legs. Some kinds curl up into little balls when they're disturbed. You may call them pill bugs or sow bugs but they're really not bugs at all. If you want to be correct, call them land crustaceans.

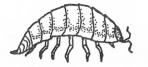

Pill bug x10

CHAPTER 16

Animals with Jointed Appendages: Insects

How DO YOU feel about insects? Do you automatically step on caterpillars and bugs without stopping to think of the parts they play in the balance of nature? Or even worse, do you reach for the nearest spray can of insect killer and fill the air with it without thinking that it might be dangerous to you and your family or to birds that might eat the poisoned insects? Of course there are some insects we'd just as soon never see in our houses and gardens, but there are also others which are very necessary to our lives. Without honeybees to help with pollination, for instance, we would not have fruits such as apples, peaches and pears.

Once you begin to study and appreciate insects a whole new world will open up for you. For instance, did you know there are more than eight hundred thousand kinds of insects in the world? This is more than all other kinds of living things combined. Let's take a brief look at the orders of insects from the most primitive wingless ones to the most highly developed. Generally speaking, insects have six legs, two pairs of wings and a body made up of three parts; a head, thorax and abdomen. Remember that some insects have no wings and some have only one pair. There are exceptions to every rule even in nature.

Silverfish

Now let's begin to take a systematic look at the groups of insects you can find if you know how and where to look. We will leave out the groups too small to be seen without a microscope. Have you ever gone to turn the water on in your bathtub and seen a small silvery gray insect running around in the tub? If you try to catch him, he's very quick and if you succeed in catching him you'll discover he's very delicate and will probably fall apart in your hand. This little creature is a silverfish and has a close relative called the firebrat. Living in warm places, they feed on starch in wallpaper, cloth and old newspapers.

Springtails

Next come the springtails. They're usually much smaller than silverfish, but when you find them you're apt to see thousands in a large gray mass on your lawn or sidewalk. Sometimes you'll even see them on the surface of a pond like a gray scum. Another good place to find them is under flowerpots you've had on the windowsill for a long time. Just lift up your pot and look for tiny things jumping around. They really do have a little "spring" under their bodies that they use to propel themselves into the air. Special springtails, called snow fleas, are one of the few insects to be found in Antarctica. Some members of this group may cause damage to mushrooms and tender seedlings, but most are harmless.

Mayflies

Mayflies are just one of the many groups of winged insects. These delicate creatures with gauzy wings often gather in huge numbers near water and are especially attracted to lights. Their eggs, laid in the water, hatch into nymphs which mainly eat plant matter on the bottom. In this stage the mayfly lives from one to three years. When it climbs out of the water, sheds its skin and flies away as an adult, it lives only a few hours. Another order called stone flies has a similar life history.

Dragonflies and Damselflies

Everybody knows about dragonflies—those curious colorful insects flying back and forth over fresh water, occasionally landing with spread wings. And some people have grown up learning to be afraid of dragonflies because they've heard things that aren't really true. In various parts of the country these beautiful creatures are called horse stingers, snake feeders, snake doctors and devil's-darning-needles. In reality they lead very useful lives, eating mosquitoes and other insects; they do not sting or have anything to do with snakes as the sayings go. We have learned from studying fossils that dragonflies have been around for as long as 35 million years. In prehistoric times some dragonflies had wingspans of two feet. The largest we have today measure seven or eight inches from wing tip to wing tip.

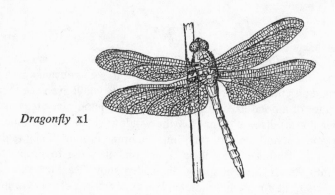

Dragonfly x1

If you have spent much time watching life around the edges of ponds or along streams, you have also seen slender green and blue dragonfly-like insects which hold their wings together over their backs when they are resting. These are damselflies and though smaller, just as beautiful and interesting as the larger dragonflies.

Like the mayflies and stone flies, dragonflies and damselflies lay their eggs in streams and ponds and pass their larval stages there. The larvae (also called nymphs or naiads) feed on smaller insects and insect larvae, and have a remarkable hinged lower jaw which they quickly thrust out to grab their prey as it passes by. As you walk around a pond in the summer look on tall grasses or the pilings of piers for the molted skins of dragonfly and damselfly nymphs and you can see how this jaw worked. Or if you spend some time scooping along the pond edge with a net or strainer and dump piles of mud on the bank, you will find live nymphs crawling out of the mud. Take a close look at their hinged jaws and other interesting features. Also look on the undersides of rocks in streams where some kinds pass their lives.

Dragonflies and damselflies have regular runs back and forth along the edges of streams and ponds and are fun to watch as they hunt for insects.

Termites

Even if you've never been to the country to see dragonflies, you've probably heard of termites, which do a great deal of damage to houses.

Termites are sometimes called "white ants" because they look similar and live in colonies as ants do, but they are not related. You may see termites with or without wings, but if wings are present, there will be four (two pairs) exactly alike. If you find an ant with wings, there will be one large pair and one small pair. Another easy-to-see difference between ants and termites is that termites have thick waists while ants have thread-like waists.

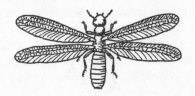 

Termite and ant x20

If you have had a termite problem in your house, you probably don't feel kindly about these insects, but if you just take one termite and look at it closely you can find out many interesting things. For instance, have you ever wondered how termites are able to digest wood? In their intestines are some tiny one-celled animals which break down the cellulose in wood, making it available as food to the termite. Termites can be found wherever there is wood. Sometimes you'll even find them under an old board that has been lying on the ground for a long time. And, if you break a piece off an old stump in the woods, you're likely to see them too. They don't like the light and will try to hide quickly. The ones with big heads are soldiers that guard the nest and there are many smaller workers as well. You're not likely to spot the queen, as she stays in the center of the colony laying eggs. Termite activities are amazing. They make little covered tunnels to get to the wood they want if there is brick, stone or cement in their way.

Grasshoppers and Their Relatives

Next we come to the insects with straight wings: cockroaches, grasshoppers, crickets, praying mantes, walkingsticks and katydids. Everybody knows about cockroaches and how hard they are to get rid of once they come to live with you! They eat practically everything and leave a disagreeable odor where they have been so it's hard to think of anything kind to say about them. But if you take just one cockroach and put it in a jar of flour, you will see that it spends most of its time trying to clean itself. Over and over again it will draw each long antenna through two feet to scrape off the flour. Besides the several kinds of roaches that are bothersome in homes and stores, there are others that spend their lives in the woods and never come inside. Keep an eye out for them when you're exploring under rocks and logs.

There are many kinds of grasshoppers living in many different habitats. Wherever they live they are well camouflaged. Along sandy beaches you may see sand-colored grasshoppers or if you're exploring an area with gray rocks, grayish grasshoppers will jump as you walk. The ones we see in grassy fields are a combination of green, yellow and brown. Grasshoppers have short antennae but katydids and crickets may have antennae longer than their bodies. They eat grass and can be pests in farmers' fields if they are too numerous. The crop-destroying locusts in the Bible were a species of grasshopper.

Did you know that there is a monument to a seagull in Salt Lake City, Utah? It was erected in honor of a flock of seagulls called Franklin's gulls who, in 1848, devoured a horde of insects that was about to destroy the Mormons' first crop of wheat. These insects were grasshoppers of the same kind referred to in the Bible as locusts.

The most curious creatures in this group are the mantes (also called mantises). The most well-known is the praying mantis, named for the

Praying mantis x½

way it holds its front legs up in a praying position. Of course, it's actually waiting for its prey—some unwary insect—to come along. Then it unfolds its front legs and grabs its meal. Praying mantes can be green or brown, up to four inches long and have even been known to grab at hummingbirds. Their long straight top wings cover another pair folded like fans. You may come upon them sitting on a bush or see and hear one flying through the air from one bush to another. Because of their insect-eating habits, mantes are highly prized by gardeners. The egg cases of mantes resemble little brown sponges fastened to the branches of shrubs. Look for them along the edges of roads and fields in the winter after the leaves have fallen. Snip them off and tie them to bushes in your yard. In the spring dozens of tiny baby mantes will hatch out and spend all summer growing while devouring aphids and other harmful insects in your yard and garden. Some enterprising people collect mantes egg cases and sell them by mail. So if you can't find any near you, look for an ad in a garden magazine and order some. There are hundreds of eggs in each egg case so even one will provide good protection for your garden. Of course, not all the baby mantes that emerge from the egg case grow up to be adults. Some are eaten by birds or even other insects. If you bring a mantis egg case into the house and leave it lying on a window sill, you'll be very surprised some February or March day to discover little crawling things all over the floor, furniture and curtains! If you want to watch some hatch, put an egg case in a jar with a piece of cheesecloth or screen on top and set it on the porch or other cool place where the babies will come out at their proper time when other tiny insects are available for food. Watch them hatch and then let them go in a bush. If they hatch in houses during the cold months, they're all doomed to die because their regular food, live insects, is not available. When this happens, the huskier baby mantes will eat their weaker brothers and sisters and finally die themselves. Mantes are such fascinating creatures that they've been drawn and painted by many artists who admire their large eyes, praying pose and lovely green color. Be careful if you should decide to hold one. They don't bite but can pinch with the sharp claws on their front legs.

Crickets are known for their cheerful chirps on the hearth or in the

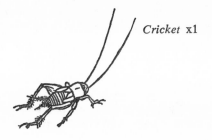

Cricket x1

fields on summer evenings. Did you know that you can figure out how hot it is on a summer night by counting the number of times a cricket chirps in fifteen seconds and adding forty? It's also amazing to find out how crickets sing. Only the males make sounds and they do this with their wings. On the underside of the upper wing is a scraper. When this is rubbed against a roughened area on the upper side of the underwing the chirping results. And if that bit of information astounds you read on! The female cricket listens to the song of the male with an ear that is on her leg! It's very easy to tell a male from a female cricket as the female has a long spear-like ovipositor on the end of her abdomen. She inserts this in the ground to deposit her eggs. For food, field crickets eat plant or animal matter and may even eat each other. If they invade your home they may chew holes in clothes but usually are not abundant enough to do much damage.

Tree crickets sing their shrill song on summer evenings in trees and bushes and can be white, green or brown. In the fall, female tree crickets lay eggs in the twigs of trees by puncturing them. These twigs may then dry out and split open, making it possible for fungus infections to get in. Where there are a large quantity of tree crickets damage may occur to trees and bushes.

The most mysterious cricket is the mole cricket. Though they're common insects, few people have seen one or even know that they exist, because these animals spend most of their lives underground. As a child, every summer I would find these strange things drowned in our pool. Finally I took one to the local biology teacher but even she could give me no clues. Years later in graduate school when I took a course in entomology I finally found out what they were. Even though they are insects, they resemble moles in several ways. First of all, they have a dark brown furry appearance due to the hairs on parts of their bodies; secondly, their front feet are well adapted for digging; and thirdly, you rarely see one above ground. Their eyes are sometimes greatly reduced. If you're digging for fishing worms in a swampy place, you may dig up some mole crickets. In fact, one of their favorite foods is earthworms so it's not surprising to find them in the same habitat.

Katydids are in another group which also includes insects called long-horned grasshoppers and green grasshoppers. Insects in this group usually have green bodies and antennae longer than their bodies. It is the males in this group that rub their wings together, producing the sounds we hear on summer nights. If you concentrate long enough, you can really hear the syllables "Katy did" and "Katy didn't."

Have you ever seen a small stick moving in the woods? Walkingsticks are long, thin relatives of grasshoppers and crickets and may be green or brown. Our native kinds are about four inches long, but in the tropics some walkingsticks reach sixteen inches. Since these insects cannot fly, they walk or run or leap to get from tree to tree. During the day, perched on branches, they may pull their legs and antennae close to their bodies and stay still. At night they move about feeding on tree leaves but don't do much harm unless there are huge numbers of them. If you happen to be in the woods as walkingstick eggs fall from the trees onto dry leaves, you may think it is raining.

Earwigs

There are several kinds of earwigs in the United States. The little earwig is less than a quarter of an inch long and in the northern states is sometimes attracted to lights at night. Another one, originally from Europe, is found under piles of seaweed on the beach at the high-tide mark. When you first see an earwig, you may wonder which end is the head. There's a pair of sharp-looking forceps on the tail end and a pair of antennae in the front but at first glance the forceps on the tail reminds you of the sharp jaws of some other insects. People used to think these insects crawled into the ears of sleeping persons, and that's how they got their name.

 Earwig x2

Another European earwig appeared in the United States in 1911 and has become a pest in many places because of its fondness for green plant shoots in the spring and various parts of flowers later in the season. It hides in any available crack or crevice during the day and comes out at night to do its damage. Sometimes it invades homes and hides under cushions and dishes and clothes, emerging at night to crawl over everything.

So, just as with the cockroach, one earwig is fascinating to watch but too many are a nuisance.

Book Lice

Have you ever picked up a book that hasn't been used in years and opened it to see holes in the pages and some tiny creatures wandering around? They are book lice. These insects usually look like whitish, brownish or grayish specks running across the pages. Due to their small size, they often go unnoticed and don't really cause much damage.

Biting Lice

These insects are called biting lice or bird lice and are small—from one twenty-fifth of an inch to one tenth of an inch in length. They live as parasites on birds and various other animals, eating particles of hair, skin and feathers. There is another group of lice that sucks blood. We'll find out about them later. Biting lice, wingless and small with large heads, are rarely found anywhere but on the birds and mammals on which they live. You may have been warned not to touch a dead bird because you might get lice from it. You needn't worry as the truth of the matter is that bird lice cannot live on people.

Thrips

Have you ever taken a walk on a cold winter's day and stopped to feel the woolly leaves of that common roadside weed, the great mullein? If you pulled the smaller leaves in the center apart, do you remember seeing some tiny black creatures about one fourth of an inch long? These are thrips spending the winter in a snug, warm woolly bed. Another place to look for them is in some of the shelf fungi, where you may see both black shiny adults and red baby thrips (and by the way, the same word is both singular and plural—one thrips or fifty thrips). Thrips, which have four fringed wings that look somewhat like tiny feathers, feed by sucking juices from various plants. The kinds of thrips found on farm and garden crops cause much damage. There are onion thrips, citrus thrips, gladiolus thrips and pear thrips, to name just a few of the one thousand six hundred known kinds. If you find your onion crop being ruined by thrips you naturally won't be very fond of these little animals, but if you use your hand lens to get a better look at some thrips spending the winter in a mullein rosette, you'll be astounded at the marvelous way Mother Nature has provided for her own.

Sucking Lice

Unlike the biting lice which parasitize both birds and mammals, sucking lice only attack mammals. Members of this group occur on people, monkeys, rats and mice, squirrels, elephants and even seals. They are all very small, wingless and equipped with sucking mouthparts. They feed by forcing two sharp stabbers through their host's skin, injecting their saliva into this wound and then pumping blood from the host into their bodies.

True Bugs

Many people call bugs everything that creeps, crawls or flies and has more than two legs. But if you want to be a good entomologist, remember that true bugs, besides having six legs, have wings that overlap at the ends. They also have a triangular plate between the bases of the wings. If you've ever seen a squash bug or a stinkbug you know what a true bug looks like. People with gardens may have the sad experience of going to check their squash plants and pumpkin vines only to find them wilting and dying with lots of little gray bugs running around on the stems and leaves. The adult squash bugs hibernate in cozy places for the winter, showing up in summer to lay eggs on the undersides of squash and pumpkin leaves just when they're at their best. When the babies hatch and stick their sharp sucking beaks into the plant stems to drink sap, the plant does not usually last very long. Squash bugs are an inch long and gray. If you only have a few squash plants, you can usually avoid catastrophe by keeping a sharp watch for the eggs and adults and destroying them as soon as you find them.

Stinkbugs can be brown or green and are more often smelled or tasted than seen. Were you ever in a raspberry patch stuffing luscious berries into your mouth when suddenly you tasted one that was horrible? That was probably one recently visited by a stinkbug.

Bedbugs are true bugs too and live on blood they suck from people rather than on juices from plants as some of their relatives do. With our high standards of living and cleanliness, we don't hear much about bedbugs in this country any more but they are still a problem in some poorer parts of the world.

Some bugs are beautiful. The lace bugs, for instance, are small but really do look like moving bits of lace on the plants where they live. Other bugs such as the harlequin bug and tarnished plant bug have lovely colors. Ambush bugs are interesting because they are carnivorous (capturing other insects that happen to visit the flowers in which they are hiding). One very large and curious bug is the wheel bug, so-called because of the structure on its back that resembles half a cogwheel. This creature can give you a painful bite by sticking its sharp beak into you, so if you happen to find one, be careful.

Many interesting members of this order live in or on water. Have you ever watched water striders skimming around on a pond or stream? These insects are called "water spiders" by some people, though they only have six legs (true water spiders have eight). It's hard to believe water striders are bugs, but they are. You may not have seen them fly although some of them do. The next time you see some on a sunny day, look at the bottom of the stream or pond where the water striders live. For each insect you'll see six shadows on the bottom. These are shadows made by the air bubbles on each of the water strider's feet. It is these air bubbles that hold the insects up as they skim around looking for smaller insects to eat.

Another interesting group of true bugs to watch are the back swimmers. They're small (about one half inch long) and really do swim on their backs! Their long, hairy legs are used like oars to push themselves around. Water boatmen are other insects that live in the same kinds of places as back swimmers, but they swim right side up.

If you're exploring along the edge of a pond and see a long, thin six-legged creature in the shallow water, you may think it's a walkingstick. It can't be because walkingsticks live in the woods. What you see in the pond is a true bug called a water scorpion. Because it looks like a dead stick that might have fallen in the water it is able to lie quietly on the bottom and capture smaller insects that swim by.

The giant water bug is also in the true bug order. You're more apt to find these bugs at night around lights to which they are attracted than in the ponds where they live. They can be two or three inches long and are broad, flat and brown. In the water they feed on other insects and even small fish.

Cicadas, Aphids and Scale Insects

After the true bugs comes another, similar group which also has sucking mouthparts. In addition, these bugs have wings which come together
like a tent over the abdomen. Included in this group are the large cicadas commonly called seventeen-year locusts, aphids, scale insects,
leafhoppers and treehoppers.

Even if you don't know much about nature, you probably know
about the seventeen-year locusts. Most people use this name for them
even though cicada is the correct name—their story is remarkable. The
baby cicada hatches from an egg its mother laid on a twig high above
the ground. The baby falls to earth and tunnels downward. There it
spends seventeen years feeding on juices from roots. In its seventeenth
summer the young wingless cicada crawls out of the ground, often making a little dirt chimney around its hole. Climbing up a nearby tree
trunk, it comes to rest. In a short time a slit appears behind the head
and out crawls an adult cicada with very damp wrinkled wings. At this
stage, the insect is very pale but as its wings expand and dry, color
comes into its body and it becomes a greenish creature often having red
eyes. Then, if it is a male, it climbs to a treetop and begins to "sing."
When thousands of these insects emerge in the same block the noise
they make can be ear-splitting for a week or two. During that time they
mate with the females attracted to the scene and gradually die off, some
being eaten by birds. People become excited about the seventeen-year
cicada and often don't realize there are other broods of cicadas with
shorter life cycles so that some emerge every summer. By the way, the
seventeen-year cicada has the longest life cycle of any insect known.

Leafhoppers and treehoppers are curious little insects of many lovely
colors and intriguing shapes. In the adult stage, leafhoppers move
quickly when disturbed so it is often hard to get a good look at them. In
their immature stage some of them are known as "spittle" bugs. These
bugs are easily observed, as they stay on certain plants inside little
bunches of bubbles made from plant sap which they have sucked up. In
these bubble houses, the insects are protected from being eaten by birds.
When they become adults they leave their "spittle" houses and fly to
various trees and bushes. Some people call these little white bubble piles
"frog spit" or "snake spit" and think that a frog or a snake really did
come by and spit! But the truth is much more fascinating. Just pick a
plant with "spittle" on it and gently poke the bubbles. Inside you will

see one or maybe more tiny green or brown baby bugs with dark eyes. They look a bit like tiny frogs and are sometimes called froghoppers.

Aphids in large numbers can do great damage to roses and other plants, but one aphid by itself is an amazing creature to observe. Once I was looking at my sweet potato vine on the window sill and noticed a little green aphid on the stem. While I was watching, a baby aphid, an exact miniature of its mother, popped from her abdomen and walked a little way down the stem. In the next few moments several more babies were born and joined their brother. Female aphids have the unusual ability of being able to reproduce without mating at certain times of the year.

There are thousands of different kinds of aphids. Many are known to be pests on various flowers and vegetable crops. Green aphids blend in so well with the plants they're on that they are hard to see, but often you can find red or black ones that show up well. Stalks of goldenrod often play host to red aphids. Take a close look to see aphids of many different sizes. The babies just stick their sharp beaks into the goldenrod stem and suck out juice for food. As they get too big for their skins, they shed them and emerge in new ones. You can also see aphids with lovely transparent wings. In some cases ants visit aphids, stroking their abdomens and drinking drops of honeydew the aphids exude. Another insect found where there are aphids is the ladybird beetle. Because these helpful insects eat aphids, it is a good idea to introduce them into your garden if you have an aphid problem.

Scale insects are just as much hated by gardeners as aphids, often becoming so thick on ornamental shrubs that the plants sicken and die. In general, there are three groups: armored scales, soft scales and mealybugs. There is one armored scale that looks like a little oyster shell and is called the oyster-shell scale. Others are serious pests on citrus fruits. Mealybugs can move about, whereas in the other two groups the insects are often degenerate (lacking legs so they cannot move). When you see a scale on a plant stem in winter, what you usually are seeing is the body of the dead female with the eggs under it. Ladybird beetles are natural enemies of these insects as well as of aphids.

Beetles

Now we come to the largest group of insects—one with which everybody is familiar. You can tell a beetle from other orders of insects by the fact that its top wings are hard and meet in a straight line down its back. Immature beetles don't look like beetles at all but are soft-bodied larvae with six legs. The ladybird beetle that can be such a pest and the Mexican bean beetle that can make lacework out of the bean plants in your garden are the most well-known. As in other groups of insects, any one beetle can make a fascinating study but large numbers of the ones that are pests may fill you with a desire to kill.

Everyone knows what a lightning bug or firefly is, but not everyone knows these are beetles too. Glowworms are actually the larvae of the firefly. You may see them on a summer's night shining in the grass and wonder why they're not flying. If you investigate, you'll find a wingless creature about one half inch long with a glowing abdomen and six legs, biding its time until it changes into an adult that can fly.

There are many kinds of ground beetles which usually hide under something during the day and come out at night to feed on smaller insects. Sometimes they're found in basements of country homes.

Tiger Beetles

You'll miss seeing tiger beetles unless you're very quick, but you'll know they're around when you hear something fly up noisily on a hot day as you walk along the road or near the sand. They like the sun and feed on other insects. It's worth trying to stalk one and get a good look at it, as they are brightly colored with metallic hues—blues and greens.

Water Beetles

There are many beetles that live in the water. One of these is the whirligig beetle, so-called because it swims around and around in circles on the surface of ponds and streams. They are fun to watch and will dive straight to the bottom when disturbed. If you can catch one, you'll find that it has a delicious apple odor.

Rove Beetles

Rove beetles are another interesting group. You'll often see them when you turn over a log or rock. They're long and slender with short wings which do not cover their abdomens. When alarmed, a rove beetle turns up the end of its abdomen and looks like a miniature scorpion trying to sting. In reality, they are harmless.

Carrion Beetles

Carrion beetles, as their name implies, feed on dead animals. They are very beneficial as well as being attractive to look at if you're not repulsed by the dead animals under which they are usually found. The background color of most carrion beetles is black, but they have bright orange, yellow and red markings.

Carrion beetle x1

Household Beetles

In another group are some common household pests such as larder beetles and carpet beetles. The former attack ham, cheese, beeswax and feathers left lying around in the pantry. A tiny black carpet beetle that sometimes appears in spring on the floors of older houses is the same as the Alexander beetle in A. A. Milne's famous poem. (Remember the little boy who had put his beetle in a matchbox and was upset that his nurse accidentally let it escape?)

Click Beetles

Click beetles are among my favorites because they can turn somersaults. They also make a clicking sound by snapping their head and thorax back and forth if you hold them up to your ear. The one usually seen is shiny and brown, but the most spectacular kind is the eyed elater. This insect is gray and an inch and a half long. On its thorax it

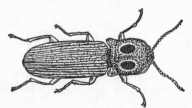

Eyed elater (Click beetle) x1

has a pair of false eyes which may serve to scare its enemies away. If you take a click beetle and turn it upside down on the palm of your hand, you'll probably see it turn a somersault. You can spend quite a while trying to figure out whether when it lands right side up it is heading in the same direction in which it was facing while it was upside down, or in the opposite direction. In Jamaica there is a very large click beetle with false eyes that glow in the dark. The larvae of click beetles are called wireworms but can be told from true worms by the fact that they have six legs. The larvae of some kinds of click beetles cause damage to crops by feeding on their roots.

Scarab Beetles

In the next beetle group are the scarabs, worshiped by the ancient Egyptians. The shiny brown June beetles appearing on window screens in late spring and early summer are scarabs, as are Japanese beetles. The larvae of these beetles are the so-called white grubs you often find when digging for fishing worms. Also in the scarab group are the dung beetles, which lay their eggs in balls of manure. To see a beetle rolling a ball is a strange sight.

Leaf Beetles

Next come leaf beetles, of which the Colorado potato beetle is one of the best-known. Many beetles in this group have yellowish wings with black spots or stripes on them, and many are pests on garden crops. The cucumber and asparagus beetles belong here. One curious beetle in this family, which isn't a pest, is the tortoise beetle. It is small and when alive has a golden color, looking like a miniature turtle.

Adult longhorn beetles are startling to see, as they are often large, with antennae longer than their bodies. Larvae of many beetles in this family do damage by boring their way around young trees, including many fruit trees. Woodpeckers help by eating the larvae.

The lady beetle family is made up of small but mostly beneficial creatures that feed on insect pests such as aphids and scales. An exception is the Mexican bean beetle, which feeds on the leaves and fruits of bean plants.

Darkling Beetles

Mealworms sold in pet stores as food for lizards are not true worms but the larvae of darkling beetles. Near the head of a mealworm are six legs, showing that it is truly an insect. On farms, mealworms are often found under feedboxes or grain sacks, where they feed on bits of oats, wheat and corn. If undisturbed they eventually become pupae and then blackish beetles about half an inch long. It is interesting to raise mealworms. All you need is an empty container such as a cottage cheese carton, some dry oatmeal, some slices of raw potato and a few mealworms to get things started. Keep the lid on with a few holes punched in it and check every day or so to see what's going on. As they eat, the mealworms get larger and in a week or so turn into beetles which mate and lay eggs. These eggs hatch into mealworms and the cycle repeats itself.

Snout Beetles

The snout beetle group is a large one that includes many pests. Its members do not really have long noses as their name implies, but rather have their mouthparts way out at the end of long extensions from their heads. The famous cotton boll weevil, immortalized in song, belongs here. One snout beetle I've enjoyed watching for years lives in hollyhock seeds. It's really a pest on hollyhocks, but the beetles are so tiny and comical to watch it's hard to be angry about the damage they do.

Engraver Beetles

Engraver beetles make up the final important beetle family. Have you ever stripped the bark from a dead elm tree and noticed interesting patterns underneath on the wood? Usually there's a main tunnel with several shorter tunnels coming off on each side. What happened here is that the female engraver beetle laid her eggs at intervals along the main tunnel which she chewed out. When the larvae hatched, each one chewed out a side tunnel of its own as it fed on the dead wood. After going a certain distance, it was full-grown, turned into a pupa and later chewed a hole through the bark and emerged as an adult engraver beetle. Some naturalists look for these natural engravings, cut them out carefully, shellac them and glue pins on the back to make lovely and unusual ornaments for themselves and their friends. Engraver beetles living on elm trees carry the deadly Dutch elm fungus disease that is wiping out the American elm.

Nerve-winged Insects

After beetles, the next order of insects is called Neuroptera or nerve-winged insects. Their wings are transparent and covered with a fine network of veins. The lacewing, a lovely pale green creature with golden eyes, belongs to this group as does the fisherman's favorite bait, the hellgrammite. The hellgrammite, in case you've never seen one, is two or three inches long, black and ugly and lives under rocks in streams. It is the larva of a large insect called a dobson fly, which you may see some summer night near a lamppost. Another famous member of this group is the ant lion. These small larvae have sharp jaws and hide in the bottom of little pits they make in dry dirt. When an ant comes along and falls into the little pit, the ant lion grabs it with its sharp jaws. There are many country people who know these creatures by such names as "yooey bug" or "doodlebug." They can take you to one of these pits and call "yooey, yooey, yooey" and sure enough, you may see some activity at the bottom. Even though the country people will tell you that these insects come when called, the movement is probably caused by vibrations in the ground which make the ant lion think some ants have fallen into his trap. After eating enough ants, these larvae turn into adults with four lacy wings.

Caddis Flies

In the next group, the caddis flies, the adults resemble small moths while the larvae look like caterpillars spending their days on stream bottoms. Caddis fly larvae are marvelous architects and begin to build their homes as soon as they hatch. Some kinds use grains of sand cemented together to make little cases to live in; others use bits of old leaves; still other types use pieces of small sticks or old veins of leaves to build log cabin-type homes. Some caddis fly larvae fasten their cases to the undersides of rocks in the stream and others can move around in their cases. They stick their heads out to feed and pull them back into their cases when danger threatens. When the larva is full-grown, it forms a door of sorts across the opening of its case and spends some time as a pupa.

After the adult caddis fly emerges from the pupal stage, it swims to the surface, holds onto a rock or plant sticking out of the water long enough to dry its wings and then flies off. The next time you have a chance to explore an unpolluted stream, look for these interesting little creatures.

Scaly-winged Insects

Next we come to a huge group, the moths and butterflies, which are actually insects with scaly wings. When you see a moth or butterfly, do you always remember that it used to be a caterpillar? Some people love moths and butterflies for their beauty and graceful flight but can't stand caterpillars.

Caterpillars

How do *you* feel about caterpillars? Do you dislike the sight of them and try to get rid of one as soon as you see it? Or do you look upon it as another of nature's endless wonders and take the time to admire its decorations and colors, watching to see how and what it eats; how it spins its cocoon or makes its chrysalis? Think back to what a caterpillar used to be—a tiny egg laid on just the right kind of leaf. And how it has grown by eating lots of those leaves and shedding its skin several times as it grew. If the caterpillar you watch is a tent caterpillar, you can think how it spent all winter as an egg in a shiny waterproof cluster of eggs on a twig, emerging only when spring came and the leaves on the cherry and apple trees it needed to eat began to grow. Other caterpillars may spend only a week or two as eggs before they hatch and then after eating their fill over the summer may spend the winter in snug silk cocoons rolled up in leaves or hanging from twigs.

Some caterpillars are so numerous that they are detrimental and can completely defoliate a forest if left unchecked. The gypsy moth caterpillar is one of these. Another familiar caterpillar pest is the larva of the clothes moth which eats holes in your woolens. But most of the caterpillars you see on casual nature walks munching away on leaves or crawling across your path are harmless and fascinating creatures to watch. There are some with irritating hairs so be very careful which you handle. Sometimes you'll see tiny greenish caterpillars hanging by long silk threads from trees and swaying back and forth in the breeze. Or you may find an inchworm creeping along your arm, hunching its back as it goes.

Caterpillars make good food for many birds and some of them eat weeds which are pests. Don't forget that silk is made by special caterpillars which feed on mulberry leaves in China and Japan. We have some relatives of the true silkworm here in the United States. One of them, the hickory horned devil, is truly spectacular to see. If you find one, you may think you've come upon a miniature Chinese dragon. These caterpillars are green or bluish green and can be up to six inches long with several orange spiny horns up front. In spite of their fearsome appearance, they are harmless, eating nothing but leaves of trees such as hickory, walnut and sweet gum. After eating their fill, these caterpillars tunnel into the ground for the winter and transform into shiny black pupae. In the summer large, beautiful moths called royal walnut moths emerge. They are tan with lavender and yellow markings. Another impressive caterpillar is that of the Cecropia moth. It is also green but has red, blue and yellow knobs on it. Its cocoon is made of tough tan silk and is fastened to a twig lengthwise. The moth which emerges in the spring is large and brown with beautiful designs in various colors on its wings and abdomen.

I'm sure you've heard people calling caterpillars worms because they're long, thin and wriggly. But if you remember that caterpillars are the larvae of moths and butterflies, insects with six legs, you won't get confused. In caterpillars, the six legs, usually small and dark, are up front near the head. Caterpillars may also have several pairs of false legs toward the end of their bodies. These fleshy appendages help the animals creep along.

Butterflies and Moths

Adult butterflies and moths are just as fascinating as caterpillars but much harder to study as they flit about from flower to flower or, in the case of moths, fly at night. Most butterflies and moths live only a short time—long enough to mate and lay eggs to ensure the next generation. Some moths are not able to eat in the adult stage and must do all their feeding as caterpillars. A few butterflies, including the monarch, migrate, and others, such as the mourning cloak, hibernate in cabins over the winter. Several perform useful services in pollinating plants. The female yucca moth is one of these, scraping pollen with her specially adapted mouthparts from the stamens of one flower and carrying it to another.

In recent years, many monarch butterflies have been tagged with a tiny band on a forewing as they migrate south. Much information has been collected in this way as to how far and fast they fly and where they go. A few monarchs live to return north in the spring. In the town of Monterey, California, there is a monarch festival each year as the butterflies cover the trees, stopping over to rest on their way south for the winter. If you find a black, yellow, white and green striped caterpillar eating milkweed leaves you may want to capture it, supply it with fresh milkweed leaves to eat until it turns into a beautiful pale green chrysalis studded with gold, and watch a week or two later as an adult monarch emerges.

Monarch x1

Another fascinating member of this group is the hummingbird sphinx moth. This is one of the few moths to be seen flying in the daytime. It is smaller than a hummingbird, but acts very much like one as it whizzes from flower to flower sucking out nectar with its long tongue, which is rolled up when not in use. Its wings are transparent and its body is covered with greenish hairs.

Most people abhor the sight of bagworms because of the damage they do in stripping leaves off trees and bushes. But one bagworm by itself does very little harm and makes another fascinating nature lesson. The female bagworm moth has no wings so she cannot leave her home. All she can do is get far enough out of her little bag on the tree to mate with a male bagworm moth. Then she retreats into her bag and dies. The eggs are kept dry and safe all winter long. When spring comes, they hatch into tiny caterpillars which crawl out onto the tree and build their own little bags from pieces of leaves or evergreen needles. They live in their bags, emerging only to feed, and eventually fasten their bags to twigs, staying inside to pupate. When the male moths emerge they fly to mate with a wingless female and so begin the cycle over again.

Bagworm x1

True Flies

After the butterflies and moths come the true flies. This is another large and very interesting group, though most of its members are small. The largest fly known is just a little more than two inches long. The main thing that sets the flies apart from all other groups of insects is that a fly has only two wings (one pair). These wings are usually clear. A fly's mouthparts are adapted for sucking or piercing. When a fly "bites" you it is really piercing your skin with its sharp mouthparts.

Housefly x25

Speaking of being bitten brings up the subject of mosquitoes, which along with houseflies are probably the most well-known members of this group. About the only good thing that can be said about mosquitoes is that they are food for many birds such as swallows, swifts and nighthawks. People spend much time and effort to protect themselves from being bitten by these pests. Only the adult female bites and there are many devices and preparations on the market to keep her at a distance. In many warmer countries certain human diseases are spread by the bites of mosquitoes but in our area we are mainly concerned with the discomfort caused by the bites. The salt marsh mosquito along the

Atlantic and Gulf coasts has ruined summer vacations for thousands. It is very abundant and very hard to control. Mosquito larvae are called wrigglers and live in water, where they are preyed upon by small fish and other aquatic animals.

Other true flies are crane flies, midges, horseflies, deer flies, black flies, gnats, botflies, flower flies, fruit flies, blowflies and flesh flies.

Fly Larvae

Fly larvae are called maggots and may hatch from the egg stage in ten to twelve hours. They thrive in garbage and manure piles as well as in decaying animals, and in their way are helping to recycle organic matter. Larvae of many flies live in wriggling, writhing masses but some, such as crane fly larvae, live singly in damp soil or water. Crane flies look like giant mosquitoes and unfortunately many are killed by people with fly swatters. They are called crane flies because they have long legs like the birds called cranes. You'll see them along streams hanging onto plants or in cabins or tents when you're out camping. They are absolutely harmless and fascinating to watch. A crane fly that is especially interesting is called the phantom crane fly. It resembles a tiny black and white ghost as it flits around.

Fruit Flies

Fruit flies are also interesting creatures in spite of their small size. Look closely the next time you see one and you may notice that it has red eyes. These flies seem to appear out of nowhere whenever you have grapes or bananas left in the fruit bowl too long and are widely used in science classes to study heredity. Fruit flies are very easily grown in small jars or test tubes. All you have to do is mix up mashed bananas and oatmeal, add a male and a female and you're in business. The female soon lays eggs so small that you can't see them. These hatch in a few days into tiny, squirming, white worm-like larvae. After they've eaten their fill of bananas and oatmeal, they climb up on the sides of the glass to pupate. From these pupae the adults emerge in a few days to begin the cycle over again. It is at this stage that you can put the fruit flies to sleep for a few minutes with a little ether and check them under a microscope to see what characteristics they have inherited. Differences in the color of the eyes, the wings and the color of the body are easy to see. By studying these tiny flies, scientists have learned much about the way in which you and I inherited the various characteristics we have.

Flower Flies

Flower flies, which often resemble yellow jackets, are fun to watch as they visit gardens. Probably because they resemble stinging insects they are not eaten by birds. Another fly which may escape being eaten by the same trick is the bee fly. At first glance you'll think it's a furry bee visiting a flower, but if you look more closely you'll see only two wings, making it a harmless fly.

So try not to let pests such as houseflies, horseflies and deer flies bother you too much and look for some of the more interesting kinds such as fruit flies, flower flies, crane flies and bee flies. Remember, whenever you see an insect with only one pair of wings it's a fly.

Fleas

Fleas are one group of insects that you probably already know about, especially if you've ever had a dog or a cat for a pet. They have piercing-sucking mouthparts and spend their lives as parasites on birds and mammals. Fleas are so small and move so quickly, jumping about with their long hind legs, that they are hard to see. Usually you realize your pet has fleas if you see it scratching or if you suddenly discover mysterious bites around your ankles. Fleas are able to move around on mammals and birds because their bodies are flattened sideways, making it easy for them to creep between hairs and feathers.

Flea x100

The female flea lays tiny white eggs, either on the bird or mammal on which she lives or in its nest or den. The eggs hatch in about two weeks into small worm-like larvae which feed on organic matter. This matter can be the droppings of adult fleas or other odds and ends of food in the host's den, carpeting or cracks in the floor of a house. Some fleas spend only a few days as larvae while others may spend six months. The weather, the abundance of food and the kind of flea are all important influences on the length of the larval stage. After the larva is full-grown, it spins a silken cocoon and spends from a few days to several months in it before emerging as an adult flea.

Since it was discovered that fleas may carry the bubonic plague, their control has become extremely important. Fleas can pick up these harmful germs by feeding on the blood of infected rats. If a person is bitten by a germ-carrying flea he is often infected by the droppings or partly digested blood left near the bite. When people scratch a fleabite, which is the natural thing to do, the plague germs get into their bloodstream and are often fatal. So control of rats is essential and controlling the cat and dog population is too. It is also important to keep your pets flea-free for their comfort as well as yours.

Membrane-winged Insects

Last but not least in our exploration of the huge world of insects, we come to the group including those which sting in self-defense. Many in this group are social insects, such as ants, bees and wasps, which live in large gatherings rather than singly. This group's scientific name is Hymenoptera, which means "membrane wings." Most of the group have two pairs of clear wings with the hind pair being smaller, and mouthparts modified for chewing, biting or sucking. Females usually have a sting.

Sawflies

Most sawflies are small, dark and differ from bees, ants and wasps in having thick waists. Their larvae resemble small caterpillars and some kinds do great damage to various plants. Many of the sawflies which are pests have been accidentally introduced from Europe and other countries. Birds help keep their numbers down by feeding on sawflies and sawfly larvae. Incidentally, sawflies get their name because their egg layers (ovipositors) are equipped with sawlike teeth.

Ichneumon Flies

Ichneumon flies are unforgettable creatures. Some are two or three inches long and can penetrate through the bark of trees with their thin egg-laying apparatus. If you've ever seen one of these insects, it was probably on the trunk of a tree laying eggs through the bark. Even more amazing is the fact that the eggs are laid on the larvae of another insect, the pigeon horntail. The pigeon horntail is related to the sawflies, and spends its larval life in a burrow under the bark of a tree. No one has yet found out how the female ichneumon fly can tell where the pigeon horntail larva is under the bark so she can aim her ovipositor directly through the bark to deposit her eggs on the larva. When the larva of the ichneumon fly hatches, it feeds on the body of the pigeon horntail larva and destroys it.

Gall Wasps

Another most interesting group of hymenopterans is the one to which gall wasps belong. The tiny female gall wasp lays her egg in a certain part of a particular plant. The plant responds by growing a gall, a special swelling around the egg, making a cozy home for the baby wasp as it develops. The young wasp feeds on the plant tissue around it in the gall, then pupates, chews a hole in the gall and emerges as an adult wasp ready to mate and repeat the cycle. There are many kinds of galls on oaks—some on the leaves, some on twigs, some on buds and still others on the roots. You will notice the galls first, but if you keep the gall in a container covered with fine cloth or wire, you may see the tiny wasp when it emerges. Of course if you find a gall with a hole in it, that means the insect has already come out or that a bird has pecked it out for food.

If you really become interested in galls and gall wasps, you will have a great time looking for them and find out many interesting things. For instance, besides the rightful inhabitant of the gall you may find a number of other insects living there. Some of these may be guests causing no harm, others may be parasites doing damage to the host.

Parasitic Wasps

Just as curious as gall wasps are certain tiny parasitic wasps. One which you may have noticed in your tomato patch lays its eggs in the body of large green caterpillars known as tomato hornworms. These caterpillars eat tomato leaves, weakening the plants. If left unchecked they complete their life cycles by pupating in the ground and emerging as five-spotted hawk moths. Female moths then lay eggs on more tomato plants and more tomato hornworms hatch out to do more damage. If the little parasitic wasps are around laying their eggs in the caterpillars not so much damage will occur. The wasp larvae hatch out inside the caterpillar and feed on its flesh. Soon they emerge through the hornworm's skin as dozens of white cocoons less than one quarter of an inch long. At this stage the hornworm may still be alive but is so weak that it dies in a day or two. In a short time the adult wasps come out of their cocoons and mate. Then the females go off to parasitize more tomato hornworms. Thus these little wasps are one of Mother Nature's means of biological pest control.

Velvet Ants

Another interesting wasp is the velvet ant. If you're lucky enough to see one of these it'll probably be a female running across bare ground. The female velvet ants do not have wings and can give a painful sting. Their bodies are covered with short brightly colored hairs giving the appearance of velvet.

Digger Wasps

Digger wasps dig holes in the dirt or sand, then go hunting for other insects which they sting and paralyze. They bring their prey back to their holes, stuff them inside, lay eggs and cover up the hole. When the larvae hatch, they have fresh food to eat until they become adults. The cicada killer is a huge, yellow-striped wasp which catches and paralyzes cicadas to put in its holes as food for its larvae.

Mud Wasps

Several interesting wasps use mud in building their homes. One of these, the potter wasp, actually builds tiny jugs with little balls of mud. Only people with very sharp eyes ever find these little jugs although they're probably quite common. One of my friends found several of these little jugs on her Benjamin fig tree when she moved it back into her living room after a summer on her apartment balcony.

On and in old buildings in the country you can often see various thin tubes made of mud. These are made by wasps called mud daubers, of which there are many different kinds. Each type makes a distinctive home by putting together little mud balls which they have made along the edges of streams and puddles. Into their mud homes they stuff small paralyzed spiders on which they lay their eggs. When the baby mud daubers hatch, they live on live spiders until ready to pupate and transform into adult wasps.

Social Wasps

The wasps with which most people are familiar are the social wasps—the kinds that live together building and sharing a common nest. Some, called paper wasps, make open nests under eaves of buildings or in trees.

Did you know that wasps and hornets can make paper? They do it the same way people do—by mixing chemicals with mashed-up wood. They chew wood from old boards, dead trees or fence posts, mix it with their saliva as they fly back to their nests and then spread it on the nests in thin layers to dry. White-faced hornets and yellow jackets build paper homes, which are enclosed, with layers of cells inside and an entrance near the bottom. In the cells, the queen lays eggs which hatch into larvae. These larvae are fed by workers until they are ready to pupate. Then a thin paper covering is put over them. When they have changed into adult hornets or wasps they chew their way out and join in the work of the colony.

Ants

Other social insects which live together in large numbers are ants and most bees. There are many kinds of ants in the United States, all of which are interesting to study. Some live in houses, some in the ground, others in dead trees or in large mounds. Each colony has a queen and several groups which perform different jobs. Many fascinating hours can be spent just watching ants going about their daily chores. Some drag home food items larger than themselves, others attack intruders and others work on the nest.

Bees

Honeybees, which usually live in hives but sometimes live in holes in trees, are the most familiar type of bee. When the weather permits, bees are always busy and like the ants, have various groups doing various jobs—some gathering pollen, others nectar, still others fanning their wings to keep the hive cool, feeding the larvae or tending the queen as she goes about her egg-laying inside the hive.

Besides honeybees there are bumblebees, carpenter bees and many others. One kind that you don't see very often lives in colonies in clay walls, excavating tunnels into the clay and extending clay tubes out into space with the mud each brings out from the wall. Bumblebees live in small colonies under old boards or trash piles while carpenter bees chew tunnels into porch railings, picket fences and shutters. In these tunnels, they store pollen for their larvae to eat.

CHAPTER 17

Animals with Spiny Skins

EVEN if you've never been to the ocean you know something about starfish, sea urchins and sand dollars. These interesting beings have some less well-known relatives: serpent stars, sea cucumbers, and sea lilies. All of them live in salt water and many have long-lasting skeletons which people bring home from the beach for souvenirs.

Starfish

Let's take a look at a starfish. Because it doesn't have a backbone, it isn't in the fish group at all. First, notice the central disc with a mouth on the underside and a number of arms radiating from it. The usual number of arms is five, but among the more than a thousand kinds of starfish in the world there are some with only four arms and others with twenty-five. These animals have the amazing ability to grow new arms when some are lost due to accident.

A starfish's skeleton is made up of a network of limy plates embedded in its flesh. These provide the animals with flexibility as well as protection. Limy spines stick out from the bony plates, giving the starfish a very prickly appearance.

Have you ever watched a starfish move? It's fascinating—especially if the one you're watching is moving across the glass side of an aquarium and you can actually see its hundreds of tube feet in action from under-neath. These tube feet work by means of water pressure and only do well on something hard such as rocks. When a hungry starfish finds a clam, it climbs up on the shell and actually pulls it apart with the suction devices on the ends of its tube feet. Of course, the clam tries to hold the two halves of its shell tightly together but the starfish eventually pulls them apart. Then the starfish pushes the lower end of its stomach out through its mouth, takes in the soft parts of the clam and digests them. Also unique is the fact that starfish have three separate nervous systems.

Sea Urchins and Sand Dollars

Sea urchins don't really look much like starfish but they are close rel-atives. Their spines and tube feet are much longer and they feed on algae and decaying plant matter. When you find a sea urchin skeleton washed up on the beach, it probably will not have any spines but will look like a slightly flattened bony ball. When these animals die and get tossed about in the waves, the spines soon break off. Sea urchins use their spines to help them move about. The spines also give a lot of protection and in some kinds of sea urchins are poisonous to touch.

Sea urchin x½

Classified with the sea urchins are some other curious animals called sand dollars, so-named because they can be about the size of a silver dollar and are often found in the sand. When sand dollars are alive, they are covered with short spines and move about by these and also by tube feet on the tops and bottoms of their bodies. They feed by swallowing sand and digesting organic matter in it. On the beach you will usually find just the skeletons of sand dollars with the spiny skin worn off. If you find more than one, it's fun to crack one open and see the five tiny white structures inside which look like little doves.

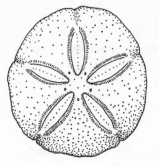

Sand dollar x½

Sea Cucumbers, Serpent Stars and Sea Lilies

Sea cucumbers look very little like the other members of the spiny-skinned group, as their spines are tiny and embedded in their skin. They move about on the ocean floor by muscular body motion and can often be seen in shallow pools left when the tide goes out. The most amazing thing about sea cucumbers is that when they are bothered or attacked they throw out their inside organs. After escaping from their enemies they grow a new set of inside organs. For food, they swallow sand or mud and digest plant and animal matter in it. In China, dried sea cucumbers are used in making soup.

Sea cucumber x¼

Serpent stars have long, thin arms that twist and writhe about, resembling snakes. They are also called brittle stars because of the fact that they lose arms easily when bothered by man or other enemies.

Sea lilies look more like plants than animals. Many have been found as fossils. They are animals which live attached to the ocean bottom with long stalks bearing branched arms at the top. They do not have spines but do have a limy skeleton made of plates like most other members of this group.

PART IV

Animals With Backbones

CHAPTER 18

Birds

ANIMALS with backbones (or vertebrates) belong to the phylum Chordata. Included are people, dogs, cats, horses, birds, snakes, fish and most of the animals wild and tame with which we are familiar. All these animals have bony skeletons and brains encased in a skull. The phylum Chordata is divided into five main classes (groups) as follows:

Pisces	(Fishes)
Amphibia	(Amphibians)
Reptilia	(Reptiles)
Aves	(Birds)
Mammalia	(Mammals)

I have listed these classes in their evolutionary order but let's discuss birds first and fish later. It is easier to make observations about birds than it is to study fish. Most of us see at least a few wild birds every day but seldom see fish except in aquariums.

Feathers

First of all—how do you know a bird is a bird? What does it have that none of the other classes of vertebrates has? The answer, of course, is feathers. No other group of animals has feathers. Much can be said about feathers and their functions. They give birds warmth and protection and make it possible for most birds to fly. In some birds, feathers have become adapted for other purposes. The peacock has a handsome crest while the tufted titmouse has a perky little topknot. These feather structures are ornamental but may also serve other purposes during courtship. In woodpeckers and chimney swifts, modified tail feathers give support as the birds cling to the insides of hollow trees or chimneys.

When you begin to think about the kinds of feathers you know, you'll probably think first of big stiff feathers on wings and tails of birds. These are called contour feathers and have been used by people in various ways. Quill pens were made from goose wing feathers and Indian headdresses used tail feathers from eagles. Down feathers are found on baby birds and underneath the contour feathers of adult birds. Ducks and geese have large numbers of down feathers and pluck out some to use in their nests. The warmest sleeping bags and comforters are filled with down. A very small bird, such as a ruby-throated hummingbird, may have fewer than a thousand feathers, while a large whistling swan has twenty-five thousand. Books have been written about feathers so you'll be able to find more information if you decide to make a study of them. (See Books I Use and Like, page 218.)

The wing feathers of owls are soft, enabling them to fly silently as they pursue their prey. Wing feathers of most other birds are stiff and are noisy during flight as the bird pushes against the air. Ducks and some other birds waterproof their feathers with oil from a gland at the base of the tail.

Ways to Study Birds

Each bird watcher you meet will probably give a different reason for his interest in birds. Some people seek the brightly colored birds such as orioles, tanagers, goldfinches, indigo buntings and bluebirds. Others like to hear beautiful bird songs. With birding as a hobby there is always the possibility of learning something new. If you live in the eastern United States, you may discover that the "common goldfinch" is the last bird to build its nest. Since it uses thistledown in its nest it cannot nest until thistles go to seed in late June and early July, after most other birds are through nesting.

Bird watching can make changes in your life! Birds wake up early and you will too if you want to see and hear them at their best. Getting to know the songs and calls of birds is fun but rather difficult. And if you really want to learn about nests and eggs and how long it takes the eggs to hatch, you have to have patience and persistence. A few hours of watching a pair of house wrens bring food to their young will convince you of the value of birds as insect eaters. Or if you are lucky enough to be able to watch some barn owls bring rats and mice to their youngsters, you'll realize they're more efficient than any traps.

Golden garden spider

Oysters and barnacles

Blue crab

Damsel flies mating

Grasshopper

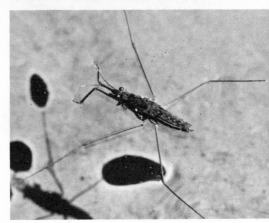

Water strider

Annual cicada

Wheel bug on chicory

*Praying mantis
on sneezeweed*

Goldfinch on thistle

There are birds to watch and hear almost everywhere. Even in the middle of a city there are always pigeons, starlings and house sparrows. In fact, these birds have adapted to city life so well that they have become pests in many places. Part of this problem is due to the fact that all three are birds native to other countries where their numbers are kept under control by natural enemies which do not exist here.

Unfortunately, some of our modern inventions such as picture windows and TV towers have caused the death of many birds. Hanging a thin piece of net outside your picture window during the fall and spring migration will help in keeping birds from killing themselves though it may interfere slightly with your view for a few weeks. Taping the silhouette of a hawk on the window may also help.

Bird Sounds

Maybe you'll become interested in the different sounds that birds make. Not all birds sing—some scream, some seem to laugh and others make various brief sounds. Most birds make several different kinds of noises for different purposes. The wood thrush, for instance, has a beautiful bell-like song but also makes a "put-put" sound when alarmed.

In some species of birds only the males sing. At different times of the year you may hear more singing than at others. For example, in the spring when many birds return to their nesting grounds from the south, the males often arrive first and set up their territories by singing. Redwinged blackbirds do this and so do house wrens.

Most birds sing in the daytime, but there are some that are heard only at dusk and others only in the night. Some mockingbirds sing in the day and also at night but whippoorwills sing mainly in the evening and most owls at night.

When you first start to listen to birds, you may become very discouraged and think that you'll never be able to learn their songs. Just find one that's singing and watch and listen to him for a while until you get the song or call down pat. Early in the day birds usually call over and over again so once you track down one that's singing you'll probably have many chances to hear him. Try to put some words to the song or call or whistle back to the birds. An easy bird to learn, if you live near woods, is the rufous-sided towhee. He sings "Drink your tea-ee-ee" or sometimes just the last two words. When alarmed, the towhee calls, "Che-wink." The eastern meadowlark sings in a very high voice, "Spring is here," usually from the top of a tree or a telephone wire.

Nest Finding

If listening to bird songs doesn't appeal to you, why not track down some nests? This can be a very rewarding hobby and you may even add to scientific knowledge about birds by keeping records. If you are careful you needn't worry about harming the birds.

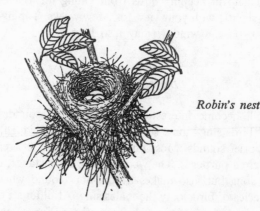

Robin's nest

Many nests are found by accident. As you're walking through a field a meadowlark may fly up from her nest, giving you a chance to spot it if you're quick enough. If the bird happens to be a killdeer, you'll have problems—the mother killdeer usually leaves the nest and runs along the ground before she flies up and starts saying "killdee, killdee, killdee." She'll land and pretend to have a hurt wing just to lure you on. After you've tried to catch up with her she'll take off and wheel around. By then, you'll be so far from where the nest really is that you might as well give up. A killdeer's nest is just a depression in a field or along the edge of a gravel road. The nests of barn swallows and other birds that nest in or on buildings and bridges are not hidden and are easy to find. House wrens, bluebirds and others which build in birdhouses are also easy to study. You can park yourself quietly in a lawn chair nearby and watch to see what nesting materials the birds are bringing in; how many trips they make in an hour; or what food they're bringing to the baby birds. If you want to become an expert in identifying birds' nests, there are helpful books in your library. You can keep busy finding out which birds use mud and which use mosses and grasses in nest building. Someday you may find a chimney swift nest which has fallen into your fireplace and see how it is made of twigs held together with saliva.

If you see a bird disappearing into a hole in a tree carrying a snakeskin in its beak you can check off great crested flycatcher on your bird list. Some experts think the snakeskin in the nest may help to scare away predators but no one really knows. In areas near cities where snakeskins are scarce, these birds have been known to use cigar wrappers instead.

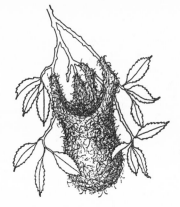

Northern oriole's nest

It's best to study birds' nests right where they are. Some birds use the same nest year after year and even in nests that aren't used again there may be biological pest control going on that should not be interrupted. When birds leave the nest often some of their parasites remain. In addition there may be beneficial insects in the nests preying on the parasites, thus helping to keep their numbers down.

Migration

If you really get into bird watching, it won't be very long before you learn that some birds live in your area all year round but others only spend the summer. Some only come in the winter and still others will be seen only in the spring or the fall when they are migrating. You may become interested in learning more about migration—where birds go; why and when. Try to keep track of the birds in your back yard. Spotting the brown thrasher that lives in your yard the first day he comes back from his winter home in the south is exciting. Trying to record the last day you see him in the fall is harder. And if you live on a flyway where wild geese, ducks and whistling swans pass overhead spring and fall, there is more excitement in store for you. The first hint you get is the sound from the huge flocks flying overhead. If you're lucky you'll have a few minutes to watch and wonder as the birds head north in the spring or south in the fall. Their V formations, constantly changing, are marvelous to watch.

"V" formation of migrating geese

Someday as you're looking up you may see a flock of crows wheeling around and swooping down on another bird either flying or perched in a tree. This is how crows behave when they discover a hawk or owl. It is interesting to watch as the crows dive at the bird of prey trying to drive it away. They instinctively recognize hawks and owls as enemies.

Distribution

If you travel, you'll soon become aware of the fact that there are different birds in different parts of the country. When you go to the beach you'll see gulls, terns and other birds that you probably don't see at home. The same is true of the mountains. At the zoo you can see birds from various parts of the world. Birds such as flamingos and penguins are almost unbelievable until you actually see them!

Birds as Pets

Maybe you'll become so fond of birds you'll want one for a pet. Many people these days have a parakeet, parrot, canary, finch or mynah to keep them company. Some of these birds pick up a large vocabulary, not because they're superintelligent, but because they are good mimics and someone has spent time talking to them, saying the same things over and over again. Don't go out and buy a bird without considering all aspects of bird ownership carefully. They do need some care. Parrots

Parrot

are fun but messy and apt to bite when displeased. They also chew on bookshelves, candles, curtains and other household items due probably to a constant need to keep their beaks in condition. They also need to have their toenails clipped two or three times a year and this means wrapping the parrot up in a thick bath towel and getting a friend to hold him while you clip the toenails. But then, all pets require some care and have their drawbacks as well as their rewards. Just remember to consider these things when you're thinking about a bird as a pet.

Feeding Wild Birds

Food habits of birds are also interesting and something you'll have to find out about if you decide to put out bird feeders. It takes certain foods to attract certain birds and some won't come no matter what you put out. Most people think of putting out bird feeders in the winter when natural food for birds is scarce, but you can keep a feeder filled with food all year round and have some very interesting visitors.

Most birds that are attracted to feeders are seed-eaters such as blue jays, chickadees, tufted titmice, cardinals and nuthatches. For these the favorite seeds are sunflower seeds. Unfortunately, these are also the most expensive. You can grow your own but unless you harvest them as soon as they're ripe and store them away for winter, the birds will beat you to it and devour them right from the sunflower head. If you buy bags of mixed seed, you will find that the birds usually eat up the sunflower seeds right away and kick most of the other seeds onto the ground. This way you get some interesting plants coming up around your bird feeder in the spring, but you also have a lot of wasted seed. Birds that are too small to handle sunflower seeds well are very fond of finely cracked corn. So a good thing to do is to buy a few pounds of cracked corn plus a couple of pounds of sunflower seed and mix them together. Put out a few dabs of peanut butter too in case a mockingbird comes by. Chickadees and titmice also like peanut butter. Big hunks of suet—also popular with birds—cost very little at the supermarket though you usually have to ask for them. You can also get suet by trimming most of the fat from roasts and steaks before they are cooked. Put this fat on your feeder and watch for various woodpeckers to come. The red-bellied woodpecker is spectacular to watch even though you'll wonder how he got his name. Even adult males have only a faint red tinge on their bellies. Identify them by the red on the top of the head and neck, black and white stripes across the back, and their large size.

Value of Birds

When you begin to think about it you'll come up with a long list of useful things birds do. Here are some:

1. Birds of prey such as hawks and owls eat rodents which damage crops.

2. Vultures and some other birds including crows perform a valuable service in cleaning up dead animals on our highways and elsewhere.

3. Seed-eating birds such as sparrows eat many weed seeds.

4. Many birds live on insects. Purple martins, chimney swifts and various swallows eat small flying insects all day long and others including the cuckoos eat caterpillars. Without birds we might well be knee-deep in insects. Many birds that eat seeds when adult are fed insects while in the nest.

5. Of course many domesticated birds such as chickens, ducks, turkeys and geese are used for food. We also depend on chickens for eggs.

6. In some parts of the world there are huge quantities of valuable fertilizer known as guano deposited by sea birds.

7. Birds' feathers are also used but fortunately not to the great extent that they were some years ago. Then some birds such as egrets were killed for their feathers and almost became extinct. Now there are laws protecting birds. Down feathers for some sleeping bags and warm jackets come from commercially raised ducks.

These are only a few of the ways in which birds are useful but sooner or later you will be reminded that some birds do damage to fruit trees and cornfields as well. And others make unsightly messes on public buildings. In the long run the damage birds do is far outweighed by the good that they do in eating insects and weed seeds and giving us pleasure.

Bird Banding, Blinds and Societies

One of the most interesting ways to find out more about birds is by bird banding. There are several thousand people in the United States and Canada who have banding permits. In order to get a permit a person has to be over eighteen, show a thorough knowledge of the birds in his area and have a research project concerning birds. Permits are issued by the United States Fish and Wildlife Service and each bander is given a supply of numbered aluminum bands of various sizes. The bander captures birds with special traps or nets in ways which do not harm them. He then writes down important information about each bird, places a band carefully on the bird's leg and lets the bird go. Vari-

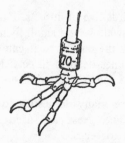

Bird's leg with band

ous parts of the bird are measured. The bird is weighed. A check is made under feathers of certain parts to see how much stored fat is under the skin. Also, if any parasites such as lice are found on the bird, these may be collected for further study. The records of the band numbers put on each bird are sent to the Bird Banding Office at the Patuxent Wildlife Refuge in Laurel, Maryland, and kept in a central file. Researchers often use these records and whenever a bird wearing a band is found, it can be tracked down. If you find a dead bird that has been banded, and it isn't a pigeon (pigeons are more or less tame birds and are banded by their owners), take off the band and tape it to a letter. Write as much as you know about the bird—what kind it is, where and when you found it, why it died if you can tell. Send the information to the banding office and they will let you know who banded the bird and when and where it was banded. They will also let the bander know. Through banding much information has been discovered on such subjects as how long birds live, where they go in the winter and how fast they fly. If the band you see is on a live bird, don't take it off, just jot down the number and send it in along with the rest of the information. Of course, sometimes you see a banded bird at your feeder but can't get close enough to read the number so you can't do anything about it. If you do find a banded pigeon and want to know more about it, look in the phone book under "Pigeon" and you may find the name of an organization you can call.

Besides banding, there are other ways to find out more about birds.

Have you ever heard of a bird blind? It resembles a little tent, has small holes in the sides and you can hide in it to get a closer look at birds. People usually set their blinds up near a nest they've found and watch the parents bringing food to the young birds. Some people who want to find out more about hawk and owl nests put blinds up in a tree near the nest tree. In England, blinds are called hides and bird bands are called rings. If you're trying to get closeup pictures of birds, you can take your camera in the blind with you.

If you're really interested in birds, sooner or later you'll want to meet other bird watchers. One of the best ways to do this is to join a club. Most states have an Audubon Society, Ornithological Society or similar group. These groups conduct field trips, have films about nature and special bird counts during the Christmas holidays and on the first Saturday in May.

CHAPTER 19

Amphibians

AMPHIBIANS are animals that spend some of their time in the water and some on land. Frogs, toads and salamanders are all amphibians. The eggs of all three groups are usually laid in the water. Some native salamanders lay their eggs under rotting logs or in damp earth and in the tropics some tree frogs lay eggs on leaves over water.

a. frog   *b. toad*   *c. salamander*
Amphibian eggs x⅔

Frogs

Varieties of frogs include bullfrogs, green frogs, leopard frogs, pickerel frogs and wood frogs, which are fairly common in the eastern United States in and around fresh-water streams or ponds. They live on flying insects, which they catch by sticking out their long tongues. Frogs move so quickly that you often hear the splash when they jump in a pond but miss seeing the frog. They spend hours sunning themselves on the bank by the water and catching insects that come too close. Not all frogs are green. The bullfrog and green frog are mostly green; the pickerel frog and the leopard frog are spotted; and the wood frog is brown

Leopard frog x⅔

with a black mask over its eyes. Sometimes the wood frog changes color and can be very light brown or almost black.

All frogs in the temperate zones hibernate during winter in the mud at the bottom of ponds or in damp areas near ponds. When spring comes, they gather in the ponds to breed. Each kind of frog has a certain time for mating and egg-laying and also makes its own particular sound during that time. So if your ears are tuned in to frog calls, you can tell by the sounds you hear coming from a nearby pond what kinds of frogs are breeding there on a spring evening. If you visit the pond the next day after hearing frogs calling, you may see masses of frog eggs. Some kinds of frogs lay eggs in jelly-like masses that float on top of the water and others fasten their eggs in globs on sticks under water. If you become a frog expert you can tell different kinds of frog eggs apart as well as the tadpoles that hatch from the eggs.

Frogs lay thousands of eggs each spring. A female bullfrog may lay as many as fifty thousand, while the smaller kinds may only lay two or three thousand. When the eggs hatch, tadpoles emerge. These tadpoles feed on very tiny pieces of plant and animal matter they get from the pond ooze and if they are bullfrog tadpoles, may take as long as two years to change into frogs. Many tadpoles do not survive long enough to grow up, as they are eaten by fish, turtles and birds who get their food in the pond.

Have you ever tried raising tadpoles? Usually they don't get along in homes as well as they do in the pond. Often children try to keep dozens of tadpoles in a small container only big enough for two or three. When some die they sink to the bottom and decay and make the water unlivable for the rest. If you want to try raising tadpoles, take only a few and give them lots of pond water. A gallon of water to every inch of tadpole is a good rule. Feeding is a problem too, but a lettuce leaf left floating on the water so that it decays around the edges is one way to keep tadpoles happy. They nibble on the edges and get what they need. You should try to take a plant or two that is growing in the pond and put it in your container. Plants help keep a healthy balance in any aquarium and the tadpoles can also get some food by eating tiny things that grow on the surfaces of plant leaves and stems.

Toads

Many people are confused about the differences between toads and frogs. Here are a few points to keep in mind that will help you tell one from the other.

1. Most frogs live in and around the water—an exception is the wood frog, which comes to ponds in the spring to breed but later returns to the woods.

2. Frogs have damp, smooth skin but toads have drier, warty skin.

3. Toads spend their lives on land except for a few weeks in the spring when they go to the ponds to breed and lay eggs.

4. Frog eggs are found in flat or round masses of jelly-like material while toad eggs are laid in long strings of jelly which resemble thick, transparent spaghetti.

5. Frogs, with their long legs, can move quickly but toads have shorter legs and travel more slowly.

Toads eat insects as frogs do and often are seen in the evening in gardens or under lighted windows to which insects are attracted. Even though they have drier skin than frogs, they still cannot stand much heat, so during the day toads rest under bushes and in other damp, cool, shady places. There are not as many different kinds of toads as frogs. The common toad in most places is the American toad, which usually has one wart in each of the dark spots on its back. The Fowler's toad, found mostly on the coastal plain, has more than one wart in each of the dark spots and has a different call in the spring.

American toad x⅔

In spring the male toads come out of hibernation first and head for shallow breeding ponds where they swim around and trill. You can hear this trill from quite a distance and if you follow the sound to the pond you'll see the toads, sometimes by the hundreds. Only their heads will be sticking out of the water and if you're there in the evening with a flashlight their eyes will shine gold. As they trill, their throats balloon out just like bubbles blown with bubble gum. The females eventually arrive at the pond; mating begins and then the long strings of eggs are laid. One female toad may lay as many as eight thousand eggs at a time. The parents leave the pond for woods and gardens, leaving the eggs to hatch out alone. Toad tadpoles are very black and small. In a few weeks the tadpoles transform into tiny toads about two thirds of an inch long and leave the pond to live on land.

You've probably heard the superstition about toads giving you warts if you pick them up. Well, like many other such sayings this is not true, but it is easy to understand how it might have gotten started. Those little warts all over a toad's back are really little glands that can put out a poisonous substance. The two large glands on a toad's head can do this as well. Some toad-eating animals are discouraged by the poison, but many others are not. The hog-nosed snake lives almost exclusively on toads and screech owls eat them occasionally too. Toads have other ways of discouraging their enemies. If you have ever picked one up, you may have noticed that it blew itself up as fat as it could. This trick may keep it from being eaten by some creatures. A toad is likely to discharge large quantities of liquid on your hand soon after you pick it up, encouraging people to leave it alone.

Toads, frogs and salamanders have an unusual bit of behavior in common—they eat their castoff skins. When I first heard this I suspected it was a superstition, but after seeing it happen I know it's true. Snakes shed their skins and leave them behind, but amphibians pull them off over their heads and stuff them in their mouths.

Spadefoot toads are smaller than American or Fowler's toads and belong to a different family. There are only a few warts on their skin and on their hind feet are sharp, black horny structures which they use in digging into loose dirt. Like their relatives, spadefoot toads meet and breed in ponds during a heavy spring rainfall. The females are attracted by the characteristic call of the males, which is quite different from the calls of other kinds of toads. Although common, these interesting animals are not seen very often due to their habit of burying themselves in the ground. Their name comes from the fact that they use their hind feet as spades.

Tree Frogs

In another family are the tree frogs, which include spring peepers. Tree frogs can be over two inches long but the peepers are smaller, usually little more than one inch. Both have tiny suction cups on their toes which help them hang onto tree trunks, blades of grass or the sides of a terrarium. As do the larger true frogs and toads, tree frogs hibernate all winter and come out in early spring. A cheerful and sure sign that spring is on the way is the "peep, peep, peep" of the spring peeper on a March evening. There are many different kinds of these fascinating little animals, especially in the southern states.

If you live near a peeper-breeding area, an entertaining way to spend a spring evening is to put on your boots, grab a flashlight and covered bucket and head for the sound of the calls. As you get closer to the swamp, the calls will become louder and you'll probably think that catching a few spring peepers will be easy. But what usually happens is that you can slosh around in the water for half an hour shining your flashlight in the direction of the peeps and not see one spring peeper!

Once you see the first one, though, it's easier to see more. They cling to plants sticking out of the water and occasionally will swim from one plant to another, but they are so small and brown that in the muddy water they are almost impossible to see. When they call, their tiny throats expand like little bubble gum bubbles and that makes them easier to see for an instant. If you take them home to observe for a few days they'll start making their peeping sound right in your living room. You can also see them get lighter or darker in color. They should be returned to the place you found them so they can get on about their business of mating, laying eggs and eating insects. After spring is over spring peepers seem to disappear and you do not hear them any more, but the larger common tree frog may be heard calling from trees off and on during the summer. It has a great variety of color changes from gray to brown to green.

Salamanders

Salamanders are very common animals and yet many people have never seen one, or if they have seen one they've called it a lizard. Both salamanders and lizards are long and thin, have four legs and a tail. Lizards are *reptiles* with dry skin, scales and claws and spend much of their time out in the sunshine. Salamanders are *amphibians,* have damp, smooth skin, no claws and spend their time in cool, dark, damp places. To find salamanders, all you need to do is to turn over logs or rocks in woods near streams. Take a look and then replace the roof of the salamander's home. If its skin dries out it will die.

Dusky salamander x2

The red-backed salamander is a common variety but its name can be misleading as some of the time its back is not red. Then you have to call it the "lead-backed phase" of the red-backed salamander! Under rocks along streams you'll find another type, the dusky salamander. There's one salamander that spends its adult life in ponds but for the first year or so of its life it wanders around in damp woods. In this land stage it is orange with red spots on its sides, but when it returns to the pond, it is green with the same red spots on its sides. The land stage is called the red eft and the adult water form is the spotted newt.

Most salamanders are just a few inches long and eat insects and worms, but the mud puppy and the hellbender, which live in rivers and large streams, can be up to two feet long. The hellbender feeds on crayfish. The largest salamander in the world is found in Japan. It is usually about three feet long but can be five feet long. It can weigh more than eighty pounds and has been known to live more than fifty years!

Many kinds of salamanders lay their eggs in water in spring but the marbled salamander lays her eggs in the fall in damp earth in the woods and curls around them to protect them until they hatch. The eggs of the red-backed salamander are laid under wet wood and also guarded by the mother.

Although they are of little economic value, salamanders make interesting terrarium pets, usually getting food from little creatures coming out of the moss and soil. The giant salamander of Japan is used for food by the Japanese, and is eaten by large animals as well. Salamanders never make a sound. You never know that a salamander is around unless you come upon one, or some of its eggs, as you turn over things in damp places.

Frogs and toads will go through their routines faithfully year after year as long as they have the right habitat in which to exist. Bullfrogs are raised commercially and their hind legs sold for food. But the other amphibians are just part of our natural world. Man may well have descended from some ancient salamander-like creature that came out of primeval waters and adapted to life on land. That's something to think about the next time you see a frog, toad or salamander.

CHAPTER 20

Reptiles

REPTILES are fascinating, from the smallest lizard to the largest crocodile. They are all covered with scales or bony plates and live in a wide range of habitats from the ocean to the desert.

Crocodiles and Alligators

Unless you live in Florida you probably won't meet one of these animals on a nature walk. Always be prepared, though—I heard of a hunter once who found an alligator in a Maryland swamp one cold December. It turned out to be an escaped pet belonging to an amateur herpetologist (a person who studies reptiles and amphibians). One place you can usually see alligators and crocodiles is at your local zoo. These animals are having a hard time everywhere because of the high prices their skins bring on the black market. Even though it is illegal to kill them, poachers shoot many anyway. They need protection and we can help by refusing to buy anything made from crocodile or alligator skins. These animals lay their eggs in piles of decaying plant matter with the heat from the rotting plants helping to hatch the eggs.

Lizards

Among the many kinds of lizards are the geckos, interesting because of the little suction discs on their toes. These discs enable the geckos to hold onto smooth surfaces such as ceilings where they hunt for insects at dusk. Two kinds of geckos are native to the southwestern United States and another, the Turkish or Mediterranean gecko, lives happily in several cities in the South. This small lizard spends its days in a crack or crevice and has the unusual ability to wash its eyes with its tongue.

Many people know about chameleons because of their outstanding ability to change color. There are Old World and New World chameleons, some of which can extend their tongues six inches when capturing insects.

The chuckwalla is a large lizard, about a foot long, which lives in the Southwest and eats plants. For protection the chuckwalla hides in a crack in a rock and blows itself up with air to fit so tightly that its enemies cannot get it out.

Eastern fence lizard x½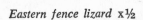

The eastern fence lizard and the horned toad of the Southwest are both in the iguana family and very useful in their territories as insect eaters. Both can be kept as pets but cannot endure too much heat and light. Another lizard looks much like a snake and is called the "glass snake."

How can you tell a snake from a lizard? In most cases, a lizard has legs and a snake doesn't. Actually, true lizards have ears, eyelids and scaly bellies, while snakes have no external ears, no eyelids and just one row of scales on their bellies. So a "glass snake" is really a legless lizard and gets its name from the fact that it looks like a snake and often breaks in two when grabbed. Some people will tell you that each piece will grow into a new snake or that the two pieces can be put back together again. What really happens is that the tail part dies and the head part grows a new end. These interesting animals live in the southern United States, feeding on earthworms and insects.

The only poisonous lizard in the United States is the Gila monster of the Southwest. Specimens are often seen in zoos. It has to turn over on its back in order to inject poison when biting; however, human death from its bite is almost unknown.

The six-lined race runner and the blue-tailed skink are other interesting lizards. They eat insects and lay eggs with thin rubbery shells. The female race runner covers her eggs with warm sand and leaves them, but the female skink stays coiled around her eggs until they hatch. Then the babies are on their own.

Snakes

There are probably more superstitions about snakes than any other group of animals. You've probably heard all of these:

Snakes will chase you.

Hoop snakes grab their tails with their mouths and roll down hills.

Milk snakes steal milk from farmers' cows.

All snakes have poisonous bites.

Snakes use their forked tongues to sting people.

It's dangerous to walk through tall grass because it's full of snakes.

As with many other groups of animals, people are afraid of snakes because they don't understand them, and probably picked up misinformation about them as children.

Snakes, like other reptiles, are covered with scales and have cold blood. They do not have ears and use their forked tongues to help find out about their surroundings. A hungry blacksnake uses his tongue to help locate a warm-blooded mouse for his next meal. One fascinating fact about snakes is that they shed their skins from time to time. You can tell when a snake is getting ready to shed by looking at its eyes. If the eyes are dull and whitish, it is about to shed its skin. Even the skin over the eyes is shed. When you find a snakeskin, notice that it's inside out just like your socks are when you pull them off in a hurry. Usually snakes crawl between tree trunks, rocks or other rough objects which help pull off their old skins.

If you are afraid of snakes it's never too late to try to overcome your fear. Begin by remembering that everything in nature has its place and that many snakes are helping man by eating rodents and insects. Also, try to put yourself in a snake's place. Then you'll realize when you suddenly come upon a snake in the woods, field or garden that he's probably just as startled as you are and will leave quickly if you give him a chance. You should find out what poisonous snakes there are in your area and how to recognize them. Your local county agent, high school or college biology teacher or natural history museum are good sources for the correct information.

All snakes can bite, but being bitten by a non-poisonous snake is no more dangerous or painful than being scratched by a rosebush. Children who love to explore ponds often panic if they get bitten by water snakes they pick up, thinking that they've been bitten by a poisonous water moccasin. Of course in southern Virginia and the southern states, there are moccasins and they are dangerous. Never pick up a snake unless you are positive you know what kind it is. It's usually best to leave all animals in nature where you find them, just observing them until they disappear. Water snakes, even though they're not poisonous, are always mean and never make good pets.

Hog-nosed snakes are often killed because they put on such great acts in self-defense. They spread out their necks in cobra fashion, hiss loudly, vibrate their tails in dry leaves making sounds like rattlesnakes and often roll over and pretend they're dead. But they're really quite harmless and feed only on toads.

Eastern milk snake and northern copperhead

Milk snakes are killed too because their coloring reminds many people of copperhead snakes. Get some good pictures or go to a museum and look at some specimens of the two to see the differences. The copperhead has hourglass-shaped markings down its back while the milk snake has irregular-shaped blotches. Both are valuable rodent eaters. Years ago when farmers found snakes in their cow barns and at the same time noticed a cow that gave less milk than usual, they thought the snake had milked the cow and called it a milk snake. Now we know the snake was in the barn catching mice and not drinking milk.

There are many more non-poisonous kinds of snakes than poisonous ones, so chances are most snakes you see in your wanderings are harmless. Try to remain calm when you see a snake and avoid the impulse to scream or to kill the snake with the nearest stick or stone. Take the time to do a little reading and you'll find out that snakes are very interesting as well as useful creatures. Like other reptiles, they are cold-blooded and hibernate all winter, sometimes getting together in large groups.

This is only one of the intriguing things you can find out. With each new fact you learn you will understand snakes better and be less afraid.

Turtles

Turtles are definitely more popular members of the reptile family. Maybe it's because they don't have teeth and move slowly that they seem friendlier. In many homes there are baby red-eared turtles though since the recent salmonella warnings pet stores no longer sell them. Be sure you follow the common-sense rule of washing your hands with soap and water after playing with any pet.

In the East, the box turtle is the one you're most likely to see as it crosses from one side of the road to the other. Or you may find one in the woods munching a mushroom, or in your garden taking bites out of your best tomato. A box turtle has a hinge and can close up the front part of its bottom shell tightly against the top shell, pulling in its tail, head and legs. In this position it is protected from almost all of its enemies and is as safe as if it were in a box. That's probably how it got its name. Of course, a turtle's worst enemy is the automobile and many get killed by speeding cars as they're slowly crossing roads.

In nature one of the few animals that can hurt a box turtle is a great horned owl. This large bird has been known to grab a turtle in its talons, drop it on a rock or other hard surface to crack the shell, and make a meal of it.

Turtles in general live a long time. Several box turtles have been known to live more than a hundred years. Every now and then an old one is found with a date and a person's initials carved in its shell. In some cases it has been possible to determine that the dates are true and not just put on by pranksters. It is not really a good idea to carve your initials and the date into every turtle you find. There are better methods of marking turtles if you want to keep track of them over a number of years. A friend of mine makes little notches along the shell edges of turtles he finds on his property.

If you spend much time wandering up and down streams or around ponds, you may come across some water turtles such as the spotted, painted and snapping turtles. The spotted turtle has small yellow or orange spots on its shell. The painted turtle is dull on top but underneath has orange and greenish-yellow stripes around the edges. If a log is sticking up out of a pond, painted turtles will sun themselves on it and fall off with loud plops and splashes when people come by.

Snapping turtle

The snapping turtle is dangerous to handle as it bites at anything when disturbed. Easily recognized by its large head, long, thick neck and sharp points on the rear of the top shell and top of the tail, this turtle's plastron or bottom shell is small compared to its over-all size. It does perform a service by eating dead fish and frogs which drop to the pond bottom but it also eats live fish and ducklings, which it pulls under as they swim by. In many parts of the country snapping turtles are made into delicious soup. They can weigh thirty pounds or more so one turtle will provide enough soup for a crowd. The largest turtles in the world are the land tortoises such as those that live in the Galápagos Islands, and the giant sea turtles which may weigh over three hundred pounds.

All turtles lay leathery-shelled eggs in sand or dirt and depend upon the sun to hatch them. Baby turtles have an egg tooth which helps them break out of the shell and disappears a short while after hatching.

CHAPTER 21

Fishes

FINDING FISHES to observe is not as easy as finding plants, birds and insects and you have to work harder to understand them. But whether you're watching minnows dash by in a country stream; angelfish swimming around in a tropical fish store; a four-hundred-pound jewfish in a large public aquarium; or the assorted fishes for sale at your local supermarket, you're seeing examples of the oldest important group of vertebrates. Scales and bones of fossil fishes have been found in rocks which are 400 million years old.

Modern fishes, of which there are about twenty-five thousand kinds, vary greatly in size, color, shape and ways of living but all have cold blood. Most have scales (except when newly hatched), fins and gills. Incidentally, don't confuse aquatic *mammals* such as whales, porpoises and dolphins with fishes. Although they live in the same environments they are different in many ways. Remember that *mammals* breathe with lungs, have hair and provide milk for their young.

Some fishes are so strange-looking they don't appear to be fishes at all. Take the sea horses, for instance—their heads really do resemble tiny horse heads as they swim through the water in an upright position. And eels superficially resemble snakes more than they do fishes. When I was a girl I used to go fishing with my brothers in a nearby millrace and catch eels which we took home, skinned and fried for supper. Then I never thought of eels as fishes. But they have fins and breathe with gills and are fishes even though at first glance they look more like snakes.

The lives of eels are amazing. Adult eels in the fresh-water streams along the Atlantic coasts of North America and Europe migrate to the Sargasso Sea to lay their eggs. This is an area around Bermuda where there are many floating marine plants. In the case of the European eel the males begin to migrate at the age of four to eight years and when they are about twenty inches long. The females are five feet long and twelve years old when they leave Europe. It takes them one year to swim the three thousand miles to the Sargasso Sea and they do not eat during this time. As soon as the eggs are laid the adults die. The baby eels take three years to reach Europe swimming up the same streams from which their parents came and are about three inches long when they get there. Our American eels behave in the same way but it only takes the young one year to reach the fresh-water streams from which their mothers and fathers came. If you ever go eeling and decide to prepare your catch for eating be very careful not to get any eel blood in an open cut as it contains a powerful nerve poison.

Another fascinating fish story concerns the coelocanth. Fishes of this kind were thought to have been extinct for 70 million years until one was brought up from very deep water off the coast of Africa in 1938. Since then fish scientists (ichthyologists) have been trying in vain to catch one and keep it alive long enough to make some scientific observations. Other specimens of this strange fish have been brought up, but as it has proved impossible to duplicate the conditions of high water pressure under which they live, they die in a short time.

In the world of fishes there are many other fascinating examples of special adaptations to certain environments and ways of living. Once, while on a ship in the Pacific Ocean, I watched dozens of flying fish about a foot in length. They leaped out of the water and like little birds, skittered along the surface for several yards before diving into the waves. One misjudged its distance and landed on the ship's deck, giving me an opportunity to admire its beautiful blue color, show it to friends and snap a few fast pictures before returning it to the sea. Besides flying fishes there are sailfishes, swordfishes, walking catfishes and many others with unusual adaptations. Lampreys are fishes with horny teeth which can attach themselves to other fishes and suck their blood.

Fishes are divided into two main groups—the cartilaginous fishes which are the sharks, skates and rays; and the bony fishes with which we are most familiar. Sharks, skates and rays have skeletons of cartilage hardened by lime, tooth-like scales and parallel slits covering their gills. Most of their time is spent in salt water but occasionally a few kinds venture into fresh water.

So much has been written about man-eating sharks that people tend to think all sharks are dangerous. But of the 250 kinds of sharks in the world only a few are known to be harmful. Some eat octopuses and squid, some eat fishes and others feed on minute plants and animals floating in the ocean.

Skates and rays are flat-bodied fishes with eyes on top of their heads. Even if you've never seen a skate you have probably seen a skate's egg case as you walked along a beach looking for shells. These egg cases are usually black, rectangular and leather-like with a long, thin projection at each corner. Some people call them "mermaids' purses." Skates are harmless but many rays are armed with a venom spine on the upper surface of the tail and so can be dangerous.

With about thirty thousand kinds of bony fishes known, it's difficult to find many characteristics that they all have in common in addition to their bony skeletons. Most have scales on which you can see growth rings, making it possible to tell how old certain fishes are. Bony fishes come in many shapes—some round, some flat, some long and thin. There is a gill opening on each side covered by a bony flap.

One well-known bony fish is a sturgeon. You may not know what it looks like but you've probably seen and tasted its eggs served as caviar. This delicacy originally came from several kinds of sturgeons in Europe but now is also obtained from American species. Under a sturgeon's snout are four long whiskers which just touch bottom as it swims along and help it locate the small animals upon which it feeds.

Another famous bony fish is the shad. Unlike the eel, which leaves fresh water to spawn in salt water, the shad leaves the ocean to lay its eggs in rivers. At this time many are caught for food. Shad belong to the herring family and so do the little fish we call sardines.

Trout and salmon belong to the same group of fishes. Both are sought after by fishermen, who are constantly devising new lures to attract them. Several kinds of trout are commonly raised in hatcheries and released into streams at the beginning of fishing season. Many of our streams and rivers where trout used to abound have become polluted to the point where these fishes can no longer survive. Unfortunately this is true of almost all bodies of water and rivers and streams which are near populated areas. Whether they live in fresh or salt water, fishes are adversely affected by changes in oxygen, temperature, current speed, silting and dissolved substances.

Just as starlings and house sparrows brought over from Europe have made themselves at home here, there are some introduced species of fishes. Those huge carp who come up to grab bread dropped into your local reservoir originated in Asia. They came to America via Europe about a hundred years ago and are now widespread. Because carp feed at the bottoms of lakes and in slow streams, stirring up mud and silt, many aquatic plants cannot grow. Without aquatic plants other kinds of fish do not fare well. Here then is another example of an introduced species having an adverse effect on native species. Goldfish are in the carp family and sometimes grow to large size when released in ponds with a good food supply.

There are many curious bits of knowledge about fishes and more information is being gathered all the time. Recently in the newspaper I read about some rare seashells that have been found only in the bellies of fishes! It seems that the little animals in the shells are eaten by the fishes and live in such inaccessible places that only the fishes can get to them. Shell collectors pay high prices to fishermen in South Africa, the Philippines and Brazil who catch these fish and extract the shells from their stomachs. Another interesting thing about fishes is that some kinds travel in large groups called schools. Being part of a school helps fishes to find mates, escape from predators and gather food.

If you go fishing see what observations you can make about fishes and their behavior. Many fishermen nowadays are returning their catch to the water, getting their enjoyment from being outdoors and outwitting

Milkweed bug on milkweed pod

Tiger swallowtail on thistle

Oak apple galls

Red-backed salamander on sphagnum moss

Peregrine falcon

Carolina wren

Hickory horned devil which becomes the royal walnut moth

Goldenrod ball gall

Tadpoles

Anole on branch with pixie cup and awl lichens

Black rat snake

Skin shed by
black rat snake

Box turtle eating grape

the fishes. Strange as it may seem fishermen outnumber baseball and football fans. With so many people involved there's a great potential for finding out more facts about fishes.

CHAPTER 22

Mammals

THE MOST FAMILIAR and well-known animals in the world are mammals. We are mammals and most of the animals we keep as pets and see in zoos and circuses are as well. All mammals are warm-blooded, have some hair and feed their young milk. Some mammals are carnivorous (meat-eaters), others herbivorous (plant-eaters) and others omnivorous (eating all kinds of food).

The blue whale, weighing almost two hundred tons and measuring over one hundred feet long, is the largest mammal. A tiny shrew living in southern Europe and less than one and one-half inches long is the smallest.

Egg-laying Mammals

One of the most fascinating mammals is the duck-billed platypus of Australia, which lays eggs, lives in tunnels along streams, eats earthworms and provides milk for its young. Other egg-laying mammals are the spiny anteaters which live in Australia, Tasmania and New Guinea.

Pouched Mammals (Marsupials)

Australia also has many other strange mammals such as kangaroos and koala bears which carry their young in pouches. These and other mammals with pouches for carrying their young belong to a special order, marsupials.

The most familiar marsupial, or pouched mammal, in the United States is the Virginia possum. Possums do most of their roaming around after dark searching for a wide variety of foods. They are especially fond of persimmons. Unfortunately, many are killed by cars as they move rather slowly across roads. Grayish white fur covers their bodies but their tails are long, pinkish and practically bare. On their hind feet the big toes are opposable (can make a circle with the next toe, as our thumbs can with our forefingers). With these toes and a tail that is prehensile (can wrap around a branch) possums clamber around in trees with ease. When the baby possums are born they are very small and undeveloped. A dozen or more newborn possums can fit into a teaspoon. In spite of their size, the front legs are strong enough to hold onto the mother possum's fur. Using these, the babies crawl into their mother's pouch and each latches onto a nipple. There they stay for five weeks. If there are more than thirteen baby possums born, the extras die, as each mother possum has only thirteen teats in her pouch. In addition to all these amazing things possums have two more unique features. One is that they have more teeth (fifty) than any other North American mammal, and the other is that they often "play dead" when threatened by a dog, person or other enemy. A possum does this by rolling over on its back, shutting its eyes and lying until it thinks the enemy has gone away. Then it quickly comes alive and scrambles off. The only other animal that's well-known for playing this trick is the hognosed snake.

Bats

Bats belong to an unusual, little-known and greatly misunderstood order of mammals. Many people find it hard to believe that an animal that flies is a mammal and not a bird. But as bats are covered with hair and feed their babies milk, they have the two qualifications necessary to be mammals. These creatures come out at dusk from their daytime sleeping places behind shutters, in caves and under eaves. One species, the red bat, is unusual in that the sexes are colored differently and it prefers hanging upside down in shady trees to sleeping in caves. Also it can be seen flying earlier in the evening than many other kinds of bats.

Many people are afraid of bats because they believe the superstition that bats will literally "get in their hair." Actually these amazing animals use a form of sonar to keep from bumping into people and things, making tiny high-pitched sounds that we can't hear as they fly around. These sound waves bounce off people, walls, trees and back to the bat's ear, causing the bat to fly in another direction. The one danger bats do present is that they frequently carry rabies. Of course if we use common sense in enjoying and finding out more about nature we never approach or try to pick up a wild animal that is acting strangely. Leave it alone and call the Humane Society or S.P.C.A. to pick it up. Bats infected with rabies have been known to bite people, especially children, with no reason. It's best to do your bat observing at a distance and to stay out of places where large numbers congregate. Try to understand bats enough so that you can reassure yourself and your friends and help them realize that bats, by eating flying insects such as mosquitoes, play a very important role in the balance of nature and should be protected.

Moles and Shrews (Insectivores)

Moles and shrews make up the next order of common mammals but because they spend most of their time underground most of us don't know much about their life history and habits. Often moles are incorrectly blamed for eating flower bulbs. Actually they eat only insects and earthworms so the blame probably rests with other creatures such as field mice. Of course, the mice may use the mole's tunnel to get to the flower bed! Many people get to see moles when their cats or dogs bring them in. Don't try to handle a live mole as it has very sharp teeth; but if you get the chance to touch a freshly killed one you'll find that the fur is very soft—in fact there's a material called moleskin which is soft and used by hikers to protect tender spots on their feet. Also take a look at the specially adapted front feet which look like small shovels and are used in digging, and notice that there are no visible eyes. If your pet brings home a live mole you can carefully, with gloves on, put it in a box of fresh dirt and watch it dig quickly out of sight. Besides the common mole of lawns there's another variety, the star-nosed mole, which lives in swampy places and is seldom seen. This mole looks very much like the common mole but around its pointy nose are several fleshy projections.

Shrews are even more mysterious creatures than moles. During the day they travel in runways under tangles of honeysuckle or beds of leaves, but at night they're more apt to come out in the open in search of their food, which is mostly insects and earthworms. They are small but fierce and can tackle an animal twice their size. Shrews are very hard to keep in captivity even for a short time, as they are constantly in motion and need huge quantities of food to keep going. They may eat as much as twice their own weight every day just to stay alive. The smallest mammal in the world is Savi's white-toothed shrew, which weighs about .09 of an ounce and lives along the coast of the northern Mediterranean Sea.

Even if your cat brings home a live shrew do not handle it, because some have poisonous bites. Just make what observations you can from a safe distance. Notice that your cat does not eat the shrews he catches, probably due to their unpleasant odor.

Flesh-eating Mammals (Carnivores)

This order, the carnivores, includes many familiar domesticated mammals such as dogs and cats, many native wild mammals such as raccoons and skunks as well as the bears, wolves, lions and tigers we commonly see in zoos.

Raccoons

Raccoons are carnivores that almost everyone has seen. They've become more common in recent years than when America was mostly wilderness. Other animals have become extinct or very rare in areas where there are many people, but because raccoons have adapted to a new way of life and learned to find food in garbage cans, they have increased in numbers. Also they are unusual in being able to return to the wild after spending some time as pets in homes. In many cases where a family has taken in an orphan raccoon and then gradually let it have its freedom as it grew older, it has gone back to the woods for longer and longer periods, finally disappearing for good.

Raccoons are active at night and spend their days sleeping in hollow trees. Often on walks along streams or around ponds, you can see their footprints in the mud looking very much like tiny human hands and feet. With their black masks and ringed tails, raccoons are easy to recognize even if you only get a quick look by the light of your headlights before they amble off into the bushes along the road. Their curious habit of washing their food is well-known. They also are experts at feeling around on the bottoms of streams and ponds with their front paws and coming up with delicacies like crayfish. People who've had their chickens killed and eaten by raccoons or their corn crop ruined by them are understandably unhappy. But under most circumstances they are fascinating animals to watch.

Weasels

Weasels are in this order but less often seen than raccoons, even though they are active by day and night. They can be up to eighteen inches long and are very slender and fast-moving. If you're lucky enough to see one you'll probably get just a quick look as it dashes across the road or under a bush with a mouse in its jaws. Weasels do a great job of keeping down the small rodent population. Occasionally a weasel will get into a chicken house and wreak havoc by killing many chickens, feeding on warm blood from their necks and then leaving. The northern weasel is interesting because it is brown in the summer and pure white in the winter, when it is known as ermine.

Skunks

Skunks also are carnivores. This is one animal we can identify without even seeing it. Even though skunks only give off their unpleasant scent if bothered by dogs or some other enemy, people associate skunks with the strong odor and grimace at the thought of any skunk. If not disturbed, skunks go about their nightly business of eating insects, fruits, mice and many other things. You can tell where a skunk has been hunting by looking for freshly dug holes about two inches deep and an inch or so across. They dig these holes with their sharp toenails while looking for grubs to eat. Many of the grubs they find are those of the Japanese beetle (skunks also are one of the few animals that will eat adult Japanese beetles). Once in a while a skunk may invade a chicken house and eat a chicken or some eggs.

Among country people there are many favorite ways of getting rid of skunk odor on your clothes or your dogs. Lemon juice, tomato juice and raw potatoes are just a few of the recommended remedies. Skunks only spray their scent, which comes from glands under their tails, as a last resort, and first give two warning signals. When you surprise or try to approach a skunk he'll raise his tail straight up in the air. If you don't go away he'll stamp his feet and then if you still persist in annoying him he'll squirt in your direction. There's a saying that if this liquid gets in your eyes it'll blind you but that's not so.

There are three kinds of skunks in the United States. Most common is the striped skunk, which is found in every one of our states except Alaska and Hawaii. Another, the spotted skunk, is found in one form or another in the South, Southwest and Northwest. A third kind, the hog-nosed skunk, lives in Arizona and New Mexico. With the top of its head, back and tail being white it is the handsomest of our skunks. It is also the largest and uses its turned-up snout as pigs do, to root around for food.

The worst natural enemy of the skunk is the great horned owl, which swoops silently down on it at night. Old groundhog holes make fine skunk homes and so do holes under porches and outbuildings on farms. Young skunks, descented, make interesting pets and can be trained to walk along on a leash.

Wolves, Coyotes and Foxes

Another group of flesh-eaters is the dog family. Wild animals in this family include wolves, coyotes and foxes. Because these animals are predators and kill other animals for food, there are many people who think they are bad and should all be destroyed. But those who understand the balance of nature realize that predators play an important role and are necessary to keep certain animal populations from becoming too large. For instance, when predators of deer in an area are destroyed more deer are able to survive. These large numbers use up the available food and ruin the trees and grass so that soon there is nothing to eat. When this happens many deer die of starvation. When foxes, wolves and coyotes catch and kill an animal for food it is most likely to be one that is very young, very old, sick or weak. So what's really happening is that the predators are helping keep animal populations strong and healthy. Many experiments have been conducted to prove this. In Isle Royale National Park in Michigan where there are wolves and moose on an island, scientists have discovered their numbers have remained constant over the years.

But out in the western states owners of large flocks of sheep have declared war on coyotes and have shot, trapped and poisoned them. As a result of the killing of large numbers of coyotes there has been an upsurge in the rabbit, mouse, rat and ground squirrel populations. This is just another example of what happens when the balance of nature is upset. Coyotes do kill an occasional sheep, most likely one that's old, ill, injured or newborn, but they also do ranchers a great service by killing many rodents. They are very clever, and have shown an amazing ability to survive in spite of all the pressures against them. To hear coyotes howling at night on the desert is truly to hear the call of the wild.

Fortunately nowadays, more and more people are beginning to realize the need to preserve our mammals. Years ago wild animals were looked upon as an unending source of meat, leather and fur and this attitude has led to the extinction of such animals as the Steller's sea cow. Others, including the plains bison, polar and grizzly bears, wolves and coyotes, have been eliminated from much of their original range and face various threats in the areas in which they remain.

Primates

Primates are the order of mammals to which we belong together with apes, monkeys and lemurs. Since we are discussing animals you may see in the wild in the United States we will not go into any detail here. There are no native lemurs, monkeys or apes in the United States. The zoo is the place to go if you want to study members of this order at close range.

Anteaters, Sloths and Armadillos

Another order, the edentates, includes anteaters, sloths and armadillos. Even though the word edentate means "without teeth" the anteaters are the only ones in this group who really have no teeth. And of this group, armadillos are the only ones you're likely to meet on your nature travels in the United States unless you go to the zoo. To see an armadillo in the wild, take a trip to Florida or the south central states. There are many interesting things to observe about armadillos. They always have four young of the same sex and live in burrows, usually coming out to forage for insects in the evening. While hunting for food, which besides insects includes some berries and eggs, they make sounds like pigs. They do not hear or see well and are often killed by speeding cars along highways at night. Because armadillos are covered with a scaly shell it is sometimes hard to remember that they are mammals but if you look closely you'll see hairs. This, combined with the fact that the young live on milk from their mother, makes them mammals.

Rabbits, Hares and Pikas

Another order, the lagomorphs, includes rabbits, hares and pikas. If you've ever been hiking on trails in the mountains out West, you may have seen the curious little pikas who live in crevices in the rocks. They make hay by drying piles of grasses in the sun and storing them in their burrows for winter eating. Pikas resemble little rabbits with no tails and short ears.

It's hard to get the differences between rabbits and hares straight in one's mind because they have become confused in this country. In Europe the hare lives in a shallow depression and bears its young covered with fur and with eyes open. The European rabbit lives in burrows and has young that are naked and blind. Here in the United States our cottontail rabbit resembles the hare in not making a burrow and resembles the European rabbit in having young that are blind and naked.

Rabbits and hares used to belong to the order of rodents and do seem to be like rodents because of their gnawing incisors. But they have an extra pair of tiny round teeth behind the upper gnawing teeth and also they cannot turn their front paws inward to hold food as the squirrels, groundhogs and chipmunks can. In North America there are thirteen kinds of rabbits and ten kinds of hares. The cottontail rabbit is a true rabbit. The famous jackrabbits of the West and the snowshoe hares of the North are true hares.

Rodents

Rodents, or gnawing animals, make up an order of mammals which everyone knows. Members of this order are distinguished by long gnawing teeth in front—two above and two below. Even the best-run households have a visiting house mouse now and then; Norway rats are a common problem of city dwellers and farmers. Both these species have been introduced from Europe and have become pests which need to be controlled. Hawks and owls are helpful but cannot completely control rats and mice—especially in cities where garbage and hiding places are plentiful. One rat or mouse can be a fascinating creature to observe but thousands of them in a small area are not only a nuisance but a threat to health.

Rats and Mice

There are native rats and mice that also can do damage to homes and crops. The white-footed or deer mouse is a lovely little animal with large eyes and ears, a brown back and white underparts. Have you ever put some mattresses away for the winter in your summer cabin and then found holes in them and a little round nest of mattress stuffing, grass and leaves when you unrolled them? That's evidence that deer mice enjoyed themselves in your absence. Occasionally a white-footed mouse will carry warm materials into an abandoned white-faced hornet's nest and use it for a cozy home.

Meadow mice or voles, as they are also called, have small eyes and ears and short tails. By girdling trees and eating some vegetables and flower bulbs they cause damage. Each vole eats its own weight in plant material every day. Many of these little animals are eaten by foxes, hawks and owls and also by house cats.

Pack rats, also called cave rats or wood rats, are curious because of their habit of hoarding large quantities of nuts, acorns and other food. They also gather bits of tinfoil, coins, old shotgun shells and other shiny objects.

Chipmunks

Chipmunks are rodents too and great fun to watch as they dash in and out of rock or wood piles or disappear into underground tunnels. They make a sharp squeak when disturbed. If you're a bird watcher, chipmunks may fool you when you try to track down a new sound in the woods. You may look and listen for several minutes before you find the noise is coming from a mammal and not from a bird. The only people who don't appreciate chipmunks are gardeners who have too many of them tunneling through their bulb plantings and azalea nurseries. These busy creatures gather seeds, nuts and berries and store them underground. They are especially fond of sunflower seeds and will even visit bird feeders and make off with their cheek pouches stuffed full of seeds. Because they are so fast they can make quick getaways when danger in the form of a hawk, owl or fox comes near. As do many other rodents, chipmunks hibernate in very cold weather.

Prairie Dogs

Out West, prairie dogs are rodents that are fun to watch because they live together in "towns." Unfortunately with the wide-open spaces being developed in various ways, many prairie-dog towns are being eliminated. Their populations have gone up and down with the advance of civilization. A hundred years ago prairie dogs were kept under control by wolves, hawks, coyotes, black-footed ferrets and other predators. Then when many of these predators were killed off by well-meaning ranchers, the prairie dogs increased dramatically and did tremendous damage to crops. Now the pendulum is swinging the other way and prairie-dog numbers are down.

Squirrels

Squirrels come in many varieties but the best-known are the gray, the red and the flying squirrels. The gray squirrel is very adaptable, being equally at home in the forest, your yard or a city park. People are often glad to have them around to watch as they chase each other around tree trunks, sit up on their haunches eating acorns and keep busy burying walnuts and hickory nuts for winter use. Some people consider gray squirrels a terrible nuisance because they are so fond of sunflower seeds that they can clean out bird feeders in no time. There are numerous devices to keep squirrels from getting into bird feeders but many times the squirrels figure how to get in anyway. If you're a squirrel watcher and keep looking, you may find black squirrels and white squirrels. They are just color variations of the gray squirrel but delightful to see.

Red squirrels, smaller than gray squirrels, have gotten a bad reputation for eating bird eggs and a few baby birds as well. Around farms they make nests in attics, garages and similar places, chewing up old rags, grasses and leaves and storing away huge quantities of nuts in the same locations. Red squirrels, which chatter angrily when disturbed or alarmed, are especially plentiful in evergreen forests.

Flying squirrels are hardly ever seen by most of us who are up and about in the daytime as they sleep all day in hollow trees and come out to glide about and find food at night. Some people say that if you wander through the woods knocking on all the dead trees you come to, sooner or later you'll wake up a flying squirrel who will stick his head out a hole and look at you curiously. (Unfortunately, most of us aren't in a position to do that.) They are beautiful little animals with large eyes and make fascinating pets if captured while very young. If you are driving in wooded areas at night, keep an eye out for flying squirrels leaping from one tree trunk to another with the membranes between their front and back legs stretched out. Because they glide rather than fly, they lose altitude after they take off and always end up lower than they started out. As do red squirrels, flying squirrels like to live in attics and can be a problem chewing up stored materials to make their nests and rolling nuts around in the middle of the night.

Beavers

Beavers, which can weigh up to seventy pounds, are the largest rodents in North America. The capybara of South America may weigh 160 pounds and is the largest rodent in the world. Like all other rodents, beavers have two long yellow gnawing teeth above and two below. The front feet are small, clawed and used as hands while the back feet are larger and webbed. Beavers spend much time in and under the water and are famous for their engineering ability in building dams. If you can visit a beaver pond, stand on the dam and notice how various sizes of tree trunks and branches have been fitted together to hold the water back. And look around in the vicinity of the pond to see the stumps remaining after the logs were chewed off. It's impressive to see how much work these comparatively small animals accomplish. They sleep most of the day, actively working in the early morning and evening hours. When not building dams they are busy gathering bark, cattails and other water plants for food.

The broad flat tail of the beaver is something no other animal in the world has. It is used in various ways; as an alarm signal the beaver will slap its tail against the surface of the water, making a loud sharp sound just before it dives. The beaver's tail helps it steer and push along when swimming, and on land the tail serves as a prop when the beaver is standing on its hind legs. The tail is also used sometimes to help carry building materials to the dam. It is not employed as a trowel to apply mud to the dam as many people think.

In the pond backed up by the dam, beavers build their lodge and store their food supply of branches for the winter. By adding mud and stones to the branches, the animals make them sink to the bottom of the pond where they can swim out and get food as needed even when the pond is covered with ice. Canals are also built so that trees can be floated to the pond from nearby groves. Large numbers of beavers are still trapped for their fur in Canada but in the United States they are mainly valuable for their pond-building activities. These ponds help in flood control and also are useful as water storage reservoirs.

Muskrats

Muskrats resemble small beavers and are sometimes mistaken for beavers by people who see them swimming in ponds. They live along streams and in ponds and marshes over most of the United States and get their name from two glands near the base of the tail that secrete a musky odor. This odor seems to be used as a way of communicating with other muskrats and is left at landing spots along the shore. Muskrats use their chisel-like gnawing teeth to gather food, to help build homes and to fight. Amazing as it may seem, the more a muskrat uses its teeth the sharper they get. This is because the inner side of the teeth is made of a softer substance than the outside and wears down faster, as with beavers and other rodents. You won't have any problems telling a muskrat from a beaver if you check the animal's tail. The muskrat has a much thinner tail and it is flattened sideways rather than from top to bottom. Because they are more plentiful and can live in a wider range of climate and terrain, you're more likely to see a muskrat than a beaver.

Woodchucks

Some people think they're seeing a beaver when a woodchuck runs across the road in front of them. These mammals are rodents and use their gnawing teeth to chew apples and tender young plants, such as bean and squash, in your garden. Also called groundhogs, woodchucks live in big burrows they dig in various places. Around farms they may dig in fields, along hedgerows or under buildings. These holes can be dangerous if a person or large animal such as a cow or horse falls into one and breaks a leg. Hunters and dogs are the worst enemies of groundhogs. If you're not worried about your garden being eaten by them, woodchucks are fun to watch. Sometimes they sit up on their haunches and nibble on clover held in their front paws. If they see something that alarms them they may give a loud whistle before they turn and retreat down their holes. Because of this they are sometimes called "whistle-pigs." When you see one of these fat furry creatures it's fun to remember the tongue twister, "How much wood could a woodchuck chuck if a woodchuck could chuck wood? A woodchuck would chuck all the wood that a woodchuck could if a woodchuck

could chuck wood." Here again you won't have any trouble identifying
a groundhog and telling it from a beaver or muskrat if you check on the
tail. A groundhog's tail is fairly short, very furry and round, while the
beaver and muskrat have practically naked tails which are flattened in
one direction or another.

Porcupines

Porcupines, with their thirty thousand quills, are interesting but not
very intelligent rodents which make dens in trees or under rocks. In the
East they are found from West Virginia north, and in the West they live
as far south as central California. Their food consists of various plant
materials and they have a craving for salt. In their search for salt they
do much damage by chewing up tool handles and similar objects that
have been used by men. Dogs often get quills painfully embedded in
their noses when they try to investigate a porcupine. The porcupine does
not throw its quills but erects them when in danger and stands firm. A
dog is likely to come close and sniff around the porcupine. As soon as
he touches a quill its barb hooks into his nose. Then the dog's owner
has the difficult job of removing the quill. Only one baby porcupine is
born at a time and it is already covered with spines at birth.

Pet Rodents

There are several interesting rodents you won't meet on field trips in
the United States but which you will see in pet stores. Gerbils are very
popular pets these days because they are fun to watch and easy to care
for. Their original home is in the Mongolian Desert where they were noticed by a scientist who introduced them as laboratory animals. Now
you see them in many homes and schools as well as pet stores. Hamsters
also come from Asia and are fun to watch, but sleep all day and run
around at night. Nowadays there are many varieties of hamsters including panda bear, pink-eared, blue-eared and long-haired.

Guinea pigs, natives of South America, have babies that are practically
able to get along by themselves the day they are born. Baby hamsters
and gerbils are born naked, blind and helpless but not baby guinea pigs.
Guinea pigs are bigger animals and so take up more room and eat more
but are great pets. There are also rats and mice of varying kinds and
colors that are kept as pets too. You may find a chinchilla in a pet store.

This rodent, a native of South America, was bought some years ago by people who thought they could get rich raising them and selling their skins for fur coats. For most people the plan did not work. Some turned the chinchillas loose and others kept them for pets. They are nice clean pets and make interesting little noises.

Whales, Dolphins and Porpoises

Whales, dolphins and porpoises cannot smell well but do have excellent hearing even though their ears are mere slits. Only bats hear better than cetaceans (that's the group or order to which whales, dolphins and porpoises belong).

Cetaceans over the years have been noted for their curiosity and playfulness and for being unafraid of man. Probably the reason for their lack of fear is that they have no natural enemies except for the killer whale. In various aquariums throughout the country and especially on the coasts of Florida and California, dolphins, porpoises and even small whales delight visitors with their tricks and antics. Divers have conducted experiments with dolphins, teaching them to carry tools and messages to men working under water.

Because they were exploited for centuries for their oil, some kinds of whales have almost disappeared from the oceans. But their future looks a bit brighter now due to the efforts of conservationists and the research done by scientists trying to understand better their life histories.

Seals, Sea Lions and Walruses

There is another order of mammals, the Pinnipedia (fin-footed), you probably won't see unless you make a trip to the zoo, the ocean or the Arctic. Everybody knows what a walrus is but many people confuse sea lions and seals. Remember one fact and you'll be able to keep seals and sea lions straight from now on: sea lions have external ears and so do fur seals but all the other kinds of seals are earless. The next time you go to the zoo and see some graceful, streamlined animals leaping out of the water to catch the fish their keeper is tossing, look carefully to see if they have external ears. If they do, they are sea lions, which are much more often seen in zoos than earless seals.

Manatees

If you live in or visit Florida, you may be able to see a member of the manatee order. They have become rare in recent times due to hunting, unusual spells of cold weather and collisions with the propellers of high-speed power boats. Manatees, also known as sea cows, are quiet, gentle and unusual-looking animals from seven to fifteen feet long. They feed on water plants and may eat one hundred pounds a day of such things as turtle grass. They have a strange habit of sitting upright in the water with just their head and shoulders showing, so they may be what sailors have seen and described as mermaids.

Even-toed Mammals

You may never have thought of counting a cow's toes but if you do you'll discover that she has four on each foot. Other mammals with an even number of toes are pigs, sheep, goats, camels, hippopotamuses, giraffes, moose, deer and elk. As you can see there are both wild and domesticated mammals in this group.

Some even-toed mammals have long legs useful for running but others such as pigs have short legs. There are variations too in the kinds of horns and antlers some members of the group have. Deer have antlers which they shed every year but cattle and sheep have permanent horns. The pronghorn antelope keeps the inside bony part of its horns but sheds an outside layer annually.

These animals have another thing in common besides their even number of toes: they all eat plants. Giraffes, cattle, camels, sheep, goats, buffalo and bison have complicated digestive systems including stomachs with four parts. As they graze or browse these animals bite off large quantities of plants and swallow them into the first two sections of their stomachs. Here water is added, some fermentation takes place and muscle action helps make the plant material into pulp. Later the animals lie down, often in the shade, and regurgitate small quantities of this pulp to chew at leisure. In my childhood I spent hours watching our cows chew their cud and counting how many times each mouthful was chewed before it was swallowed into the third part of the stomach and a new batch regurgitated. Sometimes cows chew their cud while standing in the barn being milked. The final step is the passing of the food into the fourth section of the stomach. When wild animals retreat to a quiet place to chew their cud they not only get out of the sun but also are less apt to be killed by predators.

Even-toed mammals often have fewer front teeth and also their teeth vary in size and shape. Hippopotamuses have almost horizontal incisors helpful in rooting out water plants. These strange creatures also have their eyes on top of their heads. With this arrangement they can look for danger while almost completely submerged.

It's interesting to note that all even-toed mammals live in groups. Some, such as wild pigs, may live in small groups of ten or so while others, such as some of the African antelopes, live in herds of several hundred. In each of these groups there is a definite social structure with one animal as the leader. This is true also of herds of domestic cattle. The next time you have a chance, make some observations on groups of cows or steers you see in the country. When they are grazing, usually all the animals will be headed the same way. When they move from one part of the pasture to another they fall in line behind a leader.

Odd-toed Mammals

It's hard to believe that horses, tapirs and rhinoceroses have something in common but they do—an uneven number of toes. In ancient times there were many more kinds of odd-toed mammals but today we have only three families: the horse family, the tapir family and the rhinoceros family. Included with the horses are the asses, zebras, donkeys, burros and mules, all of which are more or less specialized for running. Strange as it may seem horses are more numerous today than they were a hundred years ago when they were necessary for farming. Most farming now is done with tractors and other machines but in a few parts of the country horses are still used. Around Lancaster, Pennsylvania, there are many Amish people who do not believe in using machinery and there you can see horses and mules out in the fields pulling plows just as they did a hundred years ago.

The numbers of riding and race horses have been steadily increasing. With more leisure time people are enjoying horseback riding and afternoons at the race track. Horses can also be seen in cities carrying mounted policemen into such difficult spots as riots and traffic jams, or hauling carts of fresh produce through the streets to be sold door to door.

If you take a close look at a horse's hoof you will see that all but the middle toe have been reduced in size and that the hoof is really the end of the middle toe. Two small useless toes are located behind the leg and several inches off the ground.

Tapirs have four toes on their front feet and three on their hind feet but rhinoceroses have three toes on each foot. To see either of these animals visit the zoo. Tapirs are found in Malaya and tropical America and rhinoceroses inhabit certain areas of Asia and Africa but are becoming quite rare.

Elephants

Elephants are descendants of those ancient beasts, mastodons and mammoths, which roamed the earth thousands of years ago. Only two kinds of elephants, Indian (Asiatic) and African, exist today. Indian elephants have been trained for centuries to carry people and do heavy work, such as pulling or carrying logs. Three thousand years ago Hannibal used African elephants on the battlefield and to carry heavy loads over the Alps.

Unless you plan to take a safari to Africa or India, the best place to observe elephants is a zoo or circus. It is spellbinding to watch them and ponder their many unique features. First of all, there is the enormous size they attain. Their weight of five or six tons is supported by a heavy skeleton. Inside an elephant's huge skull is a comparatively small brain. They are intelligent and after dogs are the most easily trained animals. Elephant tusks are overgrown teeth coming from the upper jaw and are used in rooting up food plants and for fighting. African elephants have the biggest tusks (sometimes weighing two hundred pounds). The ivory from these is highly prized for carving and other uses. Both sexes of African elephants have tusks but only the male Indian elephants do. Another difference between the species is their ears: those of the Indian species are smaller.

Elephants are sociable, traveling in herds of from five to forty animals. In Africa these herds migrate during the dry season from the plains to forests in the mountains or along rivers in search of the fruits, herbs and leaves they need for food. Elephants are good swimmers with the females sometimes carrying their young on their backs or guiding them through the water with their trunks. An elephant's trunk, with its up to forty thousand muscles, is a hand, arm, lips and nose all in one besides being used for drinks and showers.

Today elephants face two major problems. First, because of their valuable tusks many are illegally killed by poachers. Second, in many areas there are more elephants than can exist on the amount of food available. Particularly in Africa, herds are being driven from their ancestral territories by natives who need more room.

PART V

Ways To Enjoy Nature

CHAPTER 23

Non-Living Things

IN SOME PLACES and at certain times it's hard to find plants or animals to study, so it's a good idea to have an interest in non-living things as well. If you know something about stars and planets, rocks and minerals, water and weather, you'll never run out of ideas for investigation.

Moon, Stars and Planets

Even in the smoggiest cities you can sometimes see the sun during the day and the moon at night. The sun, 93 million miles away, is fascinating to watch and especially beautiful when it rises and sets. The ancient Greeks and Romans made up many fascinating stories about the sun and the moon and the stars. Even today there are many unsolved mysteries about them, but centuries ago nothing was known. Myths involving the sun, moon and stars are great reading. One I like tells the story of Daedalus and his son, Icarus, who flew too close to the sun wearing wings made of gull feathers. As the tale goes, the feathers were fastened together with wax, which was melted by the sun, causing Icarus to fall into the sea and drown.

When you look up at the moon at night it's not hard to imagine you see a face or to understand why people long ago might have thought it was made of green cheese. Today we can think of many more things when watching the moon, such as all the feats performed on it by the astronauts and projects that are planned for the future.

Watching the moon change in size and shape during the course of each month gives you many things to wonder about. Where does it get its light and why does it seem to get gradually larger and then gradually smaller every month? It's easy to understand that the moon's light comes from the sun. But when you go further and learn that the moon revolves around the earth as the earth is revolving around the sun things become complicated. The moon affects the tides of the ocean. Seeing the moon in the daytime is always a surprise but not so much so when you understand that each day the moon follows the sun across the sky from east to west.

Eclipses of the moon and the sun are phenomena that never fail to arouse interest among many people who don't pay much attention to the natural world at other times. Eclipses can be total or partial and can be predicted far ahead of time by astronomers. I have always had trouble understanding eclipses but when I consult the diagrams in my encyclopedia my confusion vanishes. Eclipses can be total with the sun or moon completely dark; partial with the sun or moon partly darkened and partly lighted; or annular with the center of the sun or moon dark and surrounded by a ring of light. Eclipses of the moon happen only when the moon is full. Then the earth is between the moon and the sun and the moon disappears from view in the shadow of the earth. Eclipses of the sun happen when the moon is new and passes directly between the earth and the sun. Astronomers interested in eclipses travel all over the world to observe them and record their findings. Some scientists watch eclipses from planes and others from ships. In recent years astronomer friends of mine have traveled to Africa and Australia to see eclipses and find new facts about them.

Learning the constellations and the stories behind them is not hard if you go outside on a clear moonless night, in a place where there are not too many interfering lights from shopping centers and freeways. If you know which direction is north you can pick out the Big Dipper.

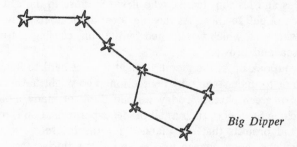

Big Dipper

The two stars on the side away from the handle point to the North Star, which is the first star in the handle of the Little Dipper. Cassiopeia is another easy constellation to pick out—just look for a lopsided W in the Milky Way. In the fall and winter the most magnificent constellation in the night sky is Orion, the Mighty Hunter. With just a little imagination you can see this giant with a sword hanging from his belt, a club raised overhead, followed by his two dogs while facing a charging bull.

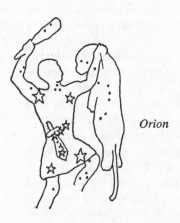

Orion

It's harder to follow and identify planets on your own as they are not always in the same place in relation to the stars. If you see something red that doesn't twinkle it's probably Mars. Jupiter is outstanding at times and with the aid of a good telescope you can pick up at least some of its nine moons. A telescope will also help to pick up Saturn with its rings.

A wonderful time for star study is as you're lying in your sleeping bag out in the open on a mountaintop. You can listen to the night sounds, try to pick out familiar shapes and begin to count stars before you fall off to sleep.

Rocks and Minerals

Rocks and minerals can be just as fascinating to study as plants and animals. Since they do not move around like animals or come and go with the seasons, they are easier to observe and study. If you plan a field trip to a quarry to look for a particular mineral, you'll probably find it, whereas you often may not find the bird you have gone many miles to see. To get started in rocks and minerals, it's best to join a group to get help in identifying your specimens. Rock and mineral clubs often conduct field trips to special places where unusual specimens can be found.

There are three basic kinds of rocks classified as to the way in which they were formed. Igneous rocks came first and were originally hot and liquid. They are our oldest rocks. As igneous rocks become worn down by weathering (the effects of the sun, frost, wind and water) they are broken into fine particles. As these particles settle down into layers they become sedimentary rocks. Some examples are particles of sand becoming sandstone; particles of clay becoming shale; and in the sea, pieces of shells becoming limestone. When sedimentary rocks are affected by tremendous heat and pressure they are changed into metamorphic rocks. Sandstone turns into quartz; shale into slate; and limestone into marble.

Much more fascinating than the rocks themselves are the beautiful crystals that occur in or with them. Collect them either from nature or by buying from or trading with other collectors. As with any other collections it is important to label each specimen with the collector's name, date it was collected and locality.

Remember that the earth we live on is really a big ball with a hard rock crust on the outside and molten rock inside. All the pieces of rock you find in your travels were originally part of this rock ball. There are many ways in which the piece you hold in your hand may have been broken off. Volcanoes erupting break off rocks. Oceans break off rocks along the shores where waves pound ceaselessly day after day. Rivers break off rocks and carry them to new places. Ice-embedded rocks are moved by glaciers and dropped in new locations as the ice melts. In states such as Maine, where much glaciation took place in times past, you can find huge boulders brought down by glaciers from the Far North.

If you're very lucky you may find a rock that came from outer space, called a meteorite. Have you ever looked at the stars and seen one suddenly shoot across the sky? At certain times of the year you may see many in one night. When in the air they're called shooting stars or meteors; when a piece of one lands on earth it is called a meteorite. There are some large meteorites to be seen in the Smithsonian Institution in Washington, D.C.

To analyze what chemicals and minerals compose a particular rock, a very thin slice of the rock is sawed off and examined under a microscope. In your home you can observe many things about rocks—notably color, hardness and cleavage. If you found your rock in a woods or field, the true color may be covered by dirt so scrape off a little of the surface with your penknife. One test for color is the streak test, in which you make a streak with your rock on a piece of unglazed porcelain. Some rocks and minerals may be one color but make a streak of a

Beaver swimming by lodge

Fishing in a farm pond

*Exploring a
bald cypress swamp*

Field trip along a railroad track

Forest floor

Birch gnawed by beaver

different color. Pyrite is a mineral that looks yellow but makes a black streak. Another test is for hardness. Talc is so soft you can scratch it with your fingernail but diamonds are so hard you can scratch glass with them. Different rocks and minerals have special ways of breaking, called cleavage by geologists. You may see a rock hunter using his hammer to break a rock when he's trying to identify it. Heat and chemical tests must be done in laboratories under controlled conditions.

If you travel by train, bus or car, get in the habit of looking at rocks as you go, particularly where the road has been cut through a rocky hill. Notice that sometimes you can see layers of rock of different thicknesses and colors. These layers may be straight or they may have been pushed into wavy patterns by tremendous forces in the earth's crust long ago. If you travel by air, get a bird's-eye view of the areas you fly over. Look for coastlines, mountains, rivers and other geologic features which will give you clues as to what has happened in these areas.

An interesting project is the collection of rocks or soil from each state in the union. An old professor I know built himself a friendship fireplace using rocks given to him by students and friends from many different parts of the country. He made a chart to help him remember where each rock came from and who gave it to him.

Many children's games using stones are played all around the world. Flat, roundish pebbles of certain sizes are just right for skipping across water. Sometimes you find a rock with such an interesting shape you just must take it home to use as a paperweight, doorstop, mantel decoration or conversation piece. Flat stones from the beach are fun to paint. Notice that rocks you find in the middle of a field often have sharp edges while those you find at the beach or along a river are smooth and rounded. Over the years water rolls stones against each other until finally all the sharp edges are smooth.

Rocks were used to make man's earliest tools and weapons. Bowls were made by grinding hollows in soft rocks with hard rocks. In these bowls grain was ground, using one rock against another. A rock held in the hand made a fine hammer and one lashed onto a stick made an ax. Sharpened rocks were used to skin animals and as arrow and spear heads.

Campers today use rocks to make temporary fireplaces or hold down tents. Certain flat rocks can be heated in the fire and used for cooking. Eggs-on-a-rock is one of my favorite camp foods. You have to be sure that the flat rock you heat in the fire does not have moisture in it. Moisture will cause the rock to explode and scatter dangerous fragments. Don't use a rock in which you can see fine cracks. Use a good solid rock at least the size of a slice of bread and about an inch thick. Heat it up in a good fire and carefully take it out with a green stick. Lay a slice of bacon on it. If the rock is just the right temperature the bacon will sizzle, smell delicious and cook in a few minutes. Push it to the edge of the rock and add a slice of bread with the middle removed. Into the hole in the middle break one egg. When the egg is cooked on the bottom flip it over. As soon as it is done on both sides put the bacon on and eat it. No pans, dishes or forks to wash!

Rocks still make good hammers when you're out in the field and need to pound in stakes or crack nuts. In a pinch you can use a rock to cut string by pulling the string back and forth across a sharp edge.

As you go about your daily life look for uses of rocks. At the breakfast table when you reach for the salt you are reaching for a mineral (part of a rock). Halite is the name for salt in mineral books. When you write with a pencil you are using another mineral, graphite. (The so-called "lead" in lead pencils is not really lead at all.) Chalk for the blackboard comes from a very soft rock made up of the shells of tiny animals that lived in ancient seas.

Sand is usually made up of fragments of rock. When you look at sand with a hand lens or under a microscope you can see little chunks of quartz and other minerals as well as some bits of shells and miscellaneous materials. If you ever visit Sand Beach in Acadia National Park on Mount Desert Island in Maine, you'll find different things in the sand there. Mixed together on the beach are mainly ground-up shells and the green spines of sea urchins with lesser quantities of rock fragments.

Mica is an exciting mineral to find in large sheets and beautiful even when you see it as tiny sparkles in a cement sidewalk. Quartz is a colorless mineral but often becomes discolored in various ways so you can find it as smoky quartz, rose quartz, rusty quartz and milky quartz. Asbestos is another interesting mineral because of the way it is composed of long fibers and the fact that it is used to insulate hot pipes.

Fossils

Since a fossil is defined as "any remains, impression, or trace of animal or plant of a former geological age" it seems to bridge the gap between living and non-living. Finding the print of a fern, shell, dinosaur foot or even a raindrop inside a rock almost makes the rock come alive. Scientists have been able to put together a pretty good idea of what plants and animals were like millions of years ago from the evidence they have found in fossils. From the fossil record the evolution of the elephant has been traced from a pig-like animal living 20 to 40 million years ago to the mastodon of 1 million years ago and finally to our present-day Indian and African elephants.

Fossil hunting can be done in various places. Along the west coast of Maryland's Chesapeake Bay are the Calvert Cliffs, full of fossils from the Cretaceous Age. Many shells, sharks' teeth and other interesting remains are found here on the beach washed from the cliff by the action of the waves in the bay. Fossils are usually found in sedimentary rocks such as shale, limestone and sandstone but not everywhere that these rocks occur. Fossils are also found in coal. Besides bones and shells and their casts or impressions, there are fossil lumps of dung called coprolites, and smooth pebbles called gastroliths that used to be inside dinosaurs' chests and may have helped them grind up their food in much the same way that the gravel in the gizzards of certain modern birds helps them grind up grain.

Water

Water in its various forms can be just as interesting to study as birds, flowers, trees and insects. And it's one of those things you can find even on days when living things are scarce. In cities, take a trip to a park and watch a fountain with water sparkling in the sun. Always keep an eye open for a rainbow any day that it rains while the sun is shining. Think of the various places you can find water: dewdrops, fog, oceans, lakes, springs, ponds, streams, rivers, faucets and puddles. Also think of the forms water comes in: frost, ice, snow, liquid and steam. If you're out in Yellowstone National Park watching Old Faithful erupt, you're seeing water turned to steam.

Clouds are collections of water droplets or small pieces of ice in the atmosphere and are constantly changing in shape and size. There are cumulus clouds which are fluffy like big pieces of cotton and feathery cirrus clouds which float at higher altitudes. Stratus clouds are low layers of fog. Watching clouds move across the moon's face at night is fascinating. Gray and black clouds tell us of approaching storms and are often brightened by flashes of lightning. Clouds of lovely colors appear at sunrise and sunset. These are the times to have your camera or your art supplies ready to try to capture the beauty of these special times of day. No two clouds or sunrises or sunsets are ever the same.

Storms of various kinds give us many more chances for nature observations. Thunderstorms, with all the noise, lightning flashes and torrents of rain, can be frightening, but if you are in a safe place to watch and understand what's happening you will gain a new appreciation of natural phenomena. Tornadoes, cyclones and hurricanes fall into a different category. If you happen to be in the path of one of these you cannot take time to appreciate nature but must quickly escape to safety.

Ice storms make fairylands out of woods and fields in just a few hours. Each little twig and blade of grass encased in a thin layer of ice is beautiful. Snow caps on fence posts, soft drifts, individual flakes on your jacket and footprints of birds and mammals are all things of beauty. And of course sledding, skiing and snowshoeing are great ways to get exercise while making nature notes. If you have very clean snow you can make snow ice cream and a special kind of candy called leather aprons. Look for these recipes in Chapter 25. With a little special equipment and great care you can even preserve snowflakes in plastic. If you'd like to try this find the directions in Chapter 25 and get your materials together now so you'll be ready when the next snow falls.

Flooding can occur when huge amounts of rain fall in a short time or thick layers of snow and ice melt rapidly, causing much damage to crops and homes in certain areas. If you've ever seen cars and houses washed away by a serious flood you'll realize how much power water can have. Watching just a small stream overflow its banks and carry trees, boards and large quantities of soil along is impressive. The next time you make observations in a heavy rain notice that little water runs off grassy fields while much erosion goes on in plowed fields or bare areas in new housing developments. Every year tons of good topsoil are carried downstream by floodwaters, leaving the fields from which it came poor in nutrients. Much of this rich soil is eventually washed out to sea or into the Gulf of Mexico but some is left on floodplains or flatlands beside rivers and streams. Floodplains have very rich soil which is added to whenever there is a flood. Some of our loveliest wildflowers grow on floodplains. Among these are Virginia bluebells and trout lilies making solid beds of blue and yellow in early spring.

Water is our most important natural resource. Remember that a large percentage of your body is water and that we cannot get along without it. I hope you have the experiences of seeing the Mississippi River and the Atlantic and Pacific oceans and of lying face down to get a drink from an unpolluted spring or stream. There still are some. We all must work to preserve the clean waters that are left in our country and to help restore those that have been polluted.

Going for a walk in the rain helps us to appreciate water. Plants are refreshed by rain especially on a hot summer day. And after a rain, drops of water sparkle like diamonds on the leaves of jewelweed, lotus and other plants. Make a water garden if you can, indoors or out, and marvel at the ways water plants and animals are adapted to their special environment.

CHAPTER 24

Habitats to Explore

WHEN you take time to think about it you'll realize that different habitats have living in them certain plants and animals. If you want to see skunk cabbage blooming you have to go to a swamp and if you want to see a squirrel you take a walk in the woods or park where there are trees. There are many different kinds of places to explore. Remember that a field trip may last several hours, days or only a few minutes; you can take one at any hour of the day or night and at any time of the year. Don't get into the habit of just going out in the spring to look for bloodroot and trailing arbutus or just in the fall to see geese flying south. Get out as often as you can and keep an open mind so that you won't be disappointed if you don't see exactly what you thought you might. If you have an enthusiastic and inquisitive attitude even the most ordinary creatures and most common weeds become fascinating.

Fields

First let's take a trip in a field. Some may be cultivated, others lying idle, though all have grass of several kinds. In the grass (try to learn some of the varieties of grass you may see) there are many insects making a variety of noises. Crickets may be chirping and flies buzzing, especially if there are cows or horses in the field. As you walk through the grass in summer, grasshoppers fly ahead of you. Other sounds may come from crows flying by, wind blowing through tall weeds or little mice and shrews scurrying along under dry grass. If you come upon a pile of cow dung you can spend time observing a whole little world of insects and fungi returning the manure to the soil.

If there are fences around the fields, keep an eye out for birds which perch there to look for insects. If there are old wooden fence posts with holes in them, watch for downy woodpeckers, bluebirds and house wrens nesting inside. If the field is mowed now and then the blooming season of flowers such as Queen Anne's lace and thistles is prolonged. Think about how persistent these weeds are in putting up new stems and buds after the original plant is cut off. And see how many different grasses you can find even though you may not be able to tell what they are.

In a cultivated field you will not find such variety, but nevertheless a walk through a field of tall corn in tassel is a great experience. The pollen-laden tassels give off a delightful fragrance as the breeze blows the pollen grains onto the lovely maroon and green corn silks on the ears below. Even in the most carefully cultivated cornfield there are some interesting weeds. Morning-glories may be climbing up the corn-stalks and Indian mallow with its curious fruits often thrives at the edges.

Open fields are good places to watch for butterflies; also check milkweeds and thistles for interesting caterpillars munching away on their leaves.

A trip through a field on a snowy day in winter brings more surprises —curious weed stalks and seed pods sticking up through the snow and interesting tracks and trails made by animals. Maybe then you'll be able to see that field sparrow's nest that you missed in the summer near the base of an old dead thistle.

Marshes, Swamps and Bogs

Marshes, swamps and bogs have one thing in common—their dampness. To clear up the confusion about what characterizes each, think of a marsh as being either fresh or salt water and near the coast. A swamp is a low, wet place often near a stream and with a few trees in it. And a bog is a place that used to be a lake or pond but which is gradually becoming filled in with plants such as sphagnum moss, pitcher plants, sundews, various members of the heath family and some grasses and sedges. When you go exploring in a bog you always get wet feet and can feel the plant layer under you shaking up and down.

Once you are reconciled to getting your feet wet, bog, swamp and marsh exploring is a fascinating experience. There are plants and animals you'll find only in these habitats. One is the larva of the Baltimore butterfly which feeds on a plant called turtlehead. Since turtlehead grows only in swamps, that is where you'll find the caterpillar and the butterfly it later becomes. Marsh fern, swamp milkweed, fringed gentian, the purple fringeless orchid, nodding ladies' tresses, poison sumac and hellebore are other plants that need to have their roots in wet soil. In many of these wet places, especially the salt-water marshes, hordes of mosquitoes may interfere with your enjoyment of nature's wonders. Just be sure to include some insect repellent in your field trip knapsack. The sights, smells and sounds of a salt-water marsh are different. The main thing to try to comprehend while you're there is that the incoming tide brings certain things from the sea and the outgoing tide takes with it rich nutrients from decaying plants and animals in the marsh. And while you're admiring the birds and crabs and shells, think of the millions of tiny animals and plants there that aren't big enough to see but which are very necessary food items for larger animals.

Beaches and Dunes

Even if you spend most of your time at the ocean jumping in the waves, and then stretch out on your beach towel to enjoy the sun, you can make many observations about plant and animal life on the beach and on the dunes behind the beach. Notice the definite lines along the beach—one where the beach grass stops growing, and one where high tide drops its flotsam and jetsam (floating wreckage from the ocean). In each zone there are certain animals living beneath the sand in very specialized habitats. Little mole crabs live where they can reach up and grab food from the receding water as it passes over their holes and then scuttle back into their burrows to wait for the next wave. Insects that live on the beach are fascinating too; even the biting flies, if you can avoid getting bitten and just watch them.

Shells are fun to find and try to identify if you have your shell book along, and so are the different kinds of seaweeds. Seaweeds are really marine algae and come in reds, greens and browns often with numerous tiny creatures clinging to them as they are dumped on the beach by the waves. When you do beachcombing, take time to think about the vastness of the ocean and its power. As each wave comes in, the force of the water moves millions of grains of sand. Tumbling around in and being ground down by the sand are pebbles, shells, algae and many other things. Some are dropped on the beach and others carried back to sea. The beach and dunes are constantly being eroded by the waves during normal tides. Under normal conditions, a certain stability is reached but if people frequently trample the beach grass which holds down the dunes, the dunes will be washed away within months. And if the dunes disappear, the ocean will go farther inland and change living conditions of the plants and animals there.

Most people, who go to the beach to lie in the sun and get a good tan, miss the really important and exciting nature drama going on all around them. There's no better place to use all your senses in getting close to nature. Smell the salt air; taste the salt on your skin after you've been for a dip in the ocean; feel the cold water and hot sand; hear the gulls and terns calling and see the sun and sand and flotsam and jetsam. Life at the beach can have an element of suspense too, for you never know when the waves will bring in a whale or a sea turtle or uncover some Spanish gold pieces!

Ponds and Lakes

There are many places to look for interesting forms of life when you go to a body of water. First take a broad look at the setting of the pond or lake to see the succession of plants from the middle of the water to the shore. There may be water lilies and other floating plants on the water's surface; then plants such as cattails and rushes growing in shallow water near the shore; various plants right at the edge; grasses and small shrubs; and finally tall trees a distance away from the water. This over-all look will help you determine how the pond was formed. Walk along the edge looking and listening for insects, fish, turtles and frogs. Scoop up a handful of mud and drop it on the bank to see what creatures wriggle from it. There may be tadpoles, diving beetles or dragonfly larvae.

If you have a rowboat or canoe you can extend your field trips farther into the water to check on plants and animals that don't grow close to the shore. Be sure to check the undersides of water lily leaves and other floating plants to see the kinds of tiny animals that live there. Snails and aquatic insects often lay their eggs under floating leaves, so if you notice what look like little blobs of clear jelly use a hand lens and maybe you'll see tiny snails growing inside. Keep an eye out for the various birds that visit water habitats. Many kinds of swallows swoop low over the water catching insects; ducks land and dabble for a while; and herons wade close to shore looking for frogs and small fish.

Streams and Rivers

In flowing water you'll find fish, insects and other animals that are often different from those living in still water, but you may have to work harder to see them. A field trip to a stream means special equipment such as boots, long-handled nets and seines (nets that hang vertically in the water). Two friends to hold the seine are important too. After noting the important features of the surroundings, check along the shore for footprints and droppings of birds, muskrats and raccoons. If you find remains of crayfish or empty mussel shells you'll know that these animals live in the stream. Then turn over some rocks near the edge and farther out to look for creatures clinging to the undersides. This is a good place to find various kinds of caddis fly larvae. Mayfly, stone fly, dragonfly and damselfly larvae live under rocks too. And if you see a long black creature with pincers rush out when you lift up a rock, that's a hellgrammite. Crayfish hide under rocks and when disturbed scoot backward by means of jet propulsion. On the bank you may find crayfish chimneys made of little balls of mud piled up, with an opening in the top, and connected to the stream by tunnels. Plants grow in flowing water too, attached to rocks or rooted in the bottom. Algae, mosses and some liverworts live on rocks. When you get ready to find out what's farther out have your friends stretch out the seine, being sure that the bottom of the seine is on the bottom of the stream or river. Then go upstream and turn over lots of rocks quickly either by hand or with a rake. Many interesting animals hiding under the rocks will be carried downstream by the current and end up in the seine where you can get a close look at them before letting them go. Listen for the rattling call of a kingfisher flying overhead.

Gardens

Whether your garden contains only two or three house plants on a window sill or rows and rows of flowers and vegetables outdoors, you can make interesting observations. Once when I was living in a garret and my only plant was a sweet potato vine on the window sill by the fire escape, I saw a tiny green aphid fly in the open window and land on the stem. As I watched, several very tiny baby aphids were born and walked on down the stem to find a soft spot in which to poke their sharp mouths and begin feeding. In bigger gardens there are many kinds of insects to observe, and always curious weeds coming up along with your plants. While you're pulling weeds notice any soil-dwelling creatures that come up with the roots. And also keep an eye out for curious fungi such as the bird's-nest fungi. These spring up on old twigs or bits of compost and really do look like miniature bird's nests with several egg-shaped, spore-bearing cases inside. Often there are robins, sparrows and other birds in and around gardens looking for insects to eat. Letting birds take care of your insect problems is a much better idea than spreading poisonous substances around on your plants.

If you inspect your vegetable garden and find your lettuce or bean plants nibbled to the ground, you'll have to look for clues to decide whether your crops are being lost to rabbits or groundhogs. A field trip in your garden at night may introduce you to some creatures living there that you don't see in the daytime. Maybe you'll find a fat toad helping keep down the insect population or some slugs that have been responsible for holes in your lettuce leaves. It's fun to explore other people's gardens and to go on trips to very special gardens, such as herb gardens or topiary gardens or those of the du Pont family (Longwood and Winterthur in Pennsylvania and Delaware). The Huntington Gardens in Pasadena, California, are famous for their wide variety, including a huge cactus garden where you can easily pretend you're on a field trip in the desert. And if you're lucky enough to travel outside the United States there are fascinating gardens to visit wherever you go.

Forests

On a field trip to a forest try to see if there are more signs of life at the edges or in the middle. From stories you have read you may have the idea that the middle of a forest is teeming with wildlife. In reality there is much more life at the edges of the forest. This is true of both plants and animals. Getting into a forest is a wonderful experience—quiet and peaceful—and there are things to see such as old fallen trees being turned into humus by the actions of innumerable tiny plants and animals working on them. But take a walk along the edge of the woods to see and hear birds and admire the wildflowers. Certain ferns and club mosses thrive in the shady interior but the most variety in plant and animal life is found at the edge of the forest. Look for different kinds of fungi in the woods and for water-filled holes in old stumps. If you have a microscope at home, take a little sample of water from a tree hole back to examine. Sometimes too you can find a tree that has been blown over with its roots pulled right out of the soil. Take a good look at the intricate root system and the depths of the various soil layers in the cavity.

Lawns

Have you ever spent some time lying on a lawn and making nature observations? If you lie on your back, you can watch the clouds, the sun and the birds but if you turn over you can find out something about what's going on in the grass and in the earth beneath it. The most interesting lawns are those with several kinds of grasses and weeds. Of course, there are people who want only one kind of grass in their lawns and spend time and money poisoning the clover and pulling up the dandelions. But if your lawn has clover and dandelions in it, you can watch honeybees visiting the flowers and going about their work. You can look for four-leaf clovers and make salad out of the dandelion leaves and tell your friends the story about how dandelions were named because the teeth on the leaves look like lion's teeth and in French lion's teeth is *dents de lion!*

You can check your lawn at night and see earthworms bringing up dirt from below and in the daytime there may be robins and other birds looking for worms and insects to eat. If there is a path across your lawn, look for the trail rush that only grows where people or animals walk often. If your lawn doesn't get mowed for a while, the grasses will have a chance to bloom and you can see that their flowers in their own way are just as pretty as those produced by larger, more well-known plants.

Stumps and Logs

Someday when you don't feel like taking a long hike but really want to get close to nature and see interesting things going on, just find a stump or a log and spend your time there.

If you settle down by a stump, here are some questions you can try to find the answers to:

What kind of tree grew here?

Did it fall down?

If it was cut down was an ax or a saw used?

How many men worked on taking the tree down and where did they stand?

How old was the tree?

How long ago was it cut?

What plants and animals are living on and in the stump helping to turn it into rich soil?

Has this stump ever been touched by fire?

What birds and animals have visited this stump?

These are just a few questions to help you start your nature detective work. Even if you can't figure out the answers to all of them you'll have fun trying.

If you decide to investigate a fallen log, use the same approach. If the log you're exploring is hollow, look for clues that will help you find out which animals have been using it for a home.

Walls

A walk around a wall makes another interesting field trip. The older the wall the more likely you are to find interesting things happening in, on and around it. Stone walls and brick walls are most common and stone walls without cement between the stones are most interesting. Look for various kinds of lichens; little gray, green, orange or yellow patches. These are the first plants to get started on bare rocks. After they have broken down, the surface mosses can get a toehold. In cracks and crevices of walls, bigger plants get started. Ebony spleenwort and wall rue are ferns found on walls and if the wall is made of limestone, purple cliff brake, another fern, will probably grow well.

Walls are good places to see ants and spiders busily going about their various activities. If you find acorn shells on top of the wall, you can be sure squirrels or chipmunks have been spending time there. In a stone wall the stones themselves are fascinating. Look for shining flakes of mica or black tourmaline crystals. If the stones are smooth, that means they've been rolled around in water. Many walls have vines growing up over them and you may find birds' nests in the vines and insects living on the leaves. Try to discover how each kind of vine manages to get a foothold on the bricks or stones. Take a book or note pad along when you go wall exploring and do a little reading, sketching or letter writing after your observations.

Roadsides

Even if you rarely or never have a chance to get into the wilderness you can have fun making nature observations as you walk, bike or ride along the road. The plants that grow along roads are usually immigrants from Europe or Asia and commonly known as weeds. But each has something unique about it. Chicory is a plant that makes roadsides blue on summer mornings. Shortly after noon most of the flowers have closed. But if you're going along the road in the morning, see if you can find an albino chicory plant among all the blue ones. A plant with white flowers really stands out in a sea of blue ones. When you get to know chicory well you can gather the young leaves and cook them to eat. In the South chicory roots are dried, ground and mixed with coffee to make a stronger brew.

Two kinds of tall yellow flowers grow well along roads. The great mullein has large woolly leaves and a tall, thick flower spike while the evening primrose's leaves are smooth and its flower spike is slender. The dried seed stalks of both these plants make fine additions to your winter bouquets.

Both kinds of ragweed also do well on roadsides. Common ragweed can be anywhere from a few inches to three feet tall and the giant ragweed may be six or seven feet tall. If there are thistles near the road then you will see goldfinches when the thistles go to seed. Tall thistles with purple flowers and fluffy white seed heads are lovely. With black and yellow goldfinches perched on them they are lovelier still. These dainty little birds eat thistle seeds and gather the down to use in their nests.

Telephone poles and wires are good places to look for birds. A little practice on bird silhouettes will help you identify what you see sitting on the wires. Birds often seen on wires are mourning doves, sparrow hawks, swallows, starlings and flycatchers. Once in a while you'll see a squirrel doing a tightrope act on a wire to get across the road.

Vultures, crows and occasional hawks come down to the road to feed on dead animals that have been hit by cars. Some birds, such as mourning doves, often gather at road edges to pick up little bits of gravel for their gizzards.

Sidewalks

It's true that you're not going to get a very long list of plants and animals when you go sidewalk exploring but you may be surprised at what you do find. Most of what you see will be living in cracks. Silvery *Bryum* is a tiny moss that does well in sidewalks almost everywhere. It grows in the country, in cities and even in Antarctica. Crabgrass is another plant that needs only a little bit of soil in a sidewalk crack to thrive. Goose grass also does well in sidewalks. Take a walk around a city block and keep a count of how many kinds of plants you see. Seedlings of *Ailanthus* or tree of heaven can take hold where you might think that no plant could survive. Ants and spiders can get along in cracks and occasionally you may chance upon a larger insect such as a praying mantis blown into the city by the wind. House sparrows and pigeons are fearless and likely to be seen on sidewalks wherever people have dropped crumbs or left food of any kind.

Vacant Lots

In a vacant lot you can expect all the plants and animals you find on the sidewalk and many others because there's more soil to support life. Also, the plants you find in vacant lots may grow bigger because life is not quite so harsh and there is more food and water. Stray cats and dogs may hide out here as well as those inveterate city dwellers, Norway rats, attracted by piles of rubbish.

Railroads

It's dangerous actually to walk close to railroad tracks, but if you live where you can wander along in a field near some tracks and take frequent walks, you'll get to know the common plants there. If freight cars use the tracks there's always the chance that exotic plants, growing from seeds dropped from carloads of grain, will spring up near the tracks.

Using flame throwers and herbicides, railroads wage a constant battle on nearby plants but they keep poking up through the gravel and cinders to try again.

Your Home

Don't overlook the possibilities for nature exploring inside your home. A fearsome-looking house centipede may show up in your bathtub or you may find a moth fly lurking around a faucet. Even ants, spiders and cockroaches in your home can make interesting studies if they're not too numerous.

Certain insects such as the housefly are usually found only in or near houses. Others—like mosquitoes—come into houses accidentally when a window or door is left open. Fruit flies appear as if by magic in homes where bananas or other fruits have been left out too long, and disappear just as quickly when the overripe fruit is thrown out. Pharaoh's ant, a tiny red ant that lives in houses, is almost impossible to eliminate. It lives in large colonies inside walls and other hard-to-reach places. You may not see any for weeks but one day as you are sitting by a window and notice a dead fly on the window sill you also notice a long line of these little red ants marching out of their hole in the wall to eat the fly and marching back again.

Other insects appear in houses at certain times of the year. Box-elder bugs do no harm but may come indoors in large numbers to hibernate during cold weather. I think they are very attractive insects with their red and black colors but most people just don't appreciate bugs of any kind in their homes.

Insects are the most common forms of wildlife to appear in houses but birds and mammals may also be found. If you have a fireplace you may hear noises coming from it some summer day. Baby chimney swifts often fall out of their nests or become so heavy they pull the nest off the wall of the chimney and land in the fireplace below. The nests are small and made of twigs glued together with saliva. The birds are dull brown with long, narrow wings, tiny feet and short tails. If there is any way you can get the young birds back up the chimney into another nest or even up onto the roof where their parents will find them and feed them that's the best thing to do. Attempts to raise baby chimney swifts by hand, using canned dog food instead of their natural diet of insects, usually end in failure.

Starlings and house sparrows will nest in any hole or crack they can get into on the outside of a building. With the advent of air conditioners house sparrows have found a new source of housing. They stuff feathers and grass into any nook or cranny left around the units and settle down to raising families. Starlings need an actual hole to nest in. Neither of these birds is desirable to have in, on or around your home so the best thing to do is to block all possible nesting sites so that they will go elsewhere. Of our more welcome birds, robins will nest on the tops of shutters and mourning doves on window sills.

The large attics of many old houses are favorite wintering-over places for paper wasps. They spend the winter hibernating in cracks but wake up and fly around on warm days and may sting the unwary attic visitor.

Certain insects falling into the category of household pests usually appear in flour or other grain products stored too long in the kitchen. The confused flour beetle is one of these. About a quarter of an inch long and brown, these little creatures wander around in flour canisters. If you see some small striped moths flying around your kitchen check that box of cornmeal you haven't used for months. You will probably find small white larvae and the silken cocoons from which the moths emerged. Infested foods like these can be put out for birds.

Most warm winter clothes nowadays are made of synthetic fibers but if you have any woolen coats, sweaters and socks beware of the clothes moth. This very nondescript little pale moth does no damage as an adult. However, when it lays eggs on your favorite woolen sweater and the eggs hatch into little white larvae, *they* proceed to eat the yarn. When you put your winter woolens away for the summer spray them with mothproofer or add moth balls or flakes to the storage box and the moths will stay away.

In addition to observing various forms of wildlife that invade your home take close looks at the materials used to build your house and the furniture in it. Speculations as to what kind of wood the dining room table is made of and where the stones in the fireplace came from can lead you on many interesting mental journeys. Make a list of natural materials in your home. In addition to wood and stone you can probably come up with leather, wool, cotton, rubber, fur, feathers, grass and many more.

When you turn on the water to get a drink think about its travels to get to your home. When the oil burner turns on to keep you warm wonder about fossil fuels and how amazing it is that plants that grew in dinosaur days are providing fuel to keep us warm. With practice you can make many more nature observations inside your home.

CHAPTER 25

Projects and Activities

THERE ARE MANY ways to carry on your nature activities at home. You may want to make some nature crafts to brighten up your room or give to friends. On field trips you'll find many items that will give you ideas for later projects. Besides making nature things for yourself you may want to help wildlife in some way. After trying the projects in this chapter you probably will come up with many others on your own.

Things to Do with Fungi

Making spore prints

This activity will help you identify mushrooms by the color of their spores and also provide you with lovely decorations.

1. Remove the mushroom cap carefully and place gill side down on paper. Use dark-colored paper for mushrooms with pale gills and light paper for those with dark gills.
2. Cover mushroom with bowl, glass or jar for several hours or overnight.
3. Remove cover and lift mushroom cap gently to see a lovely radiating pattern of spores. If you want to preserve the print spray it carefully with a fixative so that it will not smear.

Drawing on artist's fungi

1. Carefully remove the fungus from the tree without getting fingerprints on the fresh white underside.
2. Make drawing on underside with any sharp instrument. You can use a pencil, nail, sharp twig or thorn.
3. Put in a safe place to dry and your drawing will last for many years.

Carving on black locust fungi

1. Remove this big, tough brown fungus from the locust tree.

2. Using a penknife or wood carving tools carve a nature scene out of the bottom surface. These carvings also will last many years.

Making ink from inky cap mushrooms

1. Collect some of the inky cap mushroom caps and put in a jar. In a day or two you will have a black slimy mess.

2. Thin this with a little vinegar and try using it for ink. You can also thin your ink with water but the leftover ink may become moldy. Vinegar keeps the molds from growing.

Things to Do with Algae

Mounting for decoration and reference

1. Use the bigger algae you find in fresh water or some of the smaller salt-water kinds washed up on the beach.

2. Float fresh plants in a shallow pan of water.

3. Put a sheet of paper in the pan of water and bring it up under the algae.

4. Spread and arrange the algae any way you wish on the paper.

5. Lift the paper carefully out.

6. The algae will stick to the paper without glue. Cover with damp cheesecloth and put away to dry between newspapers with a heavy object pressing down on top.

7. When dry these algae can be framed and used as pictures or if you use small specimens on small sheets of paper you can use them for writing letters.

*Making blancmange, a delicious vanilla pudding, using Irish moss**

1. Collect Irish moss and carefully clean it, sorting out all the little animals living in the clumps.

2. Heat a quart of milk just to the boiling point but do not let it boil.

* Irish moss is a purplish-brown, cartilaginous alga which grows on rocks along the Atlantic coasts of Europe and America.

3. Add a generous handful of Irish moss to the milk.

4. Also add ½ cup of sugar and 1 teaspoon of vanilla extract.

5. Simmer and stir gently until milk thickens.

6. Remove the Irish moss and throw away.

7. Pour pudding into bowls and eat when cool.

Things to Do with Higher Plants

Making terrariums

A complete miniature environment—animals living in the terrarium give off carbon dioxide which the plants use and the plants in it give off oxygen which the animals use.

1. Select a container. It can be a gallon jar, an aquarium, fish bowl, brandy snifter, peanut butter jar, etc. Use the original jar lid to close jars, and use plastic wrap or a piece of glass cut to size on the other containers.

2. Think about the scene you are going to create—a miniature woods, field, desert or whatever you want. Plan ahead so that you can build up one side for a mountain—put in gravel paths, streams or even a pond. Use your imagination!

3. Get your materials together (be careful not to collect more living things than you're going to use):

   - enough gravel to cover the bottom

   - a few pieces of charcoal

   - enough dirt to cover the gravel and charcoal about half an inch deep

   - green plants or small trees, ferns, vines—anything that is still green in the woods in the fall will stay green in your terrarium all winter and may bloom in the spring

   - interesting small stones, acorns, bits of wood, mosses and lichens

   - little animals—one or two add interest and give you something special to watch for—try a spider, beetle, earthworm or salamander

4. Lay a newspaper on a table and set out all your materials.

5. Spread gravel in bottom of container.

6. Add a few pieces of charcoal.

7. Spread dirt over the gravel and charcoal.

8. Plant in the dirt any plants having roots.

9. Fill in the bare spots between plants with mosses and lichens.

10. Add stones and bits of wood.

11. Add lichens.

12. Add animals.

13. Add a teaspoonful of water in a small container—more in a big one.

14. Cover and watch. If moisture is on lid the next day it's wet enough. If you don't see any water, add some. If you see any mold in a week or two take the lid off for a few hours to let extra moisture escape.

Note: Terrariums need light but do not put in direct sunlight where heat will build up. Do not put them on radiators.

Making nature notepaper

Items you will need:
Pressed leaves and flowers (small specimens)
Notepaper (plain)
Wax paper
Elmer's glue mixture (½ glue and ½ water)
Square Kleenex (white or colored)
Glitter (optional from the dime store)
Brown paper bag and paper toweling
Narrow ribbon
Envelopes

1. Look for tiny leaves, ferns, flowers and herbs. You will find many things that will please you as you start to gather them, more so in summer than in winter.
   Gather and place your plant materials between the pages of a magazine. Use about twenty-four hours later as colors will fade if kept too long. Pine needles, grasses, hay and small seeds dry well. Fleshy flowers are not satisfactory.

2. Mark a square on a piece of paper the size of a square Kleenex.

STEPS 1,2,3   STEP 4

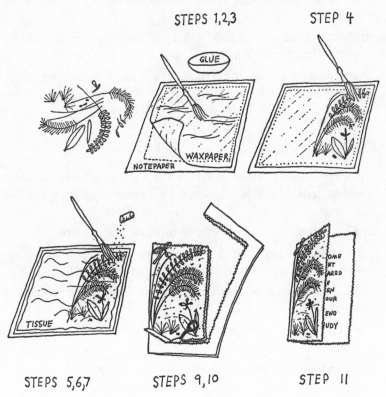

STEPS 5,6,7   STEPS 9,10   STEP 11

Making nature notepaper (see directions)

3. Place a piece of wax paper on the square of paper and brush it with the glue mixture. Be generous with the mixture. It will not spread evenly but that is okay. What you are doing is making a cover for your notepaper which is the loose sheet beneath the wax paper.

4. Now make a design with your pressed plant materials on righthand half of the wax paper. Dab some glue mixture on the design.

5. Place a single sheet of any color Kleenex on top of this.

6. Brush generously with the glue mixture (it will wrinkle but that is good)

7. Sprinkle with a little glitter if desired. Put away to dry.

8. When dry, place on a brown paper bag and cover with a paper towel. Press with a slightly warm iron on both sides.

9. Fold in half with design on top and cut around edge with pinking shears.

10. If desired make a small knot of baby ribbon and glue to paper or punch holes, put ribbon through and tie in bow on top.

11. Now you have a lovely folded note. The design is in the cover made of the Kleenex and wax paper glued together with plants in between. Inside is the blank paper on which to write.

Making nature collages

1. When you go on a nature walk take along a bag or basket in which to collect small bits of bark, lichens, little stones, grasses, seeds and little twigs.

2. Dry your specimens on a radiator or other warm place.

3. Take a piece of heavy cardboard or plywood and cut it to the size you want your collage to be.

4. Make a design with your nature treasures laid on the cardboard or plywood.

5. Use white glue to fasten each specimen in the proper place. Let dry overnight.

6. If desired spray your collage with a clear fixative.

7. Attach a hanger. Now you have an original design to hang up to remind you of pleasant walks in the woods and fields.

Making persimmon leather

1. Gather persimmons late in the fall after frost has hit them and they are very wrinkled and soft.

2. Press through food mill or sieve to remove seeds.

3. Spread pulp thinly on a clean, smooth, dry board.

4. Place in sun to dry. (Persimmon leather may be dried in a slow oven but doesn't taste quite the same.)

5. When dry cut in strips about half an inch wide and roll up.

6. Store in plastic bags. Keeps well at room temperature but can also be put in freezer.

7. Eat as desired. Good snack for hikes. Just carry a roll of persimmon leather in your jacket pocket and take a bite whenever you're hungry on the trail.

Making "sumacade"

1. Gather a few heads of the red fruits from smooth or staghorn sumac at the end of summer.

2. Pull the fruit off into a pan and cover with water.

3. Simmer until the water turns pinkish but do not boil.

4. Strain out sumac fruits.

5. Sweeten liquid to taste and serve hot or iced.

Making sassafras tea

1. If possible use the bark from a root the size of your forearm. This makes the best drink but small roots will do.

2. Dig root and wash well.

3. Slice off bark and bring to boil in water to cover.

4. Strain out bark and serve tea hot or iced.

5. Sassafras tea can be sweetened and made into popsicles by pouring into ice cube trays and freezing.

6. Drink in moderate quantities. Too much may have a laxative effect.

Making maple syrup

1. In early spring when there are freezing nights and thawing days bore a hole one-half inch in diameter through the bark of a maple tree. Sugar maples are best but you can try other maples (except Norway maples) and also other kinds of trees such as hickories and walnuts. Use a hand drill to bore the hole about three feet from the ground.

2. Insert a hollow spout in the hole. This can be a hollow metal tube or a piece of elder stem that fits with the pith pushed out.

3. Hang a bucket on the spout and arrange a cover to keep out rain and bits of bark and leaves that may fall in.

4. Collect the sap each day and boil it down when you have a quart or so. The sap is mostly water which boils off as steam so you will get very little syrup. Try making syrup from several different kinds of trees to see which is sweeter.

Making your own raisins

Sometimes on field trips in the fall you'll find various kinds of wild grapes. You can gather them and use them for juice or jelly following directions in any cookbook. Just for fun try making a few raisins too. The nicest raisins are made from seedless grapes but you don't find these in the wild so the ones you make will be pretty seedy but interesting.

1. Gather ripe grapes and remove from stems.
2. Spread on cookie sheet and set out in the sun until dry and wrinkled. (You can dry them in a slow oven also.) This project will make you appreciate seedless raisins all the more, and you'll always be able to remember that raisins are just dried grapes.

Things to Do with Snow

Making snow ice cream

1. Fill a bowl with fresh clean snow.
2. Dribble honey all over the top.
3. Sprinkle on a little vanilla extract.
4. Stir and eat quickly before it melts.

Making leather aprons

½ cup molasses
1 tablespoon vinegar
2 tablespoons sugar
pinch of salt
a little vanilla
1 tablespoon butter

Cook until brittle when tested in cold water. Dribble over new-fallen snow which has been scooped into a large pan. Eat—very much like caramels.

Preserving snowflakes

1. Before winter comes get the following items and keep them in your freezer (if you don't have all your equipment cold the snowflakes will melt before you can preserve their shapes):

small piece of cardboard covered with black velvet

toothpick

glass rod

magnifying glass

glass microscope slide

solution for preserving snowflakes (ethylene dichloride) (this can be ordered from: Edmund Scientific Co., 150 Edscorp Building, Barrington, N.J. 08007)

BE CAREFUL

It is a poisonous solution.

Do not drink it.

Do not inhale the fumes.

2. When it begins to snow take your equipment outdoors quickly and keep it under shelter such as a cardboard carton turned on its side.

3. With the glass rod get a drop of the solution from the bottle and touch it to the slide. (Be sure to close the bottle promptly to prevent evaporation.)

4. Let some snowflakes fall on your black velvet. Use magnifying glass to see which snowflakes are best. You can separate them from each other with your toothpick. Pick up the one you want to preserve on the tip of the glass rod.

5. Put it on the drop already on the slide. The solution evaporates, leaving a hard plastic casting of the melted snowflake. No matter how many you collect you will never get two alike!

6. Be sure to hold the glass rod and the glass slide by the ends so heat from your hand will not travel through the glass and melt the snowflakes.

Homemade Equipment for Field Trips

Making a net

1. First you need a handle about 3 feet long. Bamboo is best because it is lighter to carry but a piece of an old broom handle will do.

2. Next you need a piece of cloth, such as part of an old sheet. Netting is ideal because you can see through it to see what you have caught. If you are going to use your net in the water make it out of sturdy cloth.

3. A finished net about 12 inches in diameter and 18 inches deep is quite useful. Take a rectangle of cloth 2 feet by 19 inches and fold it in half so that you have a rectangle 1 foot by 19 inches. Sew into a triangular shape and cut off the excess material.

4. Next fold over an inch hem around the top edge and sew, leaving openings for the wire frame.

5. For the wire take a heavy coat hanger apart and push it through the hem at the top of the net.

6. Tape the ends of the wire to your handle with heavy adhesive tape or electrician's tape. Now your net is ready for action.

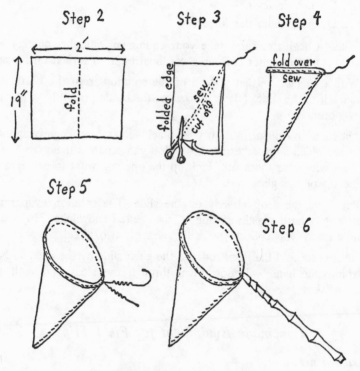

Making a net (see directions)

A carrier for field trips

A leftover soft-drink carton (from a six- or eight-pack) makes a handy carrier for plastic bags or jars of specimens on field trips. A strip of heavy tape around the carton will reinforce it and make it last longer. Specimens brought home this way will be in better shape than if stuffed in your pockets.

Collecting Spider Webs

1. First locate a suitable web and make sure that the occupant is safely out of the way.

2. Spray the web with white spray paint.

3. Bring a piece of construction paper up behind the sprayed web.

4. When the web is centered on the paper cut the lines of silk which hold the web to the bush or tree.

5. You now have a lovely work of art suitable for framing. Spraying with clear lacquer or fixative will help preserve the web.

Making an Ant Farm

1. First locate an ant colony. Look under large rocks, logs or boards that have been on the ground for a while. Brightly colored ants will show up best in your ant farm.

2. Take a gallon jar (this size is best but a quart jar will do) and a shovel to the location of the colony.

3. Dig up a shovelful of earth and ants and dump them into the jar. Be careful so you do not get bitten.

4. Put the lid on the jar. Punch a few tiny holes in it when you get home.

5. At home either wrap black cloth or paper around the jar or put it in a dark closet for a day or two.

6. When you want to see what's going on take a look and then darken the jar again. If you don't keep the colony in the dark the ants will make their tunnels in the middle of the jar where you cannot watch what they are doing.

7. Drop in bits of various foods such as candy, bacon, crackers and bread and watch to see which your ants prefer.

8. After a couple of weeks let the ants go where you found them.

Making a Crystal Garden

This is a good project for dreary winter days when nothing is growing outdoors.

1. Arrange several chunks of brick or coal in a shallow pan.

2. Mix together   4 tablespoons of ammonia
                       4 tablespoons of salt
                       4 tablespoons of bluing
                       4 tablespoons of water

3. Pour over the pieces of brick or coal.

4. Very soon you will see crystals forming. From time to time drop a little food coloring in various spots to add more color to your "garden."

Bird-related Activities

Making bird feeders

There are many simple bird feeders you can make that will bring wild birds closer to your window especially during the winter. Here are a few ideas:

1. Cut holes about an inch from the bottom on all four sides of an empty milk carton and put sunflower seeds, cracked corn and peanut butter inside. Hang the carton in a bush or tree where you can watch from inside your home.

2. Roll a corn cob in leftover fat and then in cracked corn and sunflower seeds. Cut the bottom of a coat hanger in two and insert the cut ends in the ends of the corn cob. Hang from a bush or tree by the hook and watch the birds come to feast.

3. Nail bottle caps to a foot-long piece of a branch. Screw in a cup hook and hang up for the birds after filling the caps with peanut butter.

Making a birdbath

Birds need water to drink as well as to bathe in all year round. A garbage can lid makes a fine birdbath. You can either set it on the ground or on a stump. If it has a small hole in the middle as some do just stop it up with clay and add water. If it seems to be deep in the center put in a piece of brick or a small rock.

Making birdhouses

The simpler the better is a good rule to follow in building birdhouses. First decide what kind of bird you want to attract to your yard. Then you can make just the right home for it. Each kind of bird has its own housing requirements. The easiest bird to attract is the house wren. Starlings and house sparrows move in without any encouragement. In fact in most areas they are considered to be pests.

House wrens will nest in old buckets hanging on the garage or in the pocket of a pair of pants left on the line overnight. You can make a wren house quickly by cutting a ⅞-inch hole in a plastic jug 1 to 6 inches above the bottom. Also make several small holes in the bottom of the jug for drainage in case of rain. You can put a wren house almost anywhere; hanging from a branch or fastened to a tree trunk. But a house for bluebirds must be put out in the open away from trees. Good dimensions for a bluebird house are 5 inches by 5 inches by 8 inches high. The entrance hole should be 1½ inches in diameter and 6 inches above the floor. Fasten your house on top of a fence post or on a pole out in the open. A few years ago there were many dead trees and holes in old fence posts for bluebirds to live in, but today these lovely birds need help. Tree swallows and house wrens will also use bluebird houses if they are available.

When you first see a colony of purple martins nesting in an apartment-like birdhouse in someone's yard you will probably want to rush home and build a martin house. Martins are beautiful birds to watch, fun to listen to and fantastic insect eaters. Unfortunately there is no sure way to attract a colony to your yard. You can spend hours building a martin house (or spend lots of money buying one) and erect it in what looks like the perfect place (on a tall pole out in the open) and still never get any martins to set up housekeeping. Starlings and house sparrows can always be counted on to move in and have to be discouraged. Unless you live near a vigorous martin colony which needs room for expansion don't spend your time and money on a martin house. You'll probably have much greater success with homes for wrens and bluebirds.

Going Fishing

I'd like to describe the kind of fishing I do on the farm in a pond stocked many years ago with large-mouthed bass and bluegills (a kind of sunfish). If you go fishing under different circumstances be sure to check the fishing license regulations in your area so you won't violate any local laws.

1. *Pole*   Sometimes I use a bamboo pole cut from our grove of bamboo and sometimes I use a maple sapling about half an inch in diameter. Five or six feet is a good length for a pole.

2. *Line*   Heavy-duty thread (carpet thread) is good to use but may break if you catch a heavy fish so it's best to use some nylon fishing line. Ten to twelve feet is enough to tie onto your pole —if you have too much line it will get tangled up. You just need enough to toss out from where you are standing on the bank of the pond.

3. *Hooks*   Get a package of assorted hooks. Use the small or medium-sized ones when you are fishing for bluegills and the larger ones when you try for bass, which are more difficult to catch. Tie the hook on the line with a good tight knot.

4. *Sinkers and Bobbers*   These are not really necessary for simple fishing but you can tie something heavy such as an old nail on your line to make it sink, and tie on a cork for a bobber.

5. *Bait*   Earthworms make excellent bait and can be dug for in your compost pile or garden. Keep them in an empty cottage cheese carton with a little dirt. Put the lid on or they will escape. White grubs that you sometimes find when you dig make good bait too. So do Japanese beetles, crickets and grasshoppers. If worms are scarce try little bread balls or hunks of cheese.

6. *At the Pond*   Put the bait on your hook and throw your line carefully into the water. If you have large earthworms just use a piece of worm about half an inch long. Put the hook through it lengthwise, being very careful not to hook your finger. Hold your pole very still to give the fish a chance to come close. If after a few minutes you haven't gotten a bite move to another spot. When you get a nibble hold the pole still a little longer

until you think the fish is caught then pull it out quickly to land on the bank. Remove the fish and put it in a bucket of water or on a string or thin branch pushed through its mouth and gill cover. If you catch a lot of little bluegills keep some alive and release them in a nearby stream to keep the pond from becoming overcrowded. When there are too many bluegills in one pond they are all stunted due to a limited food supply.

7. *Cleaning and Cooking* Scale the fish on both sides with a sharp knife, holding it with your thumb under the gill cover. Scrape from the tail toward the head. Remove the head by cutting off behind the gill covers (cutting through the backbone is a bit difficult). With your knife make a slit in the belly and then remove all the insides. Wash the fish thoroughly inside and out and dry it with a paper towel. If desired, shake lightly in a plastic or paper bag containing a little cornmeal or flour. Then fry in several tablespoons of melted butter a few minutes on each side until the backbone pulls out easily. Sprinkle with salt.

8. *Eating* To eat bluegills just pull the flesh off the bones in two pieces, leaving the skeleton. You will have to experiment a few times to do it just right. Bluegills are delicious except for the bones but with a little practice you can get the flesh and leave the fins, tail and bones behind.

Hints for Building Campfires

If you have plenty of matches and plenty of dry firewood building a fire in camp is a cinch. But if it has rained recently at your campground and you're short on matches you may spend much valuable time trying to get a fire started to keep you warm and dry. Here are a few tips that may help:

1. Keep a few old broken candles or pieces of paraffin in the bottom of your knapsack or pack basket. Even damp wood will start to burn with some melted wax under it.

2. Even when it has been raining you can usually find some dry wood if you know where to look. Often the bottom branches of spruces are dead and dry, protected by the green branches over them. Pin oaks

usually have dead, dry, thin branches within reach of the ground hanging down close to the trunk. With your hatchet or ax you can chop into a dead tree which is wet on the outside and find dry wood in the middle.

3. In dry weather, if you have trouble finding small twigs for tinder to get your fire started, make a fuzz stick by cutting one end of a thick dry stick into splinters and pulling these back. One naturalist I know makes a lot of fuzz sticks ahead of time and keeps some in his pack.

Tips for Cooking Without Pots and Pans

Sometimes you find yourself at a beautiful campsite with a nice fire going and suddenly you remember you forgot to bring any pots or pans in which to cook. And there are other times when you just don't want to be bothered lugging cooking utensils out into the woods. Here are a few ideas for getting along without kettles and skillets.

1. Use green sticks—thin ones for marshmallows, hot dogs and shish kebabs. Avoid sticks from poisonous shrubs such as poison sumac and from shrubs or trees which would add a strong flavor to your food. Don't use dead sticks as they will catch on fire, causing your food to fall into the flames.

2. Steaks are delicious cooked right on the coals. The trick is to build first a hot fire with good wood. Let it burn for about twenty minutes until there are no flames left, then lay the steak right on the coals. Let cook for about five minutes; turn and cook on the other side. Any ashes that stick to the meat may be easily brushed off.

3. Flat rocks are also good substitutes for frying pans. (Be sure they do not have cracks full of moisture as this kind of rock will explode when heated in a fire.) Put your flat rock in the fire to heat up. When it is hot (in about ten or fifteen minutes) fish it out with sticks and brush off any ashes. Grease with a strip of bacon and proceed to fry an egg and/or make toast.

4. Round rocks of various sizes can be heated in the fire, carefully removed with sticks and dropped into bark or gourd containers of water. This is a fine way to get hot water for tea, soup or washing your face. You cannot set bark or gourd containers over the fire without having them catch on fire so the hot rock technique is a good one to remember.

5. Many modern campers use aluminum foil instead of frying pans. This is fine if you remember to bring foil and also remember to recycle used foil or otherwise dispose of it properly. It will not decompose quickly in the woods and really spoils the wilderness when it is left lying around.

6. Potatoes, apples and whole fish can be wrapped in a layer of mud and baked in the coals.

Ways to Fight Pollution

Many containers and other discarded items can be recycled instead of thrown away. Here are some ideas:

Paper:

1. Papers that are blank on one side can be used for lists, telephone message pads and coloring.

2. Old envelopes can be used for messages, grocery lists and saving seeds.

3. Old newspapers can be tied in neat bundles and taken to a recycling center. They can also be used as mulch between rows in your garden.

Glass:

1. Take the labels and metal rings off non-returnable bottles and jars and save them until you get enough to make a trip to the recycling center worthwhile. Keep brown, clear and green glass separated.

2. Some bottles and jars can be turned into lovely terrariums with colored sand and plants.

3. If you have a glass-cutting machine you can make vases and tumblers and candleholders from beer and soft-drink bottles.

Cans:

1. Small cans such as tuna fish and cat food cans are nice to save. Spray with paint and use for dried arrangements.

2. Cans of various sizes can be used for growing plants.

3. Any cans you cannot reuse can be taken to the recycling center after having the ends and labels removed and being flattened.

Foam and Cardboard Trays:

These containers as well as the plastic and cardboard baskets berries come in make wonderful containers for keeping odds and ends neat in your bureau or desk drawers. They also come in handy for keeping various sizes of nails, screws and bolts in order on the family workbench.

Pantyhose and nylons:

Save them for stuffing young children's toys.

Garbage:

Save vegetable scraps and eggshells to add to your compost pile. To make one, layer garbage, soil, weeds, manure and grass clippings as they accumulate in a pit in the ground or inside a wire enclosure aboveground. Poke holes through all the layers occasionally to let rain and air down and turn everything over with a fork from time to time. In a few months you'll have rich compost to use in your garden and put around your house plants. Don't forget to add a few earthworms as they help speed up the compost-making process.

Old Tires:

Tires are difficult to get rid of and take years to decompose if thrown out in the woods or fields but there are a few ways they can be used.

1. Tires can be painted and used as planters for flowers.
2. Hang a tire from a tree limb using a strong rope. It makes a great swing.
3. A tire cut in half makes two circular canals when filled with water, perfect for small children to sail their boats around in.
4. If you live near the ocean you may be able to organize a collection of old tires and get some government agency or fishermen's group interested in using them to build an offshore reef. This has been done successfully off the coast of New Jersey. The stacks of tires make wonderful

hiding places for smaller fish to get away from their enemies and serve other useful purposes.

5. In some states, including Maryland, the wildlife officials
use tires for making squirrel homes but it takes special
tools and staples to hold the cut pieces together. The
homes are hung high in trees and are welcome substitutes for the holes in dead trees that are scarce these
days.

Take old toys, games and furniture you no longer need to the Good-
will, Salvation Army or some other charitable agency that can get them
to people who need them. *Don't* just take a ride in the country and
throw them out.

Do your best to keep your neighborhood clean. Collect papers, bottles and cans which thoughtless people toss along the road and recycle
them.

Report air pollution, water pollution and noise pollution when you
smell, see or hear it to your local officials. Write letters to newspapers
telling how upset you are about polluters and pollution in your area.

Writing a Nature Newspaper

Another project that might bring pleasure to you, your friends and
relatives is publishing your nature observations in the form of a little
newspaper. My sister and brothers and I did this for several years when
we were growing up on the farm. We wrote about the farm animals and
the wild animals and about what was going on in the woods, fields and
gardens. Our friends and relatives all over the country looked forward
to getting copies of *The Lone Hickory Farm News* when it came out
every three or four months.

If you'd like to try this just jot down on your calendar or in your nature notebook such things as when you see the first arbutus blooming or
wild geese flying north. Every few months write these little items up,
have copies made and send them to people you know who are interested
in nature. Pretty soon you'll probably have a long subscription list of
people who want to know what you've seen and heard on your nature
rambles.

Books I Use and Like

THE AUDUBON NATURE ENCYCLOPEDIA (12 vols.). National Audubon Society, 1965. Curtis Books, Curtis Publishing Co. New York.

THE BIRD YOU CARE FOR by Felicia Ames. 1970. Signet Books, The New American Library Inc. New York.

BIRDS' NESTS by Richard Headstrom. 1949. Ives Washburn. New York.

BIRDS OF NORTH AMERICA by C. Robbins, B. Bruun and H. Zim. 1966. Golden Press. New York. (Note: guides on SEASHELLS and TREES also in this series.)

THE BOOK OF BIRDLIFE by Arthur A. Allen. 1930. D. Van Nostrand Co. New York. (Has excellent chapter on Feathers.)

CARE OF THE WILD FEATHERED AND FURRED by M. Hickman. Unity Press. San Francisco.

EDIBLE WILD PLANTS OF EASTERN NORTH AMERICA by Fernald and Kinsey. Harper and Row. New York.

FEATHERS AND PLUMAGE OF BIRDS by A. A. Voitevich. 1966. University of Washington Press. Seattle.

FIELDBOOK OF NATURAL HISTORY by E. Laurence Palmer. 1949. McGraw-Hill. New York.

FIELD GUIDE TO WILDFLOWERS by R. T. Peterson and Margaret McKenny. 1968. Houghton Mifflin. Boston. (Others in Peterson series also good.)

FIVE DAYS OF LIVING WITH THE LAND by Sarah Brown. 1971. Addison-Wesley. Reading, Mass.

FOXFIRE BOOK and FOXFIRE 2, edited by Eliot Wigginton. 1972 and 1973. Anchor Press/Doubleday. Garden City, N.Y.

GOLDEN NATURE GUIDES (more than twenty titles—all good), various authors with H. Zim. Simon and Schuster. New York.

HANDBOOK OF NATURE STUDY by Anna B. Comstock. 1947. Comstock Publishing Co. Ithaca, N.Y.

HUNGRY BIRD BOOK by R. Arbib and T. Soper. 1965. Ballantine Books. New York.

LIVING ON THE EARTH by Alicia Bay Laurel. 1971. Vintage Books, Random House. New York.

OUR SMALL NATIVE ANIMALS by Robert Snedigar. 1963. Dover Publications. New York.

OUTDOOR ADVENTURE by Hal Harrison. 1951. Vanguard Press. New York.

PLANT GALLS AND GALL-MAKERS by Ephraim Felt. 1940. Comstock Publishing Co. Ithaca, N.Y.

TEN-MINUTE FIELD TRIPS by Helen Ross Russell. 1973. J. G. Ferguson Publishing Co. Chicago, Ill.

Index

Page numbers in italics refer to illustrations.

Acadia National Park, 184
Africa, 175, 180
agar, 64
agrimony, 54
Ailanthus, 59, 196
Alatamaha River, 35
algae, 64, 91, 200
algal fungi, 66
allergy, 28, 29
alligators, 150
Alps, 175
alternation of generations, 45
amanitas, 70
Amoeba, *80*
amphibians, 143–49; eggs, *143*
anemones, 53; sea, 82
angelfish, 155
animals, 79–176; dead, 29
ant, *101,* 125
anteaters, 165
antelopes, African, 174; pronghorn, 173
antennae, 97
ant farm, 209
antihistamines, 29
antlers, 50
ant lion, 115
ants, 125; white, *101;* velvet, 124
aphids, 109, 110, 192
Arachnida, 92–95
arborvitae, 42
arbutus, 53, 187
armadillos, 165
arrow worms, 79, 89
arthropods, 79
artist's fungus, 70, 199
asbestos, 184

Aschelminthes, 79, 88
Asiatic chestnut blight, 40
asparagus fern, 45, 46
asparagus, wild, 59
asses, 174
astronomers, 180
athlete's foot, 74
Audubon, John, 53
Australia, 159, 180
azaleas, 42

back swimmers, 108
bacteria, 76
bagworm, 118, *119*
Baltimore butterfly, 189
bamboo, 61
barberries, 42
Bartrams, 35
basidium fungi, 67
bats, 26, 61, 160, 161
beaches, 189–90
bear's head, 68
beavers, 169
bedbugs, 107, 108
beech, 6
beefsteak fungus, 69
beetles, 110–15; Alexander, 112; asparagus, 113; carpet, 112; carrion, *112;* click, 112; Colorado potato, 113; cotton boll weevil, 114; cucumber, 113; darkling, 114; dung, 113; eyed elater, *112;* firefly, 111; ground, 111; household, 112; Japanese, 113; June, 113; ladybird, 111, 113; larder, 112; leaf, 113; lightning, 111; longhorn, 113; Mexican bean, 111, 113;

rove, 111; scarab, 113; snout, 114; tiger, 111; tortoise, 113; water, 111; whirligig, 111
bees, 122, 125–26
Bermuda, 156
Big Dipper, *180*
biking, 18
bird bath, 210–11
bird blinds, 143
bird counts, 143
bird feeders, 210
birdhouses, 211
birds, 133–43; as pets, 139; banding of, *142;* distribution of, 139; feathers of, 133; feeding of, 140; migration of, *138;* nests, *136, 137;* sounds, 135; value of, 140; ways to study, 134
bird's nest, 25
bird's-nest fungi, 73, 192
birds' nests, 136–38
bison, 173
blackberry, 68
blackbirds, 135
black-footed ferret, 168
black locust, 34, 35; fungi, 200
black widow, 92, 93
bladderworts, 57
bloodroot, 53, 187
bluebirds, 188
bluegrass, 60
blue-tailed skink, 151
boats, 20
bogs, 188
boletes, 69
bones, 50
book gills, 97
box-elder bugs, 197
boxwoods, 42
Brachiopoda, 79, 89
bracket fungi, 69
brown recluse, 92, 93
Bryophyta, 33
Bryozoa, 79, 89
bubonic plague, 122
bugs, true, 107–9; ambush, 108; bedbugs, 107, 108; doodlebug, 115; giant water, 108; harlequin, 108; lace, 108; spittle, 109;

squash, 107; stink, 107; tarnished plant, 108; wheel, 108; yooey, 115
buffalo, 173
bumblebees, 125, 126
burros, 174
butterflies, 116; Baltimore, 189; monarch, 58, 117, *118;* mourning cloak, 117
butterworts, 57

cactus, *7*
caddis flies, 115
Caesar's mushroom, 70
California, 118, 192
Calvert Cliffs, 185
camels, 173
campfires, 213–15
cans, 215
capybara, 169
carapace, 97
carnivorous plants, 56–57
carp, 158
carpenter bees, 123
caterpillar, 116, 117; gypsy moth, 116; hickory horned devil, 117; tent, 116; woolly bear, 27
catkins, 42
cave rats, 167
cellulose, 101
centipedes, *96*
cephalothorax, *95*
chalk, 184
chanterelle, 71
Chesapeake Bay, 185
chestnut, American, 40; blooms, *5*
chicken polypore, 69
chickweed, 59
chicory, 195
chimney swifts, 197
chinchilla, 171
chinquapin, *5*
chipmunks, 167
chitons, 91
chlorophyll, 74
chores, 10
chrysalis, 116
chuckwalla, 151
cicada, 109
clams, 90, 91

classification, 24–25; invertebrate, 79; vertebrate, 133; plant, 33
cleistogamous flowers, 55
clouds, 185
club moss, 43, 46–47; spores, 47
coal, 185
Coal Age, 47
cockroaches, 101, 102
cocoon, 116
Coelenterata, 79, 82, 83
coelocanth, 156
comb jelly, 79, 83, 84
compost, 216
constellations, 180, 181
Cooperative Extension Service, 23
coprolites, 185
coral fungi, 68
corals, 82, 83
Cordyceps, 67
corn, 188
corn smut, 68
cow, 173, 174
coyotes, 164, 168
crab, 97; horseshoe, 96, 97
crabgrass, 60, 196
cracked Fomes, 70
cranberry, highbush, 42
crayfish, fresh-water, 97, 149, 163, 191; salt-water, 97
creeping Jenny, 46
crested flycatcher, 137
Cretaceous Age, 185
cricket, 102, 103, 104; mole, 19, 104; tree, 104
crocodiles, 150
crowfoot, 46
crows, 196
crustacean, land, 97
crystal garden, 210
crystals, 182
Ctenophora, 79, 83, 84
cud, 173

daddy longlegs, 92, 95
Daedalea, 70
Daedalus, 179
dandelion, 53, 58, 59, 193
damselflies, 99, 100
dead man's fingers, 67

deer, 173
deer mouse, 167
destroying angel, 70
devil's-darning-needles, 99
dinosaurs, 184, 185
diphtheria, 76
dogbane, 57
dogwood, 41
dolphins, 172
donkeys, 174
dragonflies, 17, 27, 99, 100
dunes, 189–90
dung, 50, 185
Dutch elm disease, 42, 114, 115

ear fungi, 68
earthstars, 73
earthworms, 86, 87, 216
earwig, 105
Echinodermata, 79, 126
eclipses, 180
eels, 156
egg-laying mammals, 159
eggs-on-a-rock, 183
elephants, 175, 185
elm, 4, 114, 115
England, 143
erosion, 186
euonymus, winged, 41
evening primrose, 55
evergreen, 38
eyes, compound, 97

fairy ring marasmius, 71
fears, 26
fence lizard, 151
fences, 188
fern, asparagus, 45, 46; Boston, 44; bracken, 44, 45; Christmas, 43; cinnamon, 43, 45; grape, 45; hay-scented, 5; interrupted, 45; maiden-hair spleenwort, 43; New York, 44; prothallium, 45; spores, 44; walking, 44
ferns, 43–46
field trips, 13–22
fields, 187–88
fir, 39
fishes, 155–59

fishing, 17, 212–14
flatworms, 79, *85*
fleas, *121,* 122; snow, 99; water, 97
flies, 119, 120
floodplains, 186
floods, 186
flower flies, 121
flowers of tan, 66
fly amanita, 71
flying fish, 157
forests, 192
forsythia, 41, 42
fossils, 129, 184–85; fish, 156
foxes, 164
Franklinia, 35
friendship fireplace, 183
froghoppers, 110
frogs, *144–45;* bull, 144; green, 144; leopard, *144;* pickerel, 144; wood, 144
fungi, 65–76

gall, 123
gall wasps, 123
garbage, 216
gardens, 191
gastroliths, 185
gastropods, 90
geckos, 150
gerbils, 171
Gila monster, 151
gill fungi, 70
ginkgo, 37
giraffes, 173
gizzards, 185, 196
glaciers, 182
glass, 215
glass snake, 151
glowworm, 111
goats, 173
goldenrod, 54
goldfinch, 59, *135,* 195
goldfish, *2*
goose grass, 196
graphite, 184
grass, goose, 196; sweet vernal, 5; timothy, 61; zoysia, 60
grasses, 60–61
grasshopper, hairworm in, 85, *86*

grasshoppers, 101; green, 104; long-horned, 104
Greeks, 179
groundhogs, 170
grubs, 113
guinea pigs, 171
gull, Franklin's, 102; monument to, 102

hairworm, *86*
halite, 184
hamsters, 171
Hannibal, 175
hares, 166
hawks, 196
hay, 60
hazelnut, 42
hedgehog, 68
hedges, 42
hellbender, 149
hellgrammite, 115
hepatica, 53
hexylresorcinol, 86
hickory horned devil, 117
hides, 143
hikes, 18
hippopotamuses, 174
home, 197–99
honeybees, 98, 125
honeysuckle, bush, 42; Japanese, 59
hookworm, 86
horn-of-plenty, 68
horned toad, 151
hornworts, 33
horse, 18, 174
horse stingers, 99
horsetails, 43, 47, 48
housefly, *119*
house mouse, 166
house plant, 2
house sparrows, 9, 135
hummingbird, 44; sphinx moth, 118
Huntington Gardens, 192
hydras, 82
Hymenoptera, 122

Icarus, 179
ice, 186
ichneumon flies, 122, 123

imperfect fungi, 74
inchworm, 117
India, 175
ink, 200
ink sacs, 92
inkycap, 72, 200
insects, 98–126; ant farm, 209; ant lion, 115; ants, *101*, 125, 196; aphids, 109, 110, 192; back swimmers, 108; bagworm, 118, *119;* Baltimore butterfly, 189; bedbugs, 107, 108; bees, 122, 125–26; beetles, 110–15; bugs, 107–9; butterflies, 116, 117, 118; caddis flies, 115; caterpillars, 116, 117; Cecropia moth, 117; chrysalis, 116; cicada, 109; cicada killer, 124; clothes moth, 116; cockroaches, 101, 102; cotton boll weevil, 114; crane flies, 120; cricket, 102, *103*, 104; mole, 19, 104; tree, 104; damselflies, 99, 100; dragonflies, 17, 27, 99, *100;* earwigs, *105;* fleas, *121;* flies, 119–20; hornets, 125; sawflies, 122; wasps, 125
invertebrates, 79–129
I.Q., nature, 22–25
Irish moss, 200–1
Isle Royale, 164

jack-in-the-pulpits, 53
jack-o-lantern mushroom, 71
Japan, 149
jasmine, winter, 42
jellyfish, *82*
jelly fungi, 68
jewelweed, 54, 187
jewfish, 155
Jew's-ear, 68
jimson weed, 62
joint-footed animals, 79
junipers, 42
Jupiter, 181

kangaroo, 159
katydid, 101, 102, 104
killdeer, 136–37
kingfisher, 17

koala bear, 159

lacewing, 115
lagomorphs, 166
lakes, 190
lamb's-quarters, 59
lamprey, 157
lamp shells, 79, 89
larch, 39
laundry soap, 28
lawns, 193
leather aprons, 206
leather fungi, 68
leather, persimmon, 204
leaves, 41; arrangement of, *36;* bay, 41; maple, 41; uses of, 41
leech, 87, *88*
legume, 34
lice, bird, 106; biting, 106; book, 106; sucking, 107
lichens, 74–76, 194; awl, 76; British soldier, 75; crustose, 74; dog, 75; flame, 75; foliose, 74; fruticose, 74; hieroglyphic, 75; lungwort, 75; matchstick, 75; old-man's-beard, 76; pink earth, 74; pixie cup, 75; reindeer, 75; scarlet-crested Cladonia, 75; script, 75; shield, 75; smooth rock tripe, 75
lilacs, 5
lily of the valley, 5
limestone, 182
Linnaeus, 24
liverwort, *52*
lizards, 150–*51*
lobster, 97
locust, black, 34, 70; clammy, 35; honey, 35; seventeen-year, 109
logs, 193–94
Longwood Gardens, 192
lotus, 187

maggots, 120
Maine, 182, 184
mammals, 159–76; egg-laying, 159; pouched, 159, 160
manatees, 173
mantes, *102;* egg cases of, 103

maples, 37; Japanese, 37, 38; Norway, 37; red, 37; silver, 37; sugar, 38, 43
maple syrup, 205
Marasmius, 71
marble, 182
Mars, 181
marshes, 188
marsupials, 159, 160
Maryland, 185
mastodon, 185
mayapple, 53, 68
mayflies, 99; nymphs of, 99
meadowlark, 136
meadow mice, 167
meadow mushroom, 72
mealworm, 114
mealybugs, 110
mermaid, 173
mermaid's purse, 157
meteorite, 182
mica, 184
mildew, 74; powdery, 67
milkweed, 57
milkweed beetle, 57; bug, 58
millipedes, 92, 96
minerals, 181–84
minnows, 155
mint, 6
mites, 52, 92, 94
moccasins, 153
moles, 161; star-nosed, 161
moleskin, 161
molluscs, 79, 90–92
monarch butterfly, 58, 117, 118
Mongolian Desert, 171
moon, 179, 180
moose, 164
morels, 67
mosquito, 57, 99, 119, 189; salt marsh, 119, 120
moss, 49–52; apple, 50; animals, 89; Bryum, 49; burned ground, 50; Ceratodon, 49; collection, 51; cushion, 50; Funaria, 50; garden, 51; hairy cap, 50; Irish, 200–1; sphagnum, 50, 188
mosses, 49–52; as indicators of pollution, 49; help in identifying, 51;

life cycle, 50; uses of, 50; where to find, 50
moths, 116; bagworm, 118, 119; Cecropia, 117; hummingbird, 118; royal walnut, 117; yucca, 117
Mount Desert Island, 184
mud puppy, 149
mulberry, 117
mules, 174
mullein, great, 55
mushroom, commercial, 72; meadow, 72
muskrats, 170, 191
mussels, 90
mycelia, 65

naiads, 100
naturalized plants, list of, 61–63
nature collages, 203
nature newspaper, 217
nature notepaper, 202–3, 204
nematocysts, 82
nematodes, 86
nerve-winged insects, 115
net, making a, 208
nettles, stinging, 28
Neuroptera, 115
New England, 43
ninebark, 41
Norway, see: Norway maple, 35; Norway pine, 35; Norway rat, 166; Norway spruce, 35
nylons, 216

oaks, 70
octopuses, 91
Old Faithful, 185
orchids, 54, 55; Adam and Eve, 55; lady's-slippers, 54; purple fringeless, 55; puttyroot, 55; rattlesnake plantain, 55; showy, 55
orienteering, 15
oriole, 20; nest, 137
Orion, 181
ovipositor, 122
owl, great horned, 154
oxalis, 60
oyster mushroom, 71
oysters, 90, 91

pack rats, 167
pantyhose, 216
paper, 215
paper wasps, 198
paramecium, *80*
parasites, bird, 106
parasol mushroom, 71
parrot, *139*
pelecypods, 90, 91
pen, of squids, 91
persimmon leather, 204
Pharaoh's ant, 197
pigeon horntail, 123
pigeons, 9, 135
pigs, 86, 173; wild, 174
pikas, 166
pill bug, *97*
pine, 38; Fomes, 70; ground, 46; loblolly, 70; longleaf, 70; Norway, 35
pitcher plant, 56, 57, 188
pith, 41, 42
planets, 181
Platyhelminthes, 79, 85
Poinsett, Joel Roberts, 3
poinsettia, 3
poison ivy, 27, 28; sumac, 28, 189
poisonous animals: black widow, 28,
   93; brown recluse, 28, 93; centipedes, 96; copperhead, 153; coral
   snake, 153; Gila monster, 151;
   rattlesnakes, 153; scorpions, 95;
   water moccasins, 153
poisonous plants: jack-in-the-pulpit,
   53; jimson weed, 62; poison hemlock, 28; poison ivy, 27, 28; poke,
   59, 60; sumac, 28; toxic mushrooms, 28, 70
poke, 59, 60
pollen, 117, 125, 126
pollination, 98
pollution, 215
polychaetes, 87
polypores, 69
ponds, 190
pony, 18
porcupines, 171
pore fungi, 69
Porifera, 81
porpoises, 172

Portuguese man-of-war, 82
possum, 160
prairie dogs, 168
praying mantes, 101, *102*, 103
primates, 165
privet, 42
pronghorn antelope, 173
Protococcus, 64
protozoa, 79, *80*, 81
Pteridophyta, 33
puffballs, 72
purslane, 59

quartz, 182
Queen Anne's lace, 46, 188
quillworts, 43, 48

rabbits, 166
rabies, 161
raccoons, 40, 162, 163, 191
ragweed, 195
railroads, 196
rain, 186, 187
rainbow, 185
raisins, 206
rats, 121
rays, 157
recycling, 215–17
red eft, 149
reptiles, 150–55
rhinoceros, 174, 175
rice, 60
ringworm, 74
rivers, 191
roaches, 102
roadsides, 195
robin, 20, *136*, 192, 193
rocks, 181–84; igneous, 182; metamorphic, 182; sedimentary, 182;
   uses of, 183–84
rodents, 166–71; pet, 171
Romans, 179
Roosevelt, Theodore, 53
rose, 5; multiflora, 42
rotifers, 88
roundworms, 79, 85, 86
rusts, 68

sac fungi, 66

salamanders, 148–49; dusky, *148;*
eggs, *143;* giant, 149; hellbender,
149; mud puppy, 149; red-backed,
148; red eft, 149; spotted newt,
149
salmon, 158
salmonella, 154
salt, 184
sand, 182, 184
Sand Beach, 184
sand dollars, 126, 127, *128*
sandstone, 182
Sargasso Sea, 156
sassafras, *7;* tea, 205
Saturn, 181
sawflies, 122
scale insects, 109, 110
scallops, 90
scaly-winged insects, 116
scarlet fever, 76
scorpions, 92, 95
scouring rush, 47
sea anemones, 82
sea cucumbers, *128*
sea horses, 156
sea lilies, 129
sea lions, 172
seals, 172
sea urchins, 79, *127,* 128
segmented worms, 86, 87, 88
seine, 191
selaginellas, 48
senses, using, 4
serpent stars, 128
shad, 158
shagbark hickory, 6
shaggy-mane, 72
shale, 182
Shanghai, 66
sharks, 157
sheep, 164, 165, 173
sheep-sorrel, 8, 60
shelf fungi, 69
shellfish, 90–92
shrews, 159, 161, 162
shrimp, 97
shrubs, 41–43
sidewalks, 196
silk, 117

silk glands, 95
silverfish, 98, 99
six-lined racerunner, 151
skates, 157
skating, 18, 19
skunk cabbage, 53, 187
skunks, 163–64; hog-nosed, 164;
spotted, 164; striped, 164
slate, 182
sleepy catchfly, 57
slime molds, 65
sloths, 165
slug, *90*
Smithsonian Institution, 23, 52, 182
smuts, 68
snail, land, *90;* tree, 90
snake, 24–27, 152–54; bites, 152;
black, 27; copperhead, *153;* feeders, 99; glass, 151; hog-nosed,
153; hoop, 27; milk, 27, *153;* water, 27, 153; worm, 40
snake doctors, 99
snow, 186, 206
snowflakes, 206–7
snowfleas, 99
snow ice cream, 206
Socrates, 25
Socratic method, 25, 44
sour grass, 8, 60
sow bug, *97*
sparrow, chipping, 4; house, 135,
198
Spermatophyta, 33
sphagnum, 50, 188
spicebush, 41
spider, 92–94; black widow, 92, 93;
brown recluse, 92, 93; crab, 94;
eggs, 94; golden garden, 93;
house, 94; jumping, 93; nursery
web, 94; poisonous, 92, 93; spiny-
bellied, 94; tarantula, 93, 94;
webs, 93, 94, 209; wolf, 93
spike mosses, 43, 48
spittlebugs, 109
sponges, *81*
spore prints, 199
spring peepers, 147
springtails, 2, 52, 99
spruce, 39; Norway, 35; standing, 46

squids, 91
squirrel homes, 216
squirrels, 168, 195; flying, 40, 168;
    gray, 40, 168; red, 40, 168
starfishes, 79, 126, 127
starlings, 9, 135, 195, 198
stars, 179, 180
Steller's sea cow, 165
stereum, 69
stinkbug, 107
stinkhorn, 5
stone flies, 99
straw, 60
streams, 191
stumps, 193
sturgeon, 157
sucking lice, 107
sugarcane, 60
sulfur polypore, 69
sumac, harmless, 28; poison, 28;
    fruits used for drink, 205
sun, 179, 180
sundews, 57, 188
superstitions, 26
swamps, 188
sweet pea, 34
swimming, 19
sycamore, 35

tape recorder, 54
tapeworm, 85
tapirs, 174, 175
telescope, 181
tent caterpillar, 116
termites, 100, 101; queen, 101
terrariums, 201–2
tetanus, 76
Thallophyta, 33
thistle, 58, 59, 188
Thoreau, Henry, 53
thrips, 55, 106, 107; citrus, 106;
    gladiolus, 106; in mullein, 107;
    onion, 106; pear, 106
tick fever, 95
tires, 216
toads, 26, 145, 146, 147, 153; Amer-
    ican, 147; Fowler's, 147; horned,
    151; spadefoot, 147
tomato hornworm, 123

tooth fungi, 68
towhee, 136
tracks, railroad, 57
trays, 216
tree cricket, 104
tree frogs, 147, 148
treehoppers, 109
tree of heaven, 59, 196
trees, dead, 39–41
trichina worms, 86
trichinosis, 86
trout, 158
trout lilies, 186
truffles, 67
tuberculosis, 76
tulip tree, 6
turkey tail fungus, 69
turtle, box, 154; painted, 154; red-
    eared, 154; snapping, 87, 155;
    spotted, 154
turtlehead, 189

U. S. Department of Agriculture, 23

vacant lots, 196
varnished ganoderma, 69
velvet ants, 124
velvet-footed Collybia, 71
Venus flytrap, 56
vertebrates, 133–76
vinegar, 200
violets, 53, 55
Virginia bluebells, 186
volcanoes, 182
voles, 167
Vorticella, 80
vultures, 196

walkingsticks, 101, 105
walls, 194–95
walruses, 172
warts, 26
wasps, 122–25; digger, 124; gall,
    123; mud, 124; parasitic, 123; so-
    cial, 125
water, 185–87
water boatmen, 108
water scorpion, 108
water striders, 2, 108

weasels, 163
weeds, 58–60
West Virginia, 43
whales, 172
whelks, 90
white ants, 100, *101*
white-footed mouse, 167
wild carrot, 25
wildflowers, 53–57; color in, 54
willow, corkscrew, 42; fantail, 42
wings, of insects, 98
wintercress mustard, 59
Winterthur, 192
wireworms, 113
wolves, 164, 168
woodchucks, 170
woodpeckers, 5, 113; downy, 188;
  red-headed, 21; red-cockaded, 70

woodrats, 167
wood thrush, 135
woolly bear, 27
worms, arrow, 89; earthworm, 86,
  87; flatworm, 85; hairworm, 86;
  leech, 87, 88; nematodes, 86;
  roundworms, 85, 86; segmented,
  86, 87, 88; tapeworms, 85; trichina, 86
wren, house, 135, 188
wrigglers, 57, 120

yarrow, 46
Yellowstone National Park, 185

zebras, 174
zoo, 2